ISBN 978-1-5280-5550-5
PIBN 10924576

1 MONTH OF
FREE
READING

at
www.ForgottenBooks.com

By purchasing this book you are eligible for one month membership to ForgottenBooks.com, giving you unlimited access to our entire collection of over 1,000,000 titles via our web site and mobile apps.

To claim your free month visit:

www.forgottenbooks.com/free924576

English
Français
Deutsche
Italiano
Español
Português

www.forgottenbooks.com

Mythology Photography **Fiction**
Fishing Christianity **Art** Cooking
Essays Buddhism Freemasonry
Medicine **Biology** Music **Ancient
Egypt** Evolution Carpentry Physics
Dance Geology **Mathematics** Fitness
Shakespeare **Folklore** Yoga Marketing
Confidence Immortality Biographies
Poetry **Psychology** Witchcraft
Electronics Chemistry History **Law**
Accounting **Philosophy** Anthropology
Alchemy Drama Quantum Mechanics
Atheism Sexual Health **Ancient History**
Entrepreneurship Languages Sport
Paleontology Needlework Islam
Metaphysics Investment Archaeology
Parenting Statistics Criminology
Motivational

PECULATION TRIUMPHANT;

BEING

THE RECORD

OF A

FOUR YEARS' CAMPAIGN AGAINST OFFICIAL MALVERSATION

IN THE

CITY OF NEW YORK,

A. D. 187.1 to 1875.

NEW YORK:

John Polhemus, Printer, 102 Nassau Street.

1875.

INDEX.

State of New York,

IN THE COURT OF APPEALS.

THE PEOPLE OF THE STATE OF NEW YORK,
Plaintiffs and Appellants,

against

JAMES H. INGERSOLL, impleaded with WILLIAM M. TWEED and others, *Defendant and Respondent.*

STATEMENT and POINTS *for Plaintiffs.*

STATEMENT.

History and State of the Case:

This appeal presents what might seem a very simple question, that is to say, what public corporate entity should be the plaintiff in an action to recover money fraudulently obtained by means of an undue or unadvised exercise of public authority where such exercise wrought no immediate loss to any individual or judicially recognizable entity, nor involved any possibility of a future injury except to such persons as might, at a future period, indicated by law, belong to a class of local tax-payers. When the action was brought, this class was, indeed, already designated ; but the designation might fairly and constitutionally have been altered at pleasure by the legislative body at any time before the levy of the tax. Either without any cause save the poverbial variety of human opinion, or from some cause or causes, perhaps not discernible, or if so, not proper to be here stated, this apparently simple question of practice under the attorney's formula, has afforded aliment to forensic effort, which has delayed judgment for more than two years. Flagitious wrong has been enabled by this means, during that long time, to hold the public demand for a remedy outside of the door, vainly asking admission to the temple of justice, and has thereby obtained a temporary immunity for itself. The immunity will doubtless become permanent and perfect if this Court shall countenance, by its high approval, the device which would commit the correction of knavery to the hands of the knaves themselves, or of the knaves' appointees.

In July, 1871, by existing laws then recently enacted, the Mayor, HALL, the Comptroller, CONNOLLY, the Commissioner of Public Works, TWEED, and the President of Public Parks, SWEENEY, were virtually the local administrators of government in the City of New York. (Fols. 49 to 52.) At this time, the frauds hereafter mentioned being in full progress, discovery thereof was made and public indignation was greatly excited by the disclosure. Eventually, on October 17, 1871, the then Governor and Attorney-General, yielding to loud demands for redress, directed counsel, residing in the City, to aid the latter in such suits and proceedings as might be deemed advisable in the premises. (Fol. 56 to 58.) No sooner was this official act promulgated than (October 19, 1871,) the local officers, who had theretofore disregarded the public will, rushed into the courts of justice with nominal prosecutions against themselves, in the names of the local bodies which they controlled. Law agents, whom the delinquents had appointed and could peremptorily instruct, were thus set in motion by them to demand the infliction of justice upon themselves for their own delinquency !

The Counsel to the City Corporation, who was also denominated by statute "law adviser" to the New York County Board of Supervisors, by direction of the

Mayor, *Hall*, promptly anticipating action on behalf of the State, commenced several and separate actions for the same causes in the name of the City Corporation and mates thereto in the name of the County Board of Supervisors against *Hall* himself, *Tweed* and *Connolly* (fols. 59, 60). For some as yet undeveloped reason, no such embarrassing legal rivalry with any possible action against *Sweeney* was thought necessary, and none was set on foot. The action now before this Court on this appeal was commenced, October 24, 1871, by the service of process against *Tweed*. Its progress and fortunes as against him are only interesting, or perhaps relevant, so far as they bring into view judicial opinions which, though not authoritative in this Court, are often cited here, and doubtless exercise such influence as the reasons contained in them may deserve. On December 5, 1871, Judge Learned, holding a Special Term in Albany, denied a motion to discharge the defendant *Tweed* from arrest. (See opinion paper marked B, p. 93 to 100.)

In February, 1872, a General Term for the Third Department, MILLER, P. J., with POTTER and PARKER, J.J., affirmed this order without delivering any written or oral statement of its reasons. TWEED then demurred ; and, at a Special Term, held by HOGEBOOM, J., on June 5th, 1872, his demurrer was overruled. TWEED appealed, and at a General Term, held for this express purpose, by order of the Executive, on July 16, 1872, the appeal was heard.

The order overruling the demurrer was affirmed, MILLER, P. J., and POTTER, J., concurring in the order. PARKER, J., dissented.

From the outset the defence has been, and it still is, that the State, as such, is not concerned in the alleged grievance, and of course is not entitled to any judicial remedy.

Sundry papers containing diverse views on this point will be furnished to the Court.

1st. An argument furnished to the City Corporation's Counsel by GEORGE TICKNOR CURTIS, Esq. It will be marked A. This is mistakenly denominated an opinion.

2d. Points printed for the use of the General Term by the State's Counsel on Tweed's appeal from the refusal of JUDGE LEARNED to discharge the order of arrest. To this is annexed Judge Learned's opinion at pages 93 to 100 and Ex-Judge GREENE C. ROBINSON's advisory official opinion as counsel to the City Corporation delivered many years ago, pages 55 to 59. This paper will be marked B.

3d. A report of the oral arguments before the General Term by Counsel for the State on the hearing of TWEED's appeal from the order overruling his demurrer in July, 1872. This paper will be marked C.

4th. A copy of the several opinions delivered by the three Judges of the General Term, when Tweed's appeal from the order overruling his demurrer was decided. This paper will be marked D.

Not venturing to stand upon his demurrer, Tweed answered, thus waiving the defect, if any there was, in not making any local corporation or body a co-defendant. No further delay could have occurred save by the device of inducing Ingersoll, the present respondent, to appear and set up in succession the same technical objections under new auspices.

After Tweed's appeal from the order overruling his demurrer had been submitted to the General Term, that is to say, on August 14th, 1872, the defendant James H. Ingersoll appeared.

His first step was a successful motion at the Albany Special Term, before INGALLS, J., to strike out, "as irrelevant and redundant," all the allegations of neglect and collusion on the part of the local authorities. This was on November 19th, 1872. (Fols. 89 to 94.) On Tweed's motion the same Judge then changed the venue to New York, and Ingersoll demurred. Only one of the causes assigned requires notice. It is the fourth, and is an alleged "defect of defendant in the omission of the Board of Supervisors of the County of New York." (Fol. 97). This demurrer was heard at the New York Special Term, before HARDIN, J., when the demurrer was allowed. The order of allowance was entered March 21, 1873. (Fol. 109.) See Judge Hardin's opinion. (Fols. 117 to 172.)

The State appealed, and at a General Term, held in the First Department, on May 5th, 1873, Judge Hardin's order was affirmed and final judgment rendered in favor of the defendant Ingersoll, with costs. (Fols. 173 to 180.)

No written opinion was filed with this decision. The State appealed to this Court May 15, 1873. (Fol. 184.)

Ingersoll moved this Court to dismiss the appeal on the ground that the plaintiffs were bound first to go through with their litigations and trials as against Tweed, and that after every thing was adjusted and settled by an unexceptionably regular and legal trial and judgment as between them and him, they might then be heard on appeal here against Ingersoll's successful demurrer, and if their views should be sustained they might go back again, rip open the settled determination as to Tweed, and have a full trial of the entire case. This conceit was not adopted here, and the appeal was heard on its merits in May, 1873.

Facts Pleaded.

The following facts are stated in that part of the complaint not referred to by Judge Ingall's expunging order:

In the laws of 1870, p. 878, § 4, it is enacted as follows: "All liabilities against the County of New York, incurred previous to the passage of this Act, shall be audited by the Mayor, Comptroller and present President of the Board of Supervisors, and the amounts which are found to be due shall be provided for by the issue of revenue bonds of the County of New York, payable during the year eighteen hundred and seventy-one, and the Board of Supervisors shall include in the ordinance levying the taxes for the year eighteen hundred and seventy-one, an amount sufficient to pay said bonds and the interest thereon. Such claims shall be paid by the Comptroller to the party or parties entitled to receive the same, upon the certificate of the officers named herein."

Hall was Mayor, *Connolly* was *Comptroller*, and *Tweed* was President of the Board of Supervisors.

These persons directed that the *County Auditor* collect from the committees of the Board of Supervisors all the bills and liabilities provided for, and "that the evidence of the same be the authorization of the said Board or its appropriate committees on certificate of Clerk or President."

This so-called County Auditor was one James Watson, since deceased, then a Clerk in the Comptroller's office. He made up numerous claims; and Hall, Connolly and Tweed, separately, in pretended compliance with the above recited act, but without any examination, certified them.

Such certifications amounted to a sum slightly exceeding $6,312,000. The Comptroller issued and sold to *bona fide* purchasers the prescribed bonds to that amount, and deposited the moneys obtained thereon with the Broadway Bank, to the credit of an account there kept by the Chamberlain of the City of New York, as County Treasurer. (Fols. 7 to 11.)

Immediately upon such pretended audit and allowance of each claim, a check or warrant on said bank in favor of the certificated claimant for the payment thereof was signed by the Comptroller, the Mayor, and one Joseph B. Young, as Clerk of the said Board of Supervisors; and such checks or warrants were accordingly paid by the bank, for and on behalf of the

County Treasurer, and to the debit of his said account. (Fols. 17, 18.)

The accounts or claims so audited were *all* false, fictitious and fraudulent ; they were made up by fraud and collusion between the said James Watson and the defendants, Andrew J. Garvey, James H. Ingersoll and Elbert A. Woodward ; and the payments on such warrants respectively by said bank were pursuant to a corrupt, fraudulent and unlawful combination and conspiracy to that end by and between all the defendants, agreed to be divided, and were divided accordingly between the defendants Ingersoll, Garvey, Tweed and others, unknown, their confederates. (Fols. 31 to 43.)

The certificate of allowance on each claim, the check or warrant for its payment, the actual payment thereof by the bank, and distribution of the proceeds among the conspirators were in each instance substantially cotemporaneous. All these frauds occurred between May 5, and September 1, 1871. (*See schedules annexed to complaint.*) A large portion of them took place after the first Monday of July, 1870. (*See laws of* 1870, *p.* 483, *sec.* 11.) After that date Tweed was not an officer or member of the Supervisors' Board; but as a private individual he continued auditor under the section in question.

The parts of the complaint directed by Judge Ingalls to be stricken out as irrelevant (case, folio 93) are the 4th, 5th, and 6th sections. These parts alleged in substance as follows :

No provision was made by the New York Board of Apportionment in fixing the amount to be raised in the year 1871 for the payment of the said bonds, and such Board, in fixing such amount, proceeded to the full extent of their authority.· The Board of Supervisors had raised by tax all the moneys which they could lawfully raise during 1871, and none of it could be applied to the payment of these bonds. There was no fund existing, or capable of being raised or levied by taxation or otherwise, which could be legally, or in fact, applied to their payment, unless it be the moneys sought to be recovered by this action. There was no property, nor any person, natural or artificial, bound by law or contract for the payment of the bonds, unless it be the wrong-doers in the complaint mentioned, save and except only the People of the State of New York in their capacity as a body politic; and the people of this State are, through such means as their State government in its wisdom may employ, bound, by reason of the pledge of their public faith implied in the Act, to provide for and pay these bonds.

After it became publicly known, and known to defendant Tweed, and to Mayor Hall and the Corporation Counsel, that the Attorney-General was about to commence suits against these defendants, and others implicated in the said corrupt and fraudulent proceedings, Hall, as such Mayor, and as President of the Board of Supervisors of the County, wrongfully and unjustly, with purpose and intent to defeat any suits, actions, or proceedings which might be instituted in behalf of the people, and thereby to enable the said defendant Tweed and his confederates to evade and escape from the pursuit of justice, did, in collusion with Tweed, and without the consent or knowledge of the Attorney-General, direct the Counsel for the Corporation to commence six actions in the First Department of the Supreme Court, by the service of a summons in each, as follows : three actions in the name of the Mayor, &c., of the City of New York, as plaintiff; one of them against Wm. M. Tweed, as sole defendant ; one against Richard B. Connolly, as sole defendant, and one against Abraham Oakey Hall, as sole defendant therein ; and also, three actions in the name of the Supervisors of the County of New York, as plaintiffs ; one against Tweed, one against Connolly, and one against Hall, as sole defendants respectively ;

which actions were still depending without any step having been taken, or in good faith intended to be taken therein, beyond the service of the summons. Said actions were intended to cover and embrace, in point of form, and apparently in substance, claims for satisfaction in respect to all frauds of Tweed, official or otherwise, in this complaint mentioned or referred to, and all other liabilities of Tweed, Connolly and Hall, for which any action could be brought against them. But such six actions will not and cannot be fairly, beneficially, or usefully prosecuted, inasmuch as they are controlled by Hall, who is in complicity with Tweed and Connolly, and has complete control over the Counsel of the Corporation. Nor can or will any other action or proceeding be had or taken by said Mayor or any other officer of the City or County, for the purpose of redressing the said frauds and wrongs against the People of the State of New York, or of recovering the public moneys so as aforesaid fraudulently appropriated by said defendants, or any of them. But, on the contrary, the said Mayor, and all other officers of said City and County, having power or authority in the premises, intend and design to prevent any such action, suit, or proceeding, redress or recovery.

The complaint demands judgment against the defendants, for the sum of six million three hundred and twelve thousand dollars, with interest from the first day of September, 1870, and costs. (Case, fols. 43 to 66.)

The Revenue bonds issued by the Comptroller in the name of the County under this section (Laws of 1870, p. 878, § 4), and sold by him for the purpose of obtaining the money in question, had not yet been paid, nor had any of them become due when this action was commenced. This fact was averred, and dates show that it must have been so.

In legislating at Albany to answer their own ends, the Tweed managers had thought it expedient to form for a term of two years a financially dominant Board, composed of their four head men. It was thought politic at the same time to flatter the hopes of tax-payers by limiting the exactions in each of those years to two per cent. on the assessed value of all locally taxable property, and also by fixing an aggregate maximum of $25,000,000. The Act to this effect is found in the Laws of 1871, p. 1268, §§ 1 and 2. This is usually designated the two per cent. Act. And in the pleadings and arguments the Board is styled the Board of Apportionment.

The complaint, as has been seen, alleged that this Act, and the proceedings under it by the Board of Apportionment, had rendered impossible the payment of these bonds.

But that was not the only vacuum produced by the swindling career of the local managers, which the taxation to the two per cent., or $25,000,000, was incapable of supplying. To obviate this difficulty two other short acts, known in the parlance of this controversy as the Consolidation Acts, were obtained in April, 1871. See *City* Debt Consolidation Act, Laws of 1871. p. 629, and *County* Debt Consolidation Act, *Ib.*, p. 631. These acts are precisely alike. They authorize City and County *stock* to be created, payable in *not less than twenty years* nor more than fifty, and its issue either in exchange for then outstanding bonds, or for the purpose of paying them. The usual clause was inserted directing an addition to the annual tax levy for the interest and principal as they should become payable. No limit was assigned to the amount thus issuable; the Comptroller was the sole and uncontrolled manager of the process. He had absolute control as to the form. Any other persons required to act in the matter were mere signers of the bonds—mere attestors. § 4. They had no more power of resistance or supervision than the county seal. And to cap the climax of Mr. Comptroller Connolly's omnipotence it was enacted, that in the swapping process, and doubtless it was understood as applying throughout, the issues were to be "upon such terms and conditions as shall be determined and offered by the said Comptroller." § 2. Calling these issues *stock* instead of bonds was a mere Wall street device to give them a factitious consequence and favor in the foreign market.

It has been uniformly asserted in this case by both sides at the bar, and doubtless may be assumed by the Court, that since the commencement of this action the bonds issued under § 4 of the Laws of 1870, p. 878, were all duly paid off at maturity by means of new *bonds*, as we will call them, issued under the above-mentioned County Debt Consolidation Act of 1871, page 631.

In other words, this six million swindle is a charge on the estates, real and personal, which may be liable to local taxes in or after 1891.

After the hearing in May, 1873, and deliberation thereon, this Court, in November, 1873, ordered a re-argument on the following two questions:

First.—Was the title to the money, which is the subject in controversy, in the County of New York?

Second.—If the money was the money of the County, can the Board of Supervisors maintain an action for the cause stated in the complaint in behalf of and for the benefit of the County?

The oral argument delivered at the bar in May, 1873, was very brief, and may, therefore, have been imperfect. An attempt will now be made to remove any obscurity which may exist.

Preliminary View of the Section and its Import and Effect.

The section in question is found in the Laws of 1870, p. 878, § 4, and is as follows:

" All liabilities against the County of New York incurred previous to the passage of this Act shall be audited by the Mayor, Comptroller, and present President of the Board of Supervisors, and the amounts which are found to be due shall be provided for by the issue of revenue bonds of the County of New York, payable during the year eighteen hundred and seventy-one, and the Board of Supervisors shall include in the ordinance levying the taxes for the year eighteen hundred and seventy-one, an amount sufficient to pay said bonds and the interest thereon. Such claims shall be paid by the Comptroller to the party or parties entitled to receive the same, upon the certificate of the officers named herein."

It will be seen that the Comptroller is sole manager of this process. No Board of Supervisors had any control in the matter. The Special Board of Audit made the certificates of allowance. The bonds were a mere form. The Comptroller must have issued and sold them, for it was *he*, and not any County Treasurer or other officer, that was to *pay* the certificate holders. On this point of construction see *Brewster vs. Striker*, 2 Comstock's R., 19.

It is said that the complaint shows this money to have found its way into a place called the County Treasury before being paid over to the certificate holders. It was gotten for the bonds fraudulently issued ; it found its way into the County Treasurer's bank ; and the defendant's theory is, that having gotten into that place it became County money. It will, however, be perceived that if it did get into any county treasury, it was without warrant of law. The Comptroller was to raise the money, and himself to pay it to the persons holding certificates of audit. Evidently there was no legal right to *make* an intermediate deposit of it in the County Treasury, if indeed any such act was performed. If the Comptroller did so deposit the money it is not easy to see how he could ever have gotten it back again into his own hands unless by a law-suit against the County Treasurer or the bank. Still, they say that this money having at some time got into the hands of a County Treasurer, it therefore belongs to the County. But it does not follow because money gets into the County Treasury that it belongs to the County. Such would not be the fact if it got there without any right or title to the money being given by law to the County.

Having got there without any legal authority on the part of anybody to pay it in, it would not thence result that it belonged to the County, or that the County could maintain an action founded on the mere fact that it was so in its treasury. The complaint alleges that:

" From time to time as such certifications were re-"spectively made known to him or his subordinates, "the said Comptroller caused to be issued bonds as "prescribed by said Act, in order to provide funds "to pay the amounts so certified, and obtained from "*bona fide* purchases thereof, prior to the 5th day of "August, in the year aforesaid, $6,312,000."

This is quite accurate. Here the Comptroller's action was in precise conformity with the Act. What follows in that paragraph affords some color for the idea that the County Treasurer became in some way possessor of this money, and here the pleading is inaccurate; that is, it does not state the precise fact in using the words, "in formal compliance with the "Statutes." There was not nor is there any statute authorizing the act alleged.

The whole of this inaccurate statement in the complaint is as follows :

"Which last-mentioned sum was in formal com-"pliance with the Statutes and usual modes of official "proceedings, in said city, deposited in the National "Broadway Bank of the City of New York, to the

"credit of an account therein kept by the Chamber-
"lain of the City of New York as County Treasurer of
"said County, by virtue of his said official character
"as such Chamberlain." (*Fol. 9.*)

That there was a bank account kept in the Broadway Bank by the Chamberlain of the City of New
York, who was *ex officio* County Treasurer, was true;
but it may not be easy to determine what the
pleader meant by saying "in formal compliance with
"statutes and the usual modes of official proceed-
"ings." As to the money being paid into that bank,
the matter of fact is assumed to be true; but so far as
he asserts that it was so paid in compliance with any
law, the Court will perceive that it cannot be true.
For so to pay it was contrary to law. The Comptroller had no authority whatever to pay it into that bank,
or into any other. He should have kept it under his
own control until payment of it by himself to the certificate holder. The County Treasurer had no power
or authority to receive it or to pay it to any one. The
law did not allow him to receive it or to pay it, and
consequently he had no claim to its custody. To that
part of the complaint the Court will properly apply a
well known rule of law.

When a pleader speaks of laws and statutes, and
concerning the "conformity" of any thing to "statutes," he is averring matter of law, and not of fact.
If that averment be erroneous, the Court knows it to
be erroneous and should disregard it. (Hymann *v.*
Cook, 2 Denio, 201; S. C. Howard's Appeal Cases,
p. 419.) Though that money may have been, in
fact, in the hands of the individual who held
the office of County Treasurer, it never was or could
have been, in contemplation of law, even incidentally
or even by accident, in any county *treasury.* If it
was blunderingly paid into a bank account kept by
the County Treasurer, so that it had a sort of nominal
locality within his personal control, that is a fact pro-

ducing no legal consequences. It was merely an erroneous or mistaken method of conducting the business.
The method was contrary to law. The statute is plain
on this point.

An English case directly in point shows how illegal,
irregular, and improper was the Comptroller's act in
paying this money into the bank account of another
person. King *v.* Halfshire, 5 Term Reports, page
341, had in its circumstances a close analogy to the
present case. It was a suit against the Hundred for a
liability imposed by statute; judgment was recovered,
and the method of execution prescribed was a process
to the Sheriff to levy the sum recovered, in certain pro-
portions upon the inhabitants, and to pay it over to the
plaintiffs. The Justices, in issuing their execution to
this officer, commanded him to levy the money and to
pay it into the hands of specified bankers until the
Court should make its further order for distribution
among the recovering parties. An attempt was made
to justify this proceeding on the ground that it was
simply for convenience. Indeed, it evidently was a
suitable and convenient method of doing the business. It would be very awkward that this Sheriff,
whenever he levied say five pounds, should go about
and make a dividend of it among the creditors. In
the present case it was also quite convenient to
deposit the money in the hands of a banker until called for. But in the case cited the Court overruled that argument, holding that the duty *imposed on the officer by law* was otherwise. As mere
convenience would not justify a course not warranted
by law, the proceedings were quashed. The case is in
point. But authority is not needed on the proposition
in hand. It is too plain. Those who undertake the
execution of laws are bound to obey them as written.
It is, therefore, quite clear that the County Government,
if there was one, or the Treasury of the County, or the
Board of Supervisors, or any other county functionary

or authority, never had, as such, any legal control over this money or any portion of it. In contemplation of law the money was always in the hands of the Comptroller until paid out by him. It was he, and he alone, that could deal with it. He was bound to get it, and he did so ; he was bound to pay it over, and he did so. His adoption of a ceremony which was usual in the transaction of financial business in his department is a fact of no significance. It was, indeed, attended with no inconvenience or evil. It was all well enough, as in the English case, that the money should go into the hands of a banker and there remain for a time; but it was not a thing that the law recognized or allowed, or from which it can permit any consequences to be deduced in favor of these wrong-doers.

POINTS.

FIRST POINT.—There is no actual necessity of considering the various points of law or practice as to the rights and powers of cities, counties or towns corporate, under the statutes, creating, organizing or regulating them, with which the debates and opinions in this and similar cases have been encumbered. Nor need resort be had to the supervisory power of the State to invoke the aid of Equity jurisdiction in preventing or redressing misapplications of the local corporate funds and property, or abuses of local corporate authority. The complaint presents a case of plain and manifest wrong against the rights, authority, power and dignity of the State committed by its own agents directly appointed by its Legislature. According to the primary and most simple conception of the ordinary common law jurisdiction, an action of *tort* by the State against such its unfaithful agents or their abettors, is the appropriate remedy.

I. The wrong was committed, or permitted, or so facilitated that it took effect, through the act or default of a special commission appointed, organized and controlled throughout its whole official course by the State itself, its own Supreme Legislature acting therein directly. The trio who performed all official functions in the matter were not the officers or agents of any local corporation, or in any way representatives of any persons or body except the State. Nor were they responsible or accountable for their acts to any local body or corporation.

Lorrillard *v.* Town of Monroe, 1 Kern, 394, 395.
Sheboygan Co. *v.* Parker, 3d Wallace U. S., 96.

II. The direct or primary injury consisted in
fraudulently procuring certain bonds to be
issued, and obtaining the money thereby for
the use of the conspirators. *Those* moneys
were not authorized to be thus raised at all.
They were not raised for the use of the county .
nor to be paid into the county treasury, or to
be applied to county purposes; nor was any
authority given so to raise, pay or apply
them. The County Board of Supervisors
never had any right to these moneys; nor
control over *any* moneys which could lawfully have been raised on such bonds, even to
the extent of holding them . in temporary
custody.

III. Aside from the State as the sovereign power,
or as the employer of these agents, who in
transacting its business under its immediate
direction received these moneys, the only persons, natural or legal, that could be supposed
to suffer from the wrong perpetrated were:
First, the bondholders; secondly, the corporate entity, if any there be, which might be
forced to pay the bonds; or, thirdly, the tax-
payers who may be assessed to pay the bonds.

    1. The bondholders took *bona fide*, and
    cannot fail to obtain their money on
    the bonds through the State's taxing
    power, 34 *N. Y. R.*, 30. Consequently
    they have no cause of action.

    2. Supposing the *County* to be a corpora-
    tion suable on these bonds, and so,
    possibly, endangered by the fraudu-
    lent issue, still its danger consists
    merely in being surety for the due levy
    of the State's tax for payment of the

bonds. In that view, this local corporation, if it be such, could have no
suitor's standing in Court, except as
such surety in an action *quia timet*
complaining that the State or the asses-
sable tax-paying class was likely to fail
in providing means to discharge the
bonds. Such an action would be absurd
and nonsensical. It could not be maintained. A State law providing a public fund by taxation for the payment of
a demand renders payment accordingly
an absolute certainty in judgment of
law.

Bloodgood *vs.* Mohawk & S. R.'R. Co., 18 Wend., 28,
77, and cases cited.

3. Conceding for the moment and for the
sake of the argument that an action
would lie on one of these bonds
against the County or against the
Board of Supervisors, nothing could
thence result save a ground of appeal
to the Legislature, *i. e.*, to the *State*,
for a special tax upon some class of the
State's own tax-payers, to provide
means for satisfying the judgment.
Neither the County nor the Board of
Supervisors has now or ever had any
means or property which could be applied by execution or otherwise to that
purpose.

See Argument in paper C, pp. 32 to 35 and pp. 37
to 40.

Also the Notes at the end of these Points.

4. The real and only injury, unless to the
State, was to that undefined, unknown
and unascertainable class of individ-

uals (23 *N. Y. R.*, 323) who, at some
unknown period, were to be assessed
under the tax laws for the payment
of these bonds. (*Laws of* 1870, *p.* 878,
§ 4; *Laws of* 1871, *p.* 1,269, § 3, 10; *Ib.*
p. 631, § 2.)

None of this class can be heard individually; nor have all of them combined any right to sue. Neither the
alleged County corporation of New
York, nor the City corporation of New
York, nor any Board of Supervisors,
nor any subordinate functionary whatever is their representative. When the
wrong was perpetrated and this action
commenced, they may have been all
foreigners. *Non constat*, that one of
them was yet born or would ever be a
corporator, or in any sense a constituent of either the alleged County corporation or the City corporation.

See Notes at the end of these Points, and authorities
there cited.

IV. As no right to seek a judicial remedy existed
elsewhere, our jurisprudence cannot be so imperfect as to deny it to the sovereign power,
in whose business, and by whose fraudulent
or negligent servants a large class of the
State's individual members were to be swin-
dled in its name. If, in any method supposa-
bly analogous, a private agent had improperly
acquired money under his employer's authority, which the employer was legally or morally bound to restore, or which his interest required him to restore, surely the employer
could maintain an action to recover it from

the unfaithful agent and his co-operating associates.

See Mr. Curtis' argument implying a doubt, paper A, p. 10.

1. The State plainly *owes* to its tax-payers, present and future, protection to the extent of its power from the frauds of its own agents. And though from many causes such tax-payers can have no coercive remedy, the State is, for all judicial purposes, and in all known and authoritative forensic reasoning, held to be under a *perfect* obligation to give that protection.

Coster *v.* Mayor, 43 N. Y., 407, 408.

2. The State is a corporate entity. Its corporate wealth and means consist of its power to appropriate to its corporate uses such portion as it may need of the individual property within its limits or jurisdiction. Consequently, whatever diminishes or unjustly interferes with the enjoyment of such property by the individual owners thereof, is an injury to the State, which it is the interest of the State to prevent or redress. Surely, when the oppressed individuals are an indefinite class, incapable of acting by themselves, or by any other legal representative, the State can complain of and correct judicially, as a wrong to itself, acts having this tendency, when permitted or committed willfully or negligently by its own servants, contrary to its will, in the *improper* performance of duties imposed upon them by itself.

V. No principle is known to the State's law
agents giving any local officer or corporation
a right of action or power to sue in such cases
as the present. But, if there be any such, it
is conceived that such right or power could
not, on principle or analogy, be pronounced
exclusive. On the contrary, it must be
deemed subordinate and ancillary to the
higher authority in the premises vested in the
State itself. Such subordinate need not be
made a formal party. In an action by the
State, the Court, were it needful, which is not
perceived, could always take such steps as
might be necessary without having the subordinate before it as a nominal party. There
are many cases, even in private controversies,
where different parties may sue separately for
the same cause. A factor, an auctioneer, or
a shipmaster may thus sue alone; so may
the owner sue alone. Either consignor or
consignee may sue alone. In all these cases,
and in all analogous cases, where two actions
are brought for the same cause, the Court can,
by special order, prevent its judgment from
working any prejudice to the defendant.

Att'y-Gen'l v. Wilson, 1 Craig & Phillips, 23.
Dunlap Paley on Agency, pp. 279, 362.
Williams v. Millington, 1 H. Blackstone, 82.
Coppin v. Walker, 2 Marshall, p. 500.
Taintor v. Prendergast, 3 Hill, 72.

VI. As to all rights and interests present or
prospective, of the present or future individual members of the State not capable of
judicial protection at the suit of the individual, or of some inferior and designated
public agent, the State, in its corporate capacity, as an immortal governing legal per-

son or entity, is the guardian or protector. So far as *ownership* in the plaintiff who may sue to vindicate such rights or interests is required to subsist by any practical rules, the State must be deemed to possess it.

See Notes at the end of these Points.

SECOND POINT.—The assertion that the money in question *belonged to* or was *owned by* a local body corporate, briefly referred to as "the County of New York," is a *petitio principii*. It is wholly incapable of proof. There is, in law or fact, no color for the assertion.

I. The so-called County bonds are a mere form. The County treasury, if there be one, is not to suffer any detriment; for the State has not charged their payment upon any county treasury, or county property. On the contrary, the State has, through its invincible power in that respect, absolutely secured their payment by imposing the duty upon a class of its own tax-payers selected by itself.

II. No debt or liability of the County appears to have been left unpaid. On the contrary, if any such existed, they have been overpaid. No purpose of the County could be served with this money if it were paid into the County Treasurer's hands by the swindlers in a spirit of repentance, and by way of amendment.

III. The County of New York has not, nor has its Board of Supervisors, any *corporate* capacity entitling it to sue in the premises. If

"the County of New York" or "the City
and County of New York," or "the Board
of Supervisors of the County of New York,"
or "the Board of Supervisors of the City
and County of New York," be a body corporate, and, as such, entitled to maintain
actions, it could not sue in respect of the
moneys in question.

1. If such a *corporate* entity exists, it has
the most narrow and restricted range
of corporate powers.

   See Notes at end of these Points.

   Brady v. Supervisors, 2 Sandf. Superior Court Law
   Reports, p. 460 ; and same case on Appeal, 10 N. Y. R.,
   p. 260.

2. Even as to the rural counties, there is no
principle of law, nor any word in any
statute, which, either expressly, or by
any fair implication, constitutes the
Board of Supervisors or the corporate
entity called "the County," general
protector or guardian of the local territory, or of its "*inhabitants*," against
excessive taxation under special State
laws. Much less has this entity any
such curatorship in respect of the *tax-
payers*, every one of whom may be a
non-resident of the County.

   See notes at end of these Points.
   Shoemaker v. Comm'rs of Grant Co., 36 Indiana, 183.

3. If the power of thus representing the
local district could be established in respect to the other counties of the State,
or its cities, towns, and villages, little
support would thence result to a claim

of like authority in that very peculiar official instrument, the New York Board of Supervisors.

See Notes at the end of these Points.

4. The unauthorized act of the Comptroller, in making a temporary deposit of the money obtained on the bonds with the bank, to the credit of the County Treasurer, could have no effect to confer upon the alleged County Corporation a title to these moneys.

See Paper C., pp. 6 to 9. Illustrated per Denio, J., in 1 Kernan, 395.

THIRD POINT.—If all that is claimed in the defendant's law-points for the so-called County Corporation were conceded, the fraud and collusion of the local officers having control of it authorized the intervention of the State to reclaim the misapplied moneys through an equitable action.

And if (which is denied *ante First Point, Division V.,*) the alleged County Corporate should properly have been made a formal defendant, Ingersoll expressly waived that objection before interposing his demurrer.

I. The right of the chief executive power in the State to pray for this remedy and the duty of Equity Courts to award it are clear in reason and upon authority.

See Mr. Tilden's arg't and cases cited by him, paper C., pp. 48 to 68, and Mr. Peckham's arg't in same paper, pp. 87 to 118.

As to certain cases in this State including People *v.* Miner, 2 Lansing, see notes at end of these Points.

II.   Such parties as the alleged County Corporate would be in the case supposed, are commonly called formal parties. They are not necessary to the relief or to any purpose connected with the administration of justice in the case, except to protect the defendant from double vexation for the same cause. They are made parties in the action, merely that they may, if needful, be restrained from molesting the defendant for the same cause, or from compelling him to render a second account. For this reason it is that, in the former practice, and more strictly still under the Code, the right to have them brought into the case as parties is treated as *a privilege of the defendant*, which he may waive.

> Edwards on Parties, p. 16, and cases cited.
> Code, §§ 144, 148.

III.   Procuring to be struck out, "as *irrelevant* and redundant," the charges against the County officers was such a waiver. These charges were only needful to show why the State sued ; and the additional formality— *i. e.*, bringing in the County Corporate as a party, was requisite or not at the option of the defendant. By moving to strike out the allegations in that behalf, he signified his election ; and, so far as this point is concerned, his subsequent demurrer should have been disregarded.

FOURTH POINT.—There is no possible aspect of the case in which it can be adjudged that any local corporation or body owns this money or is entitled to it.

I. Plainly no such right results from its having been obtained on the pieces of paper called County bonds which the State directed the Comptroller to issue. Reimbursement to the lenders is provided for by the State out of an absolutely reliable fund, not owned by any such local corporation or body. And the Supervisors or "the County" never had control over any fund or property to which the lenders could have any legal or otherwise coercive recourse.

II. The only legal authority for issuing the bonds was the certificate of audit. This certificate created a perfect right or title, as against the tax-payers, to levy the tax on them. It is clear that they never could, by any judicial process, draw in question the validity of the tax. (*Lynde* v. *The County*, 16 *Wallace, p.* 13.) After the bonds were issued and sold to *bona fide* purchasers, this must be so.

III. The *ownership* of the money during the interval between its receipt by Connolly from the lenders and its payment to the certificate holders, if not in the lenders, as seems quite clear, and not in the indefinite class of tax-payers,thereafter to be charged with the reimbursement, which seems equally clear, and not in the swindling certificate holders, which is *not very clear* to Mr. Curtis (see his argument, paper A, p. 10), would seem to have vested nowhere. No obligation on the County had resulted or could result from the transaction. It was not bound to pay the bonds; it had no ability or means to pay the bonds; and if the money could be supposed to have come into an ideal possession of the County, or of any County officer, neither could ever lawfully apply it to any purpose unless authorized so to do by some new and distinct subsequent grant of power, in that respect, made by the State.

IV. In fact Mr. Curtis's doubt as to there being any remedy, proves him to be a profound thinker. It may well be that the mere ownership of this money, or the *legal title* to it was absolutely and irrevocably vested in the certificate holders. It does not seem easy to establish the contrary by any clear or sound reasoning. It would seem that an inextricable confusion was created as to the ownership of the *res* or the money itself. In such cases the mere *title* to the *res* is in the possessor. (*Silsbury v. McCoon*, 3 *Comst.*, 393—same case, 6 *Hill*, 425 ; 4 *Denio*, *p.* 332.)

V. It results, that the remedy for the evil is an action of tort brought by the State as sovereign vindicator of all general public rights of the people, or of any undefined and unascertainable portion of them.

Colchester v. *Law*, L. R., 16 *Eq. Cases*, 253.

Such action should not be brought for the specific money ; but to recover damages for fraudulently using the State's authority in a manner tending to oppress its citizens.

The judgments below should be reversed, and the demurrer should be overruled.

D. PRATT,
Attorney-General.

NOTES.

A.

At a period not very remote certain trading politicians discovered that the City of New York might be made the Golconda of fraudulent cupidity. Vicious legislation was brought into their service for a price; and, by its use, they had attained in the year 1871 much power and measureless audacity. All the local patronage came under the control of four officials by laws of their own framing. They were Hall, Mayor; Connolly, Comptroller; Tweed, Commissioner of Public Works, and Sweeney, President of the Department of Public Parks. Tweed, whom common fame recognized under the designation "Boss," as chief of this quartette, enjoyed a plurality of benefices. He was President of the Board of Supervisors and a State Senator. Unwilling to rely upon the rule which enjoins "honor among thieves," the quartette, as they were called, made unanimity among themselves indispensable to the working of their machinery. (Laws of 1871, p. 1269, Sec. 3.) During the Summer of that year a subordinate's betrayal of confidence led to developments which attracted notice and aroused public indignation. On October 17th, 1871, a committee of citizens visited the Capitol and appealed to the Governor for official action. In an apparently accidental turn of the conversation which ensued, the latter suggested a particular course; and, by a consequence hardly anticipated, there was immediately established in the city a branch of the Attorney-General's office. Charles O'Conor, Wheeler H. Peckham, William M. Evarts and James Emott, four lawyers residing in the city, assumed the charge of it, and active proceedings were initiated with all practicable speed against various actors in the existing official corruption.

On the date referred to, October 17, 1871, the quartette had almost complete control over the local officers; and each of them was studiously protected, by the requisite of unanimity before mentioned, from any adverse action by any or all of his three equals. Local officers were, in the main, selected through an organization controlled by them; the Corporation Counsel could not institute actions on his own motion, and, in this respect, one of them absolutely controlled him. (*Laws of* 1870, *p.* 371, §§ 23, 40 ; Ib. *p.* 481, § 2.) William M. Tweed, Junior, son of the "Boss," was Assistant District Attorney. To specify in detail their other powers over the *personnel* of those in authority might be thought indecorous. It might approach too closely that line which, in the territory of facts, divides inculpatory truths that may be spoken from those whose mischevious enormity is, in this connection, best described as being *unutterable.* They had reduced nine daily papers and nine weekly papers to the condition of stipendiaries, an act designed, though perhaps without entire success, effectually to muzzle the press, that potent foe of tyranny. (*Laws of* 1871, *p.* 1232, § 1.) They had failed in only one of the efforts which a mad lust of absolute power had stimulated. They were defeated in an attempt to revive the exploded judicial power of punishing contempts at discretion.

This was the state of things when, at the date alluded to, October 17, 1871, the "Bureau of Municipal Correction" confronted the emergency which had called it into being.

The strictly local character of criminal proceedings, together with the palpable servility of the local judiciary then, as yet not purged by impeachment, forbade a resort to that class of remedies.

After careful deliberation, civil actions in the name of the State as plaintiffs, designating Albany County as the venue or place of trial, were determined upon.

And on the 24th of October, 1871, a civil action in the name of The People, as plaintiffs, was commenced against William M. Tweed, then Commissioner of Public Works ; Elbert A. Woodward, then Deputy Clerk of the Board of Supervisors, and James H. Ingersoll, and Andrew J. Garvey, the two latter being mechanics in whose favor large sums of money had been certified as due by the Special Board of Audit, which is made famous by this action.

At a subsequent date, a like action was prosecuted against Richard B. Connolly, who, at the time this general line of operations was commenced, held office as Comptroller of the City, and was still, as such, head of the Finance Department. The latter action is atissue on the merits, and yet undetermined. The former is the *leading case*, and is *the* case now under consideration.

The formation of this local bureau would seem to have been accidental. Something more of its history and action may deserve notice. It would never have been authorized but for the prevalence of that vulgar error, which is now sought to be corrected on appeal to the learning and enlightened intelligence of this high tribunal. There had not, theretofore, been exhibited in any department at the Capitol a disposition to curb fraudulent practices amongst officials ; but a canvass was pending, and it was deemed judicious then to evince such a disposition. The step taken seemed adequate to that end, and, no doubt, it was firmly believed that neither the Attorney-General nor his advisers could act independently of the local authorities. It was adopted as a "tub to the whale."

One difficulty in this movement, which failed to present itself to the governing minds at Albany, was instantly discerned in New York ; but the discernment came too late—the irrevocable step had been taken. In counsel, no less than in judges, there is sometimes to be found a commendable astuteness, which diligently seeks in the armory of jurisprudence for the means of striking down an evident fraud; and when either the lawyer or the judge is honest the search is rarely unsuccessful.

Prior to and until October 17, 1871, reiterated importunities of certain eminent citizens for the commencement of actions against the City heads of department had been disregarded by the New York City Law Department. But the instant the City officials became advised that the Governor and Attorney-General had authorized the counsel first above named to use legal remedies in the name and with the power of the State, the Corporation Counsel was *directed by the Mayor* to commence actions in the name of the City Corporation and of the supposed *County* Corporation, against *the Mayor himself* and Tweed and Connolly. Such actions were accordingly commenced Oct. 19, 1871; but of course they were of the sleepy sort. They were begun by summons merely, without complaint, warrant of arrest, attachment, injunction, or any like energetic accompaniment. These evidently collusive actions thus brought in bad faith were made to cover what attorney-wisdom judged to be the whole field of legal remedies for the alleged official frauds. And having been thus commenced by command of the chief prosecuted official himself, at the critical moment stated, not only without the assent but without the knowledge of the Attorney-General or his assistants, the object as well as the motive was and is manifest. It was to furnish the offenders with color in that technical argument against any earnest legal prosecution which still constitutes their whole stock in trade. Both in the popular and judicial forums that argument has been their whole capital. It is so on the present appeal. Without pretending to innocence, they use this argument in the Court, to "entangle justice in the net of form." Outside of the Court, they use it to discourage honest seekers for public rights, and to encourage unscrupulous political tricksters with that rogue's hope, a possible "flaw in the indictment."

This point in mere practice has hitherto held the civil prosecutions in abeyance. Forced changes in the official corps have freed the administration of criminal justice from their control, so that the defendants in this pending case are now expiating their crimes —one in the *State* Prison at Auburn, and the other in a *County* prison called the Penitentiary; yet, even now, Feb., 1874, the difference between *State* and *County* impedes civil justice and enables their confederates still to hold their plunder in trust for their use.

The New York Bureau received an apparent sanction from the Legislature. (Laws of 1872, p. 1194.) Less could not have been done; but this very anomalous statute was framed in the interest of the delinquents. It aimed at tempting the New York Counsel to imitate Tweed, by auditing bills in his own favor for his own personal services. The object was not accomplished.

In the action against Tweed, there was appended to the complaint a statement in figures which "could not lie" prepared by the Hon. SAMUEL J. TILDEN. It demonstrated the frauds, and it came in time to influence the elections; but it could not prevent Tweed's *returns* accrediting him as a Senator. Still, it produced upon Tweed a crushing effect. He never afterwards dared to confront accusation; nor did he dare to take his seat in the Senate. That seat remained awaiting his occupation for his whole term. His quondam associates in that body were too charitable, too timid, or too—something else—they dared not pronounce it vacant. "Achilles absent was Achilles still."

These astounding developments in New York produced the usual effect. The party whose nominal members were the most conspicuous among the swindlers, sank before the storm; an overwhelming majority in the Legislature was awarded to their adversa-

ries. An Act of that body three lines long would
have stripped the delinquents of their only cavil : but
neither that nor any subseqent Legislature could ever
be moved to any such action ; and thus it is demonstrated that a party *when* in power is not prone to act
efficiently in curbing the kind of villainy now awaiting
immunity or judgment at the bar of this Court.

Quite aware of this, the first named New York
counsel, resolving in the interests of truth and justice
that no faction should "grind its axe" thereat, formed
the New York local bureau equally from both of the
great parties. Its action has ever been absolutely
impartial and wholly unbiassed by personal or party
proclivities.

The course of proceedings in this action against
Tweed, Ingersoll and others is narrated *ante pp.* 3, 4, 5.

The failure of reform Legislatures to aid affirmatively
the movement against the delinquents has been stated.
Its affirmative action to perpetuate like practices remains to be noted, as it has an immediate connection
with the Attorney-General's proceedings.

The elections of 1871 and Mr. TILDEN'S development involved the fall of the Quartette. "Justice may
have leaden feet, but she has iron hands. Though her
pace be slow, it is not the less sure on that account ;
and finally her grasp is terrible." Their tallest man
has indeed escaped conviction ; but this result was not
due to his actual innocence. Unlike the rest, he was
not a "vulgar thief ;" his fault, if any, was a loose
unmindfulness as to the public interest ; and this has
been so common among officials of untarnished repute,
that to single out one for incarceration whilst the mass
went free and were enjoying power and renown, did
not conform to those notions of fair play which are
apt to prevail in simple minds. (*Hogan's State
Trials*, 59, 61.) Where are the others ? Mainly in
the State Prison, in the Penitentiary or fugitives
from justice ! !

Still, what have been the results? Mr. Tweed surrendered his omnivorous Department of·Public Works
to a member of the *incoming* party ; the Law Department was surrendered in like manner, and to one
similarly qualified. The outgoing Mayor, head of the
Quartette, though of a different party, made *these* appointments; and the Legislature, elected under the banner of reform and retrenchment, could do no less than
perpetuate in the hands of their political friends (col-
ored, of course, by the slightest possible variation,) the
powers which, in the hands of their opponents, had been
a source of profit to partisans. Individuals have, indeed, suffered in the tempest, but the atmosphere has
not been purified. Like causes must ever produce like
effects, and the plundered tax and assessment payers
of New York are not being relieved from any pressure
experienced during Tweed's regime. The writ of mandamus is coercive upon the financial officers ; the job-
ber chooses from the multitude his judge in the first
instance, and the head of the Law Department, selected
by the Quartette and appointed by its chief, Hall, can
for a long term of years, by his mere *sic volo*, prevent
any appeal. See present Charter, Laws of 1873, p.
495, § 36. It is not strange that these nicely concerted
arrangements created a belief that all things would
soon resume their usual routine, and tempted Genet to
elect himself to the present Assembly.

The criminal convictions which soon followed have,
in some degree, intimidated the jobbers, but if a favorable decision here shall point out a *refugium pecca-
torum* our birds of prey will return. The result will
dishearten all honest men, and discourage all honest
effort.

B.

In the nomenclature of juridical science a corporation is an artificial entity or person. It is "invisi-
ble, intangible, and existing only in contemplation of

law." Like a natural person, it cannot operate practically without organs; but its nature is such that it is
quite susceptible of being regarded as standing alone
in its judicially recognized artificial personality, without any individual interest entering into its composi-
tion, and without its being, in any just or scientific
sense of the words, even so much as the representative
in respect to property or private and personal rights of
any individual or individuals whatever. The State is
precisely such a corporation.

And this notional existent being may have an equal
place in judicial contemplation whether it be called a
corporation or not, and however limited its sphere of
action or its powers. Whenever an entity, capable of
appearing *in foro*, as *actor* or *reus* is recognized, that
entity has upon general principles the vital elements of
that which is commonly denominated corporate existence. Consequently, in the true and the general and
comprehensively scientific view of artificial juridical
personality, it matters not whether the entity in question be or be not endowed with a corporate name, or
with any one of those usual salient accompaniments
by which corporations are known. The failure of
stinted intellects to extricate themselves from the mere
mechanism of the attorney's office sufficiently to perceive this fact, caused the multitudinous wrangles
and conflicts, quite discreditable to our jurisprudence,
which arose under the free banking law. See their history per Harris, J., Leavitt *v.* Blatchford, 17 N. Y. R.,
526 to 535. And Debow *v.* People, 1 Denio, 9, overruled in Giffard *v.* Livingston, 2 Denio, 380.

It is consequently quite apparent that in considering
this subject largely, and upon principle, there is no
difference whatever between the most thoroughly and
perfectly endowed or caparisoned corporation, and
any *interest* which, aside from those of a purely individual character, is for any purpose recognized in the
judicial mind. That *interest* which has capacity, in any

form whatever, to stand up for *itself* in a court of justice, and is liable to be made *itself* a respondent *in foro*, differs not in essentials from any corporate entity. Not only the *quasi* corporations but the presidents, clerks, or other managing officers, who, by feasible or by "clumsy" devices of legislators or judges have been endowed with this capacity of prosecuting, òr charged with that of responding *for an interest*, while the cited person himself, individually, is held not to be for any substantial purpose either a plaintiff or a defendant, are all in this category. Per Blackburn, J., Mersey Docks *v.* Gibbs, Law Rep. 1, Eng. & Irish Appeals, H. L., pp. 108, 109.

We have said that no one definite characteristic of a mechanical nature, such, as for instance, a name, is necessary to the constitution of a judicial entity capable of representing *in foro* an interest. This we proceed to prove.

The ordinary trading corporation is hardly distinguishable in principle from the mercantile firm of continental jurisprudence. It is of course nothing more than the name or form under which a number of individuals place their capital and conduct their business. The fancy of Englishmen for the practical forms of the common law courts precluded the use of the voluntarily assumed social name *as a party*. It could not be *actor* or *reus*. It could not be used even in equity, for equity, says the maxim, must follow the law. Entangled in this net of their own creating, English chancellors found great difficulty, if not in dealing equitably with the *res* in partnership cases, at least in stating any consistent reasons for their action. It was reserved for this Court, in *Menagh v. Whitwell & al.*, 52 *N. Y.*, *R.*, 146, to solve that difficulty. An argument heretofore presented to this Court, thus speaks on this subject: "In many respects every co-partnership has the most important functions of a corporate existence. *Kaufman's Mackeldey*, § 141, 142.

True, it has not a corporate name by which it may sue; but this is a mere rule of judicial practice. It has a social name by which courts recognize its acts. True, it has no common seal; but many corporations have been created without this function. It is recognized as a distinct person; its creditors are protected by equity; neither partner can lawfully use its name for his own purpose, nor can he lawfully apply its property to the payment of his own debts or to his own use in any way, to the prejudice of its creditors or of his co-partner. Equity endows it with the utmost measure of immortality which any legislature *can bestow* upon the most favored corporation, and a much longer life than is *usually* bestowed upon such bodies. Whilst any property of a copartnership exists, be it in action or in possession, and, either as co-partners or as next of kin of a co-partner, or as creditors, there can be found as many as two persons interested in the disposition of that property, the legal entity created by the original association is regarded as existing, with rights, remedies and liabilities enforceable by judicial process. How enforced, in what form of action, in what name or in what court, we need not inquire. These things are mere form; the substance is the same, whatever form or forms may be appropriated to its development. Paterson's Eng. and Scotch Law, § 639; Bell's Com. by Shaw, 213. Cole *v.* Reynolds, 18 N. Y. R., 77. Review, 25th Vol. of Lond. Jurist Essays, p. 358. Colquhoun's Summary, § 906 to 910."

The puzzle thus disposed of in *Menagh v. Whitwell*, as to private interests, finds its parallel in the way Courts have dealt with the public interests not represented by that magical personality the full, formal corporation. It was questioned at an early period whether regularly organized civil divisions, like counties, as such, were corporations, or even *quasi* corporations, so as to be capable of holding property or as being entitled to sue or as being amenable to suit. The contrary was expressly held in *Russell* vs. *The Men of Devon*, 2 *Term R.*, 672, A.D. 1788. Yet, in that case, it was affirmed that where statutes created a liability or a right in *the inhabitants of a district*, the Courts would devise a remedy by action; and thus, in a certain very limited way, a narrow range of what the Court was pleased to call *corporate* capacity might arise. This idea is enlarged upon and explained in *Ward* vs. *The County of Hartford*, 12 *Conn. R.*, 406, 407. The growth in our country of this "judicial legislation," as our revisors of 1830 termed it, 3 *R. S.*, p. 482, Second Ed., is well summed up in *Angell and Ames on Corporations*, §§ 23 *and* 24, *Eighth Ed.* It is there said that counties, towns, hundreds, school districts, and the like civil divisions, came to be "considered under our institutions as *quasi* corporations, with limited powers co-extensive with the duties imposed upon them by statute or usage; but *restrained from a general use of the authority which belongs to these metaphysical persons*, i. e. (corporate bodies) *by the common law.*" *Levy Court* vs. *Coroner*, 2 *Wallace*, 502, 507.

The judicial annals of this State anterior to the revision of 1830 present apt illustrations of this precise doctrine. *Jackson* vs. *Hartwell*, 8 *Johns*, 425. *Jackson* vs. *Cory, Ib.*, 388.

The mode of suing in these cases, where the Courts had created, as they best could, a limping kind of remedy, was attended with much complexity.

The whole of this jurisprudence arose *ex necessitate rei*. It was based upon the very reasoning found in *Russell* vs. *The Men of Devon*. It stood upon the reason of the thing; its object was to prevent a failure of justice. The Judges never went further than imperious public need. The principle on which they placed their endowment of these divisions of the State with limited corporate powers, is well expressed in *Denton* vs. *Jackson*, 2 *Johns. Chy. R.*, 325. *North Hemp-stead* vs. *Hempstead, Hopk.*, 292.

For the sake of having our views clearly understood, we have endeavored not only to define, but to illustrate, by the most apposite instances or specimens, the juridical person of our law. We have sought to epitomize all the general principles governing in its creation, or recognition, by defining its nature and object in all its infinite varieties. Corporation is the only single word in our language which adequately describes this legal entity ; hence the practice of calling single official person or persons, &c., corporations sole. (6 Viner's Ab., p. 256, Title Corporations, A. 1.) The courts having no other word to describe an impersonal entity, have been obliged to call all that were not corporations, *quasi* corporations—that is, "as if," or near to, or something *like* corporations. In every respect in which we have considered them, they are all, on general principles, alike. Their nature and character are the same. And this brings us to the second stage in this discussion. Before entering upon it, we deem it proper to say here, and once for all, that, so far as any general principles, or general reasoning on principle is concerned, the slightest and least palpable juridical entity created for purposes of political government among those to which we have referred, and which we have endeavored briefly to describe or define, stands on as high a ground as the most perfect municipal corporation. Or, quitting the abstract for the concrete, let us say, if the fourth section, now under review (Laws of 1870, p. 878), had been passed in reference to debts or liabilities of the fully incorporated " Mayor, Aldermen, and Commonalty of the City of New York," instead of the " *County*," and bonds of the City Corporation had been the instruments directed to be employed in raising the money instead of *County* bonds, the right of the State to maintain this action, would not, *upon any general principles that can properly be invoked,* be a whit less perfect than it is. We make this statement to the end that there may be neither misinterpretation nor misapprehension of our doctrines. We shall, to be sure, by and by, show the very limited and narrow range of legitimate power bestowed upon the New York Board of Supervisors, and also examine whether it be, to any and what extent, that familiar entity known as a corporation. But we do not consider either of these inquiries necessary or even relevant. In touching them, we shall act in deference to those who may advance very narrow views upon the subject in hand, and views that we deem palpably erroneous.

We now pass to the distinction between public and private corporations, leaving out of view, as necessarily excluded from our comparisons, that great public corporation—the State.

At a period but slightly remote there could hardly be said to exist practically, and for any judicial purposes, among our European ancestors, any distinction between public and private corporations.

The *public* corporation of antiquity was essentially the same thing as the private corporation and trading firm. Juridically it was not at all distinguishable from a private trading corporation; nor, except in the unsubstantial forms before alluded to, was it distinguishable from a mercantile firm or partnership. The people of a district, usually a commercial town, associated their means, virtually as co-partners, and either usurped an independent existence as an united body, or by compact with the feudal lord of the territory or by charter of incorporation accepted or extorted from him, they gave form to their union. This was the origin of all the municipal corporations known to our ancestors. The geographical district thus became the property of the locally united body; in their own way they exercised absolute control over it, for it was their common property. They distributed the gains and advantages among their own *freemen*, as any partnership or trading corporation might do at this day in our country. This description of interest in the individual freemen of a local district, with guarantees for their preservation, varying in degrees of strength, still exists on the continent of Europe One specimen is well described in a recent publication. See "Swiss Federal Reform," British Quarterly Review, No. CXIV., for April, 1873, pp. 171 to 173 inql. Willcock on Municipal Corporations, pp. 1 to 9, contains several illustrations of this fact with particular reference to the political and judicial annals of England. That author speaks as follows:

"The institution of municipal corporations is said by Dr. Robertson to have conduced more than any other circumstance to the emancipation of Europe from the thraldom of the feudal system. That it did conduce much to this great event cannot be denied ; but the germs of liberty had long been sown, and they had already made some growth, when municipalities were incorporated.

Their establishment was the effect of that spirit of liberty which had gone abroad, and a considerable degree of power and independence already existing in the cities and towns to which charters were granted. They had already become influential and wealthy associations. Their traffic not only brought them riches, but gave them a maritime power not inconsiderable in those times. Their increasing wealth and commerce established among them the burgher watch and ward, and voluntary associations for the protection of property, not efficient at all times against the rapacity of marauding barons, but capable of repelling those bands of outlaws and disciplined robbers, with whose predatory excursions the annals of European history are frequently stained. The dangers to which their property was exposed taught them the necessity, and they soon learned the power of union.

While the barons wére wasting their revenues and retainers in wild wars, and weakening each other in mutual conflicts, the towns were gradually and silently accumulating wealth, population and power. At a very early period of our history they were defended by walls. With Italian merchandise they imported the institutes of Venice and Genoà; and commerce with the Hanse towns, then also in their infancy, introduced a similarity of internal arrangement. The grants of privileges contained in the charters were, in fact, confirmations of privileges already existing.

This sanction gave confidence and firmness to the municipalities, with little loss or concession to the lords. It requires no historical document to convince us that, had they not been already powerful, they would not have been equally favored by the barons and princes, each desiring the assistance of allies in the struggle between prerogative and privilege. The statesmen of those times had little idea of calling new powers into existence; the utmost extent of their policy was to avail themselves of those which they found at hand.

Some towns having attained this power, and given great importance to the princes and barons within whose territories they were established, operated as a strong inducement with other nobles for encouraging similar institutions. The walled towns became gradually more formidable than the royal or baronial castles, until the latter altogether disappeared among the martial nations of Europe.

While the royal or baronial banner was followed only by its feudal retainers, who owed but a temporary and rendered but an unready attendance, the towns, defended by walls and garrisoned by the burghers, assumed a far more formidable attitude than they could have ever presented under a more regular and permanent military establishment; till at length little remained to the lord besides a titular superiority and an inconsiderable tribute, rendered to secure his countenance in the council and the field.

In England many towns were enfranchised and incorporated by the greater barons, and many more by the crown. It appears that at first the right of doing so was in the immediate lord, and not in the king by virtue of his prerogative; for the earliest incorporations by the kings of England were of towns held in demesne, or by tenure *in capite*, and that every great baron who had towns within his barony incorporated them at will. The Earls of Cornwall incorporated many towns: West Love, Truro, Launceston, Liskeard, Bodmin, Lostwithiel, Grampound, and others, with franchises similar to those bestowed by the crown; the Baron of Villa Torta constituted Saltash a corporation; the Earl of Devon incorporated Plympton; John, Earl of Moreton and Lancaster (afterwards king), incorporated Bristol and Lancaster; and John, Duke of Britain and lord of Richmond, bestowed on Richmond a charter of incorporation and privileges.

It does not, indeed, appear that any regular municipal corporations, with exclusive jurisdiction, existed among the Anglo-Saxons. But the division of their judicature into townships and hundreds, under the authority of a class of officers distinct from the nobility, together with the comparative importance to which some towns had arisen at the time the feudal dominion was first imposed, conduced greatly to the early and general establishment of them throughout this nation. The commercial disposition of the Anglo-Saxons, who still composed the bulk of the people, tended to advance the importance of their towns more rapidly than that of towns established in nations of a more military character.

The municipal incorporation of St. Riquier by Louis the Sixth in France, so frequently referred to as the earliest on record, shows only that there were so many important towns so well constituted and established,

that the French monarch, by calling them to his assistance, could soon humble the mightiness of their nobility—the most powerful and turbulent of any feudal
nation. This implies not the infancy of such institutions, but their having advanced to great power, although without any direct legal sanction.

To the early importance of towns and their almost
exclusive possession of commerce, with the assumed
authority of establishing rules for their own government, anterior to charters of freedom, is to be assigned
the origin of those customs, which we call customs
against common right.

About the time of Edward the First the franchise of
returning members to Parliament was conferred upon
a great number of towns, for the most part incorporated. The writs being executed by the bailiff or other
chief officer, attracted them more within the sphere of
regal authority, and they began to assume additional
importance in a political point of view. Soon after the
crown endeavored to strengthen its control over them
by introducing the writ of *quo warranto*, by which the
judges in their *iter* were empowered to inquire by what
warrant all who claimed any franchise in derogation of
the crown maintained their title. This was doubtless
no inefficient weapon in the hands of an active and vigilant monarch. In the eighteenth year of his reign
another statute was made to render them more immediately dependent upon the crown. From that time
applications from towns incorporated by the barons,
for a confirmation of their former, or a grant of
new, charters became more frequent. Hence, as I
apprehend, grew up the doctrine sufficiently
agreeable to the king, and readily enough asserted by the dependent judges of the king's
own court, that no incorporation was valid without
the regal sanction. Certain it is, however, that some
towns neglected this precaution, or having originated
in the prerogative, and deeming it unnecessary, claim

their franchises by prescription at this day. Not that almost all, if not every one of them, have subsequently accepted charters of confirmation, but that their original constitution is not evidenced by any memento of royal or baronial concessions, and doubtless some were self-constituted, assuming the privileges of other towns without grant or authority. From the time they obtained influence in the national council by sending thither their representatives, municipal corporations became daily the subject of more imporant consideration with the Crown, which began to extend its influence over them—at first by encouraging popular elections and the spirit of freedom, for the purpose of strengthening itself against the barons, until, perceiving that to curb one rival it had raised a much more formidable opponent to its tyranny in those very representatives, it began to assume a different policy, and endeavored to procure returns of its own creatures by discouraging popular elections of the municipal magistrates, and raising a sort of burgher aristocracy. It was in the fortieth year of Queen Elizabeth's reign that the Judges, upon the application of the Privy Council, determined that from usage within time of memory a by-law may be presumed restraining to a select body the right of election of the principal corporators, though vested by the ancient constitution in the popular Assembly; and in the twelfth year of the reign of King James the Judges determined that the King could by his charter incorporate the people of a town in the form of select classes and commonalty, and vest in the whole corporation the right of sending representatives to Parliament, *restraining the exercise of that right to the select classes*, and this was the form of all new corporations. (12 Co., 120.) These doctrines, with more consideration of precedent than principle, have been carried into modern decisions to an extreme subversive of our ancient law, and established the opinion that the franchise of electing corporators can be surrendered by the commonalty not only for themselves, but also for their successors."

Notwithstanding the bold presumption upon the ig- norance and incapacity of its opponents in one paper which has been handed to the Court by the defend- ants, we feel at liberty to assert as, at this day and in this State, a truism, that any functionary or entity exer- cising, under the general regulations of the sovereign authority, powers of a public nature for the benefit of the people of the whole State or of any designated portion of it, who fails in duty is judicially corrigible in some form by the State, as sovereign, proceeding on its own motion, and in its own name. By mandamus he may be forced to act, and to act conformably to law. If he is proceeding to misapply funds, or has misap- plied them, he may, by a State action of an equitable nature, be restrained from such misapplication, or forced to reimburse. A large class of cases deter- mined in the Equity Courts of England and Ireland have declared this to be an indisputable principle of English Equity. But they are referred to in the pre- sent connection as illustrating our proposition that the ancient municipal corporation in Britain, as well as on the Continent, was not, except in some rare instances, an instrument of government, organized by the sove- reign for his own convenience in local administration, but was, essentially, like the common private trading corporation of the present day, the representative and agent of the individual members.

When Willcock wrote, such was the condition of most English municipal corporations. In what he calls his "Conclusion," p. 512, whilst admitting that bene- fits had in former times resulted from their existence, he asserted that "long ago they [had] ceased to have any beneficial operation." He adds: "If I may be al- lowed to suggest an alteration it would be *fundamen- tal;* that is, annulling all charters of incorporation and re-incorporating the whole Kingdom in extensive districts, upon the following plan: The Kingdom to be divided into a certain number of municipalities, more or less extensive, according to the populousness of the country," &c. After naming certain good results to flow from this change, he says: "And all the vexatious and tyrannous usages which prevail in corporations might be swept away." But he deprecates the supposal that he could be "visionary enough to imagine that the present will be improved—to fancy that any Parliament will be found willing to relinquish their influence over venal boroughs—that aldermen in the House will be allowed by their constituents to abandon the privileges of ancient cities and towns, however much in restriction of common right, however harassing to the subjects in general." Yet this gentleman's sound and philosophic ideas, borrowed, as they certainly were, from the system actually existing throughout this country, were soon afterwards, to a great extent, adopted. "An Act to provide for the regulation of municipal corporations in England and Wales," was passed September 9, 1835. It is Ch. 76 of 5 and 6 William IV., and is commonly known as the Municipal Reform Act. Grant on Corporations, 341. Grant, at p. 497, speaking of the law and practice prior to this Act, says: "Where a municipal corporation was seized of lands in their corporate capacity [they] annually made regulations respecting the mode of enjoyment of the subordinate right of common upon the lands which *belonged to the burgesses of the corporation*, and the sums to be paid by them for the agistment of their cattle thereon, which money, after deducting the expenses of the management of the lands, &c., *was distributed among the burgesses* who did not turn on cattle." Here we find the burgesses enjoying exactly the advantages from the corporate property which the Swiss Communists are described as enjoying in the article before referred to. Each is a somewhat rude but substantial parallel to the reception of dividends by a shareholder in a trading corporation. But all that was totally changed by the Municipal Reform Act. Its 92d section transferred all property and income to a "borough fund * for the public benefit." Power to enlarge the borough fund, when needed, by a rate or tax, was conferred upon the borough officers, and, as nearly as ancient habits would permit, the various boroughs or municipal districts were placed upon what we cannot but see is the American system of local administration. Grant, at p. 343, says this Act *made* the corporations therein mentioned "*public* corporations."

The series of English and Irish cases in equity, above referred to, explicitly recognize, and, in various forms, assert, certain propositions which are here very relevant, namely :

First. That municipal corporations, existing prior to that Act, were the masters of their own property precisely as any private individual owners were, and could not be judicially questioned touching their administration or management thereof by the crown—*i.e.*, the Executive Government.

Secondly. That, as to grants to them by Parliament for any public purposes, they could be so questioned. And, even though the public purpose was local in its benefits, an individual relator was not necessary but merely expedient in reference to costs to prevent vexation. So says that master of equity practice and pleading, Mitford, Lord Redesdale. Attorney-General, *vs.* Mayor of Dublin, 1 Blighs' P. C., New Series, p. 337, 351.

Thirdly. That after the Municipal Reform Acts *all* the funds and property of these now public corporations were placed in the same category as last described.

Attorney-General *vs.* Mayor of Dublin, 1 Blighs' P. C.,
New Series, p. 355.
Attorney-General *vs.* Aspinall, 1 Keen, 532. Acc. in
same case on appeal, 2 Mylne & Craig, 623.
Attorney-General *vs.* Wilson, 1 Craig & Phillips, 22.

" Before the Municipal Corporations Regulation Act
passed, certainly the Corporation was not subject to
any trust; the corporations might do with it whatever
they chose, and, generally speaking, no relief could be
obtained either at law or in equity for any misapplication of that property. The Municipal Corporations
Act creates a trust," per Lord Campbell, giving the
reasons of the House of Lords in Parr *vs.* The Attorney-
General, 8 Clark & Finelly, 431. In the same case,
and on the same page, Lord Lyndhurst observes:
"We are all of opinion that this is a public trust."
The Attorney-General's suit was sustained. We have
referred to the precise page where the views of the
English Judges can be found. A full review and com-
parison of all the cases and dicta is contained in Mr.
Tilden's Argument. (Paper marked C, pp. 54 to 78.)

In the year 1840, a similar Municipal Reform Act
was passed for Ireland, and in a most able and ex-
haustive opinion of Lord Chancellor Brady, the same
principles as are found in the English cases on the
same subject are distinctly asserted. The Act is 3 and
4 Vic., ch. 108. It corresponded with the English Act.
It is difficult to imagine any more perfect judicial performance than the opinion on it just referred to. Attorney-General *v.* Belfast Corporation, 4 Irish Chancery Reports, pp. 142, 144.

This brings us to our leading and fundame ntal p
osition, which presents the only question of principle
in this case, and we thus enunciate it. Whatever may
have been the proprietary rights of crown patentees in
the early settlement of these colonies, say the Duke of
York, William Penn, Lord Baltimore, or the Rhode
Island Company (7 How. U. S. R., 25), there never

has been, within the United States, since our secession from Great Britain, or, at all events, within the State of New York, any county, town, village, city, or other local district, which was, in judgment of law, anything else than a public civil division of the State's territory, formed or recognized by the sovereign power for pub lic purposes and for the more convenient distribution of the powers of government or administration. And there never was in or assigned to any of these civil divisions, a lawful office or officer, or a corpora-tion, or *quasi* corporation, or other entity, established or recognized for governmental purposes, that was not, in every sense, public and amenable to the sovereign power of the State alone, for the faithful exercise of its powers, including the receipt, keeping and disposition of all funds entrusted to it, or that was, in any sense whatever, the agent, servant, representative or trustee of any individual person, or set or class of persons.

Momentary forgetfulness or a singular blindness can alone account for a non-recognition of this proposition in any part of its whole length and breadth, by an educated American. That simple and uncultivated minds should be without a perception of it, or should actually think otherwise is not singular, for the history of our race is a history of these social aggre-gations; and, in a vague sense, the inhabitants of every city, village and hamlet have, practically, com-mon interests and apparently a common property in many things Besides, the clear and distinct constitu-tional arrangements in which the proposition just enunciated is founded, are of very recent origin.

We proceed to lay before the Court authorities for this view :

The abrogation of everything like the corporate *im-peria in imperio*, existing under royal charters, and every right and power in individuals to govern or control for their own benefit, as incorporated burgesses or otherwise, any public rights or public property was an elementary principle of the American revolution. This none will deny. The people of this State, when adopting the common law, after announcing in terms the great principles of the new government, declared that all parts of the pre-existing law, common or statute, which were "repugnant to that constitution should be, and that they thereby were abrogated and rejected." Article XXXV.

We shall presently go into all the details needful to exhibit the system formally enacted for the State whereby all communal ideas, such as may have previously had acceptance, were practically and completely displaced. But first we will invite attention to judicial recognitions of the great fundamental doctrines in American politico-legal jurisprudence for which we contend.

Statutes and decisions innumerable show it to be a general practice throughout this country to establish by public laws of the Legislature, in each ordinary civil division of the State, an official board for local purposes. Without the employment of such subordinate local agencies, civil government could not be conveniently administered. In some of the States other names have been used; but, with us, these civil divisions are counties, towns, cities and villages. This is the ordinary nomenclature adopted in our written constitutions. By positive enactment, in many cases, these local boards are fully organized corporations. Even when they are not so, the statutes concerning them, the powers conferred upon them, and the duties devolved, create, in judgment of law, a more or less perfectly developed corporate existence. When it is deduced by mere implication these legal entities are, in judicial parlance, denominated *quasi*-corporations. Though various and infinitely diversified in the nature and extent of their authority, it may fairly be assumed that any one of these boards exercising *the* power of local government within its district is, *prima facie*, the visible organ of a corporate existence. Cities are invariably created by a charter containing many grants of power, well known as the characteristics of a municipal corporation. Whether in point of expression the geographical district, its inhabitants, or the local body is denominated a corporation, the results are precisely the same.

Long familiar with these local governments, and constantly subjected to their action at his very door, and affecting his domestic concerns, the citizen has naturally contracted a habit of thought and mode of speech which might seem to indicate that each of them was an independent power in the land instead of being what it really is, a mere official agent of the State.

It has been shown that amongst our European ancestors, most of the chartered municipalities, or districts, were formerly thus regarded. Each was an *imperium in imperio* possessed of rights, powers and privileges guaranteed to it as its own independent property, by the sovereign or feudal lord within whose dominions or territory it was established. This property was enjoyed by its permanent freemen or burgesses for their private, individual benefit. No such local governing corporation ever existed in the United States. (*See paper B, pp.* 47 *to* 53, *and cases cited.*)

The formal point taken by the defendant, and suggested by the demurrer, as an objection to the suit by the State, is founded on these mistaken conceptions and obsolete usages.

Our local governments are mere *agencies* of the State sovereignty. Their official corps are merely officers of the State, appointed for local purposes; and their property, real and personal, both capital and income, constitute portions of the public treasure of the State, placed at a particular point by the will of the State for the convenience of the State. All such property belongs to the State ; and, as a mere question of *power*, it is absolutely subject to the control of the State, an inhabitant of the city, county, town or village, having no more right or title to it or interest in it than any other citizen of the State. The State is the creator, and the Local Government the creature. The latter is dependent upon the will and pleasure of the State, not only for the continuance of its powers and the possession of its property and franchises, but also for its very life and being.

The attempts sometimes made to draw a distinction between the *political* powers of a municipality and its *property*, have always proved vain and futile.

> Rice *v.* Railroad Co., 1 Black's U. S. R., 382.
> Davidson *v.* Mayor, &c., 2 Robertson, 359.

In respect to this question, there is, in truth, no difference in principle, between a county or town and an incorporated city or village. An attorney readily discovers that it is easier to draw up his process for commencing an action against a regular corporation, "*in re facto et nomine*," than it is to sue the legal entity called a *quasi* corporation. In this mere matter of form lies the whole difference : in substance there is none. The attempts occasionally made to raise distinction in this respect, in favor of cities, result from an imperfect consideration of the subject.

> 1 R. S., 384, title 3, first ed. : 1 Ib., p. 901, fifth ed.
> Bailey *v.* Mayor, &c., of N. Y., 3 Hill, p. 539.
> S. C. on Appeal, 2 Denio, 433.

The principles of government brought into practice by the American Revolution completely extirpated these antiquated communal ideas. Communal privileges are wholly unknown in the United States. Nevertheless, just as is now attempted in this case, able counsel, in a noted instance, most intensely and unto the highest court of resort, endeavored to procure their recognition. See *the State of Maryland for the use of Washington County* v. *The Baltimore & Ohio Railroad Company,* 12 *Gill & Johnson, p.* 399. Same case in error, 3 *Howard's U. S. R.,* 534.

The State of Maryland incorporated the railroad company, requiring it to locate part of its road through Washington county, and. on failure, to forfeit $1,000,-000 to the State of Maryland for the use of Washington county. The State subsequently repealed these requisitions and this suit was brought to establish a vested right to the million of dollars in Washington county. Very able arguments of counsel are reported. The following observations of the courts are instructive :

Per CUR., 12 *Gill & Johns.,* 436 : " The money being forfeited to the State as a penalty for the use of *Washington* county, one of the constituent elements of the State, the Legislature had an unquestionable right to remit it. *Washington* county is an integral part of the State, or portion of the body politic, and the money, if received by her, would belong to her as public property in her public political capacity, to be applied exclusively to the public use. As a county, she stands to the State in the relation of a child to a parent, subject in all respects to its jurisdiction and power, as well as entitled to the benefits of its fostering care and protection."

Again, at p. 438 :

" *Washington* county, by which the claim is attempted to be enforced, is one of the public territorial divisions of the State, established for public political purposes, connected with the administration of the government. In that character she would receive the money as public property, to be used for public purposes only, and not for the use of her citizens in their private individual characters and capacities. In that relation they would have no immediate interest, and could assert no title. She is one of the instruments of the government, invested with a local jurisdiction to aid in the administration of public affairs, and may be emphatically termed a part of the State itself."

On the writ of error, 3 How. U. S. R., p. 550, the Court, per TANEY, C. J., says:

"If this money had been received from the railroad company, the commissioners, in their corporate capacity, would not have been entitled to it, and *could neither have received nor disbursed it, nor have directed the uses to which it should be applied, unless the State had seen fit to enlarge their powers and commit the money to their care.* If it was applied to the use of the country, it did not by any means follow that it was to pass through their hands, and *the mode of application would have depended altogether upon the will of the State.* This corporation, therefore, certainly had no private corporate interest in the money, and, indeed, the suit is not entered for their use, but for the use of the county. The claim for the county is equally untenable with that of the commissioners. The several counties are nothing more than certain portions of territory into which the State is divided, for the more convenient exercise of the powers of government. They form together one political body, in which the sovereignty resides."

"In the country (England) from which we derive our ideas on the subject of Municipal Corporations, the charters of cities, as their name (*i. e*, the word charter) implies, were contracts, entered into between the corporators on the one hand, and the king or feudal lord on the other, by which liberties and franchises were bartered for personal services or money. The rights and powers which those charters conferred * were intended to be permanent, and [they] could not be lawfully taken away ; they were, in the true sense of the word, franchises. But the relation existing between our municipal corporations and the sovereign [power] is not the same ; and it is strange that this fact should continue to be so obstinately overlooked by their officers."

"The municipal government" of a city "is a subordinate agency for the purpose of police and good order. The laws * * which establish and regulate municipalities are not contracts. They are ordinary acts of legislation. The powers they confer are no longer franchises in the original meaning of that word ; they are nothing more than mandates ; and these laws may be repealed at pleasure, except so far as their repeal may affect rights acquired by third persons under them. They are all of the same nature, and must be construed and applied in all cases like other laws."

Per Rost, J., in Reynolds v. Baldwin, 1 Louisiana Annual R., 167.

"The corporation of a town is established for public purposes alone, and to administer a part of the sovereign power of the State over a small portion of its territory." * * · * * "The government of cities and towns * * forms one of the subdivisions of the internal administration of the State, and is absolutely under the control of the Legislature." So held by the Court per *Preston, J.*, determining that a State Legislature which had given a profitable ferry franchise to a town, might revoke the gift at pleasure, in

Police Jury of Bossier v. Corp'n of Shreveport, 5 Louis'a Ann'l R., 665.

See People v. Pinckney, 82 N. Y. R., 392 to 396, and cases cited.

The Supreme Court of the United States, to this point speaks as follows:

"A municipal corporation in which is vested some portion of the administration of the government, may be changed at the will of the Legislature. Such is a public corporation used for public purposes."

> State Bank of Ohio *v.* Knoop, 16 How., U. S. R., 380 : Reaffirmed, 18 How., 380 and 384.

"This, as are all such municipal corporations, is dependent on the legislative will for its existence, as well as all power exercised by them, and their corporate powers may be increased or contracted by the Legislature at will."

> Per cur. Robertson *v.* City of Rockford, 21 Illinois R., 458.

"Counties * * are not, strictly speaking, corpora- "tions. Still they are *quasi* corporations. They can "perform many of the functions of proper municipali- "ties. * * But because they cannot legislate, "everything done by the agents of a county must be "first authorized by the legislative power of the "State."

> Kittaning *v.* Brown, 41 Penn., 272.

"A county * * cannot sue or be sued except where "specially permitted by statute."

> Hunsaker *v.* Borden, 5 Cal., 290.

"County court cannot, even as relator, maintain an "action against the collector of the county levy on his "official bond." (*Head note.*)

Per Cur: "We know of no law which authorizes "the county court to maintain the suit. It has no cor- "porate capacity that would give it such right."

Commonwealth v. McFarland, 7 J. J. Marshall, 208.

"At common law, counties have no right to sue, nor "can they be sued. Their right depends on statutory "enactment, and where they sue or are sued, the pro- "visions of the statute must be complied with."

Schuyler Co. v. Mercer Co., 4 Gilman, (Ill.) 20.

A collector sued the county to recover the money which he had paid to the *County Court* for the State.

Per Curiam: "The county * * is liable to him "for nothing. * * The county treasury could not "become the depositee of any funds but those that the "law brings to it. * * Every attribute, duty, lia- "bility and obligation of the corporation of a county "is fixed and defined by law. She is strictly and "technically a creature of law, and by law are her "duties and obligations alone manifested and her lia- "bilities established."

Jefferson Co. v. Ford., 4 Greene, Iowa, 370-1.

An action on a treasurer's bond to the State cannot be brought by county commissioners in their own names, although the bond was intended as an indem- nity against failure to pay over county as well as State taxes.

Per Cur.: " A county may not improperly be called "a *quasi* corporation, for it is in many respects *like* a "corporation. But a county can neither sue or be "sued, except by express power conferred by statute, "and in the manner so expressed. Nor can any of the "officers of a county, by virtue of such office, sue or "be sued, except as provided by statute. It follows, "therefore, that the only power to sue possessed by "the Board of County Commissioners is conferred "upon them by statute."

Judgment for plaintiffs reversed.

Hunter *v.* Commissioners of Mercer Co., 10 Ohio State R., 520.

" The counties are corporations created for the pur- "pose of convenient local municipal government, and "possess only such powers as are conferred upon them "by law. They act by a Board of Commissioners "whose authority is defined by statute. * *

"The statutes defining the powers, both corporate "and judicial, of Boards of County Commissioners, "enumerate the powers given with care ; so that there "is little room for doubt as to the extent of those pow- "ers. * *

" While it is undoubtedly true that municipal cor- "porations, in common with all other instrumentali- "ties of government, are established for the public "good, it is *not* true that they are ordinarily left at "liberty to exercise an unlimited discretion in accom- "plishing that object, or that they are possessed of "that discretion unless there is an express limitation "imposed."

Harney *v.* Indianapolis R. R., 32 Indiana, 246–7.

A fund arising from fines in part payable to local commissioners, is the property of the State, not of the commissioners, and the fine may be remitted by the State.

Per Cur.: "The commissioners acquire no rights
"in the fund, but are to be considered as agents of the
"State. * * *

"If it is, as we believe, a fund which goes to the
"Inferior Court for County purposes, then does it be-
"long to the State, and the Inferior Court are only
"agents of the State to disburse it for the common
"benefit."

Matter of Flournoy, 1 Kelly, 609, 610.

S. P. State v. Williams, 1 Nott & M'C., 28.

"The * * vests the penalty in the Commissioners
"of the Roads. It is not given' to them in their indi-
"vidual capacities, but as agents of the State, and for
"public purposes. The money as much belongs to
"the State as if it had been directed to be paid into
"the public treasury."

State v. Williams, 1 Nott & McCord, 28.

Fines collected in counties in Wisconsin are a part
of the school fund. An action was brought in the
name of the State against a county officer, to recover
the amount of fines collected by him.

Per Cur.: "That the action is properly brought in
"the name of the State, we think there can be no
"doubt. * * * The State, *to whom this money*
"*rightfully belongs*, is the proper party to sue for it
"in the absence of statutory provisions directing the
"suit to be instituted in the name of some officer
"or corporation or citizen.

State v. Casey, 5 Wis., 322.

(In reference to the question whether a police board was a State or a municipal agency),

CAMPBELL, C. J. said : "The only confusion exist-
" ing on this subject has arisen from the custom prev-
" alent under all free governments of localizing all
" matters of public management as far as possible,
" and of making use of local corporate agencies when-
" ever it can be done profitably, not only in local
" government, where it is required by clear constitu-
" tutional provisions, but also for purposes of State.
" Illustrations of this might easily be multiplied.
" The whole system of State taxation, under our
" laws, is made to depend upon the action of town
" and county officers, who make the assessments and
" collect most of the taxes. And the whole machin-
" ery of civil and criminal justice has been so gener-
" ally confided to local agencies, that it is not strange
" that it has sometimes been considered as of local
" concern."

People v. Hurlbut, 24 Mich., 81.

" Where, under several local and public acts, the
" vestry of a parish were constituted the custodians of
" the public ways, and were empowered to take such
" proceedings as they should think expedient against
" any person stopping or impending any public way,
" and had the soil of such ways vested in them,

" *Held*, that they could not sustain a suit by bill
" filed by them as plaintiffs in the ordinary course, but
" must take proceedings, by way of information, in the
" name of the Attorney-General."

ROMILLY, M. R. " It is not intended by those acts,
" or by any clauses to be found in them, to delegate
" to the Commissioners named in the first act, or to the

"vestry, who have now delegated to them the powers
"conferred on those authorities, any powers and au-
"thorities previously vested in the Attorney-General.
" * * * Accordingly, if the vestry indict any one
"under that act, they must proceed in the name of the
"Queen, before a grand jury, who must file a bill be-
"fore it can be tried, and if they take any proceedings
"in the Court of Chancery, it must be in the name of
"the Attorney-General, in an information."

Vestry of Bermondsey v. Brown, 14 Weekly Reporter,
215; S. C. Law Reports, 1 Equity Cases, 204.

It is difficult to conceive what is meant by the argument concerning the county, as a legal entity capable
of suing in the name of its Supervisors, unless the
county, by and through its Board of Supervisors,
represents some class of persons who are, or are to be,
injured by reason of the wrongs alleged, or who might
be benefitted by this money being recovered from the
delinquents.

1. Neither the county, nor any officer of the county,
or any one else, was ever authorized by law to receive
one cent of this money, except for the purpose of paying it over to the holders of the audit-certificates.

2. No gross sum was authorized to be raised in anticipation of audits. The audit was a pre-requisite to
the issuing of a single bond.

3. No one was authorized to pay the debts contracted
by issuing the bonds, with any money, except the
proceeds of specified taxes subsequently to be levied.

4. If by any chance or accident any of the moneys
raised upon the bonds should not pass to the certificate
holders but should remain in any official hands, there
was no legal authority in "the county," the Board of

Supervisors, the Comptroller, or any one else, to make any disposition of it.

Under these circumstances it seems undeniable that, any fund, not applicable or not in fact applied to the payment of the certificate holders, would belong to the State or be a pure waif belonging to the chance-medley holder, unless it would belong to the individual tax-payers, people, or inhabitants of the county. In *Colchester* v. *Law*, *L. R.*, 16 *Equity Cases*, 253, it appeared that a public officer had accumulated considerable interest earned on the funds of individuals which had been deposited with him for their benefit, in his official capacity ; but, owing to certain peculiarities in his administration, there was an utter impossibility of properly apportioning these earnings among the persons entitled, or, indeed, of ascertaining who they were. *Vice-Chancellor Malins* decided that the earnings "belonged to the Crown for the benefit of the public."

In this view of the case, authorities were adduced showing that no city, corporation, county, board or town or village officials represented such individuals or had any right to sue in their behalf. And the manner in which this dilemma is dealt with by the only person who has ever attempted to handle it deserves notice. His answer, after all, is simply a *petitio principii*, an assertion of the very point in dispute. It is "the County's money." Thus speaks Judge Parker's opinion, Paper D, pp. 189, 190.

"It is claimed, on behalf of the plaintiffs, as another reason why it [the County] cannot sue for these moneys, that the county suffers no prejudice from their loss. 'Its debts,' it is said, 'if it had any, were not left unpaid—they were *over*paid.'

"True, the debts which it raised the money on its bonds, to pay, were paid and overpaid, but the money with which it paid them, before it was appropriated for that purpose, was *its* money, and the overplus has not ceased to belong to it.

"Again, it is said, 'its corporate treasury, if it has one, is not to suffer any detriment. The State, by its taxing power, has forced, or is to force, the payment of the bonds by the taxpayers,' and hence it is concluded that the *taxpayers*, whoever they may happen to be when the tax is levied and collected, alone are to suffer, and of those taxpayers ; the county is not the *curator*, and has no authority to bring suit to preserve or vindicate their rights. To this, the answer just made to the last proposition of plaintiff's counsel is sufficient. This suit is not brought to preserve or vindicate the rights of taxpayers, the money for the fraudulent obtaining of which from the county treasury the suit is brought, was the county's money, and the circumstances that the ultimate sufferers are the persons who shall be the taxpayers when the money shall be raised by tax to pay the bonds, is *immaterial*, and whether *they* can be represented by the corporation is *immaterial*. Defendants have possessed themselves of the money of the county, and it comes back to the same result—the county must sue for it in the manner provided by law.

"The authorities cited to show that municipal corporations have no standing in Court to protect or vindicate the individual rights of their taxpayers or inhabitants have no applicability ; and the idea upon which they are supposed to be applicable, that it is the persons who are eventually to pay the tax, by which the money, to make up the loss of the money in question is to be raised, who are the sufferers by such loss, and who are to be represented in any suit to recover back the money taken, is a mistaken one. Such ultimate and indefinite interest creates no cause of action, and such persons are not, in any respect, to be represented in the action to recover back the money."

Although the learned Judge takes this short cut, we find that in every instance, and many have occurred, where a local governing body ever undertook to remedy by judicial action in its own name a wrong to the vicinage, it went upon the idea of representing the people, the inhabitants or the taxpayers thereof.

That any such right to represent the injured people, &c., exists, has uniformly been denied by the Courts.

Local governing bodies may, like all other corporations, defend actions brought against them, and prosecute actions for the defence of their corporate or official property or rights; but they do not, in any general legal sense, represent the local population, or the local taxpayers, past, present, or to come. Nor is it their duty, nor have they any authority, to institute suits or proceedings to preserve or vindicate any public or private right of such persons. There is ample authority for this proposition.

Guilford vs. *the Supervisors of Chenago*, 3 *Kernan*, 147, was an action *by a town* to restrain the Supervisors from levying and collecting a tax from the taxpayers of the town. DENIO, J., says: "The proceeding which the plaintiff seeks to restrain is not aimed at and cannot affect the corporate rights or the corporate property of the town. It claims a contribution from the tax-payers and out of the taxable property in the town; and, for that purpose, it employs the instrumentality of certain town officers. It does not appear to me that the town, as a corporate body, can have a standing in Court to vindicate the individual rights of the tax-payers." (*Acc.* 18 *Barb.*, 636, 637.) *Acc.* 36 *Indiana R.*, 175.

The Corporation of the City of Georgetown vs. *The Alexandria Canal Co.*, 12 *Peters, U. S. R.*, 91, 99, was a bill in equity to restrain an alleged injury to the whole body of the citizens of Georgetown by obstructions in the River Potomac. The suit was dismissed. The Supreme Court, in assigning its reasons, speaks as follows : " The plaintiffs profess to come into Court for themselves, and for the citizens of Georgetown. Now, it is not even pretended that, in their character of a corporation only, they have any power or authority given to them by their charter, to take care of, protect, and vindicate, and in a court of justice, the rights of the citizens of the town, in the enjoyment of their property, or. in removing or preventing any annoyance to it. Nor does such a power attach to them in their corporate character, upon any principle of the law in relation to corporations."   *   *   *   *   *

They " seem to have proceeded on the idea, that it appertained to them, as the corporate authority in Georgetown, to take care of and protect the interest of the citizens. In this idea we think they were in error. *   * They cannot, upon any principle of law, be recognized as parties competent, in Court, to represent the interests of the citizens of Georgetown. Nor is the difficulty obviated by associating with them the citizens of Georgetown, as the persons in whose behalf they sue. *   * In this case, it has been already said, that the appellants [the corporate body] have no such interest as enables them to sue in their own name ; and *   * if the citizens of Georgetown were even parties on the record, the objections would equally lie against them."

In Ohio, the boards charged with like duties as those devolved on Supervisors in our rural counties, are called the County Commissioners. One of these boards undertook to be relators in. a mandamus to compel a turnpike company to repair, according to its duty, a bridge upon its road within the county. The court dismissed the action on the express ground that the County Commissioners had no interest. *State ex. rel. Commissioners of Ross County* v. *The Zanesville and Maysville Turnpike Co.*, 16 *Ohio State Reports*, 320. BRINCKERHOFF, J., delivering the unanimous opinion of the Court, thus expressed his views: "Have the relators any such beneficial interest in the performance of the alleged corporate duty as entitles them to prosecute this writ?　　＊　　＊

The Relators are a Board of County Commissioners, and in that character alone they appear in this proceeding. As a board they are an administrative body, and a *quasi*-corporation, with certain limited powers and duties defined by law. As individuals, the members of this Board may have an interest in common with all other persons domiciled in the State, in the repair of this bridge ; but as a Board of Commissioners, what interest have they? We are unable to find any."

————

"The Code makes it the duty of certain officers to "cause bridges to be built, and the public roads to be "kept in order, but this is a duty cast not upon the "county, the corporation, but upon certain public offi- "cers. And these officers are not the officers of the "'corporation.' They are officers of the State, pro- "vided for in the constitution, commissioned by the "Governor, and not at all under the control of the "county, or of the citizens of the county. ＊ ＊ The "law does not cast the duty upon the county, but "upon the officers, and they are officers of the *State*, "although it may be that their duties are confined to "the county."

Scales v. The Ordinary, &c., 41 Georgia, 227-8.

The charter of the City of Carrollton gave its Mayor, &c., power to sue, and imposed on its Mayor the duty of superintending its police. An act was afterwards passed embracing the city within the Metropolitan Police District, and conferring on the defendants, the Metropolitan Police Board thereby created, the power of controlling the police within that city and others.

The Mayor and council having enjoined the Board, the injunction was dissolved, and, on appeal, the Mayor, &c., contended that the latter act violated the constitutional provisions protecting the right of the people to be secure in their property, and to be free from unusual penalties and unjust taxation, &c.

Per Cur. : " Assuming that some of its provisions " do conflict with the constitution, does the act violate " any of the constitutional rights *of the plaintiffs ?* " Does it impose a tax *on the corporation*, infringe " upon *their* rights of property, or authorize the ex- " ercise of judicial powers by said board toward *them?*

" If the act subjects *the people* of Carrollton to un- " just taxation, and the strange and unusual punish- " ment complained of, *they* have a remedy through the " Courts by which to avert the infringement of their " constitutional rights. In all these matters the cor- " poration of Carrollton, in the opinion of the Court, " is without interest; *it* is not affected by any of the " provisions of the act which they say violate the ar- " ticles of the Constitution of the State and of the " United States."

"The Court cannot entertain abstract questions of " law presented by parties without interest, and wholly " unaffected by the illegalities and unconstitutionali- " ties complained of." Judgment affirmed.

Mayor, &c., of Carrollton v. Board of Metropolitan
Police, 21 Louisiana Annual R., 449.

"I agree with Mr. Justice Oakley in his opinion in
"the Superior Court, that * * 'the corporation, as a
"'body politic, possesses property, and also certain
"'corporate rights and powers in which all the citi-
"'zens have a common interest. But it does not in
"'any sense *represent the individual and private
"'property of the citizen*, and a measure intended to
"'protect or to save such private and individual
"'property cannot be said to confer a benefit upon the
"'city as a body corporate.' "

Bronson, J., Russell v. Mayor of N. Y., 2 Denio, 464.

An act *qui tam* authorized to be prosecuted by any
inhabitant of a town, one-third of the penalty recovered to be for the complainant and the rest for the
town, cannot be brought by a committee of the town in
their own names for the use of the town.

Per Cur.: "The inhabitants themselves, as a mu-
"nicipal body, could not maintain an action, neither
"can their committee professedly acting as such. * *
"The verdict must be set aside, therefore, and the
"plaintiffs be non-suited."

Vinton v. Welsh, 9 Pick., 91.

A town sued by its contractors for work on a bridge,
set up, as a counter-claim, damages to its inhabitants,
by reason of the contractors' delay, whereby some of
the inhabitants were compelled to pass over an adjoin-
ing toll-bridge.

Per Cur.: "Could the defendants sustain an action,
"in their corporate capacity, against the plaintiffs for
"the injury thus sustained by their citizens? If they
"could, the damages would go into the treasury of the
"town, and the judgment would be a bar to the

" claims of those citizens, if any claims exist. If they
" could, it is not easy to see why the defendants might
" not sustain an action for any debt belonging to any
" citizen, or, if sued, set off such debt if owed by the
" plaintiff, and the action would admit of such defence.
" Such proceedings are unheard of in courts of justice.
" * * On the whole, we are satisfied that the defend-
" ants have no right to reduce the plaintiffs' claim by
" the damages their citizens have sustained."

Kinne *v.* Town of New Haven, 32 Conn., 214.

" Another question which arises is, whether the
" plaintiffs are entitled to maintain a bill in this case.
" They have no greater rights, in this respect, than
" any individual owner of property affected in like
" manner by the bridge. The corporation claims to
" represent and protect the rights of the inhabitants of
" the town who are owners of property affected by the
" bridge; but the corporation cannot vindicate any
" such rights unless it be in some case where a corpor-
" ate duty exists. Perhaps the town might be heard
" in its corporate capacity, where the health of the
" community was endangered by a nuisance, or where
" they might otherwise be subjected to expense by
" reason of pauperism, and in any other case involving
" corporate responsibility. But nothing of that char-
" acter appears in this case, and the town cannot main-
" tain the bill on the ground that individual inhabitants
" are affected in their private interests."

Dover *v.* Portsmouth Bridge, 17 New Hampshire's
Reports, 214, 215.

" Most of the reasons on which the learned counsel
who appears in behalf of the county rely to resist the
confirmation of the report, are based on grounds of objection which do not affect in any degree the rights or

.interests of the county, but relate solely to the operation and effect of the act of legislation in establishing the turnpike as a common highway on the rights of abutters owning land over or through which the turnpike was originally laid out, and on the pecuniary interests of the several towns on which the burden of supporting the road as a highway is imposed. But this class of objections is not open to the County of Norfolk. * * *

"So far as the rights of other parties are involved in this proceeding, the County of Norfolk must be deemed a stranger to it. The validity of the act can be called in question only by those having a direct interest in the rights supposed to be injuriously affected by its provisions, and no one can interpose to ask for the interference of this Court to declare the act void or to prevent its full operation, except so far as may be necessary to support and protect their own property or rights from unauthorized injury or invasion."

Hingham and Quincy Bridge and Turnpike Corporation vs. County of Norfolk and others. 6 Allen's Rep., 356–357.

A new county (Grant) was formed out of an old one (Delaware). Delaware's officers collected and paid into its treasury, State and other taxes, within the new county, and the new county sued the old to recover the amount as having been illegally collected.

Per CURIAM: "It is clear that Grant County had no "claim whatever to this money. It was not assessed "or collected for the benefit of that county nor under "its authority. If the money was illegally collected, "it is the individuals from whom it was collected that "are injured, not the County of Grant."

Board of Com. of Grant vs. Board of Com. of Delaware, 4 Blackford (Indiana) R., 256.

"County commissioners are not agents or represen-
"tatives of the county in any such sense or manner as
"to render the people of the county justly answerable
"for their neglect. * * Such liability cannot be de-
"rived from the relations of the parties, either on the
"principles or the precedents of the common law."

Hamilton Co. vs. Mighels, 7 Ohio State, 109, 121, 124.

One of the forms in which this notion of a *communal
right* in the inhabitants or people of one of our common civil divisions has exhibited itself, and led to
much mischievous and vexatious litigation, is the notion that an action might be maintained by a tax-
payer on behalf of himself and his fellows, to redress
or prevent some mal-administration specially affecting
the county, town, city or village.

The history of this conflict in the Courts below is
given in *Wetmore* v. *Story*, 22 *Barb.*, 447 *to* 451. At
last, however, it was conclusively determined in this
Court that no such action could be maintained.

As it respects counties, this was expressly ruled in
Doolittle v. *Supervisors of Broome County*, 18 *N. Y. R.*,
67; as it respects incorporated cities, it was expressly
ruled in *Roosevelt* v. *Draper.* 23 *N. Y. R.*, 324; and
as it respects towns by the General Term of the Fourth
Department, in *Ayres* v. *Lawrence*, 63 *Barbour*, pp.
457 to 461, *Talcott, J.*, delivering the opinion. *Acc.
Sup. Court, U. S.*, 12 *Peters*, 100. *See also* 36 *Indiana R.*, 175.

Nevertheless, this notion of a right in the local inhabitants has been, and virtually is relied upon and
urged against the State in this very case.

Judge Balcom, in People *v.* Clark, 53 Barb., 177,
held that the individual tax-payers were the proper

plaintiffs. It also clearly appears that Judge Mullin entertained, and strongly expressed the same opinion in 2 Lansing, p. 397, and re-affirmed it, when it was quite irrelevant, in the *People* vs. *Albany and Susquehanna R. R. Co.*, 5 *Lansing*, 26. This latter case has been recently reviewed in the Commission of Appeals.

In fact, it was on the strength of these opinions that Judge Hardin allowed the demurrer of Ingersoll. *See* his *reasons*, case, fol. 169, *Division IV.*

The leading authority, and that mainly relied upon, was *People* v. *Miner*, 2 Lansing, p. 396. No such case was ever before the General Term, or decided by it. The Judges who held that term have been requested to certify the fact. Their respective statements are in the Attorney-General's possession, and are as follows:

SYRACUSE, May 16, 1873.

CHAS. O'CONOR, *Esq.*,

DEAR SIR : In relation to the report of the case of *The People* v. *Miner*, in 2 Lansing, 396, we would say that the appeal mentioned in the reporter's statement of facts, never came before the General Term for review or decision. We understood that the appeal was settled, and the bonds issued by consent of the parties.

There were, however, two suits commenced before that appeal was settled, one in favor of *Knox, Taxpayer*, v. *Miner*, and another in favor of *The People* v. *Miner*, in which *ex parte* orders of injunction were granted ; and, on motion to the Special Term, both were vacated. Appeals were taken from these orders of *vacation*, and came on to be heard together at the October General Term, 1868. Both orders were affirmed at the January General Term, 1869, upon grounds not involving the right of the Attorney General to institute such an action, in which all the Justices concurred,

The case of *Knox* v. *Miner*, mentioned in Justice Mullin's opinion, p. 397, was argued in connection with the case of *The People* v. *Miner*, and decided at the same time, as before stated.

The opinion of Mr. Justice Mullin was not concurred in by either of us ; on the contrary, we were both of opinion that the Attorney-General could institute such an action ; but the point was not decided, as we all concurred in affirming the orders appealed from on other grounds.

Very respectfully yours, &c.,

LE ROY MORGAN,
HENRY A. FOSTER.

P. S.—I will say, for myself, that in the case of *Knox* (tax-payer) v. *Miner*, I came to the conclusion that he could not maintain the action ; and in the case of *The People* v. *Miner*, the order of injunction having been granted by the Justice *ex parte* on affidavits, *without a complaint*, I came to the conclusion that it was unauthorized ; and upon that ground concurred in affirming the order of the Special Term which vacated it. Mr. Justice Foster can speak for himself.

L. R. M.

In *Knox* (tax-payer) v. *Miner*, I wrote an opinion, concluding that a tax-payer could not maintain such an action. And the case of *The People* v. *Miner*, my conclusions are stated in the foregoing letter.

HENRY A. FOSTER.

WATERTOWN, May 13, 1873.

C. O'CONOR, ESQ.

Dear Sir: The book containing the entry of the Case of The People *vs.* Miner is in the hands of Mr. Barbour,

the reporter, and I was therefore obliged to write to
him to get a copy of it. I have just received his reply, by which it appears that the appeal heard in the
General Term of the 5th District was from an order
made at Special Term dissolving an injunction. The
order was affirmed by the General Term with $10
costs.

How it came to be called in the Report of the case
in Lansing a judgment, I do not know. Possibly an
inadvertent slip of my own in writing judgment instead of order.

Yours truly,

J. MULLIN.

It will hence be seen that the asserted General Term
decision, reported in 2d Lansing, is a fiction. Supposing it to be a judgment, the Supreme Court of Missouri reviewed and repudiated it. See 51 Missouri Rep.,
350. *State* vs. *Saline Co. Court*, especially p. 367.

Two of the three Judges who sat when People *v.*
Miner is supposed to have been decided were actually
of opinion that the State could sustain such an
action, and that the tax-payers could not.

Nor does it appear that the other Judges in the subsequent case in 5th Lansing entertained Judge Mullin's
opinion on this question.

His opinion rested entirely on the completely and
authoritatively exploded assumption that the individual tax-payers are the proper plaintiffs.

"If one tax-payer cannot be heard to complain under
"such circumstances, neither will all of them com-
"bined, nor the *corporate authorities representing*
"*them*, be permitted to make such complaint."

City of Richmond v. Richmond & Danville R, 21
Grattan, 617.

We thus find that in both of its aspects, this notion of a local right, in the nature of the communal or burgher interest, is repudiated in our American law.

It has been repeatedly held that the Attorney-General may prosecute, on behalf of the Government, to prevent or redress wrongs affecting the people generally, or particular classes, as, for instance, the inhabitants of a particular district, be it city, county, town or village.

Davis *vs.* The Mayor, &c., of N. York, 14 N. Y. R., 526.
Davis *vs.* The Mayor, 2 Duer, 663.
Atty. Gen. *vs.* Eastlake, 11 Hare, 223.

A denial of this right in the State would render every corporate body charged with the government of a local district, as a city or county, perfectly irresponsible for any frauds upon the public committed by its officers or with their consent. The notion that the tax-payers, or any number of them, might maintain an action, though once entertained to some extent, has been completely exploded. And its twin sister of communal birth, now before the Court, on which this defense is founded, must share its fate.

The notion that the *County*, in and through the Board of Supervisors, is the general legal representative of all public or common interests of the County's inhabitants, or tax-payers resident or non-resident, past, present and future, so that acts of fraud and rapine subjecting these classes to excessive taxation or exposing them to the danger of it, cannot be judicially restrained or redressed, except through the medium of an action brought by "The Board of Supervisors of the County," has no color of support in law or reason.

The argument for the defendants might have some force if such a duty or charge had been devolved by law elsewhere than on the State itself; but to prove *this* devolution there never has been even *an attempt* by any judge or lawyer. Neither the argument of Mr. Curtis in the paper marked A, and erroneously styled an opinion, nor the opinion of Judge Parker in the paper marked D, pp. 176 to 194, contain any such attempt. They both build upon the same frail foundation,—the assumption of an individual interest in something called the County. The question propounded to Mr. Curtis by the New York Law Department was simply whether an action for damages would "lie in the name of the City and County of New York respectively, against any officer * * who * * has been instrumental in the unlawful abstraction of public money *belonging to the City or County.*" (Paper A, p. 1.) A careful perusal of Mr. Curtis's argument has not enabled counsel to detect a word indicating that the writer of it went behind this assumption. Pages 6, 10, 11, 26 contain abundant evidence that it was implicitly accepted. Exactly the like assumption pervades the entire opinion of Judge Parker.

It will readily be seen how much this assumption involves. Independently of any question as to there being a corporation or *quasi* corporation or not, it supposes that, as a legal entity having, on general principles, by its very nature and constitution, like an individual, rights, privileges, property, &c., there exists such a thing as *the County*. Whenever the counsel for the defendants, or those who espouse their cause, resort to reason, principle, or any abstract conception apart from express enactment, they tacitly assume that there is such a juridical or moral person.

The fact is not positively asserted, but is quietly assumed. This is prudent, for it relieves the defendants from showing the persons, whereof, aside from its official organs, this supposed juridical or moral entity, called the County, consists. Any such attempt would make manifest the inanity of the proposition.

No one could pretend that this being, called the County, was composed of the physical subject, that is, the land lying within its prescribed boundaries. Neither could it possibly be composed of the chattels therein, nor of both the lands and personal property. Mere inanimate things have no moral, political, governmental or social rights. Persons must be resorted to, as furnishing the constituent elements. What persons, then, could be pronounced the members or constituent elements of this moral or juridical being? Is he who may be passing through the County at the rate of forty miles an hour, as a babe in his mother's arms, a part of the County? Or does stopping for a few minutes to dine at a hotel within it constitute the diner a member? If residence or dwelling therein for a term of greater duration be pronounced requisite, will the incurable pauper inmate of a hospital, or the convict for life in a State prison, be constituent members. (Const., Art. 2, § 3.) Inhabitants of the County, people of the County, are phrases which figure through the arguments of and for the defendants. Sometimes tax-payers of the County is the term used. A politician would say electors of the County. All these classes cannot be included; many tax-payers are not inhabitants of the County, but actually dwell in another; all the inhabitants or people are not electors—some are women, some are infants, and some are aliens. In fact, these persons are not constituent elements of that entity which, whether corporate or incorporate, is known in our civil organization as a County. The people or inhabitants do not constitute the County, even in the sense in which the uncounted millions of globules which roll within its valley form our mighty Hudson. Though perpetually changing, these globules do indeed form the river; but the fluctuating populace of its territory do not, in any legal sense, form the County. If they were entirely swept away by a pestilence or by some convulsion of nature, the County would remain, and be still fully and uninterruptedly existent. It would, to be sure, have no Board of Supervisors, but that at worst would be merely an inconvenience ; perhaps it might be an advantage. The body could be supplied as soon as needed. But although the County consists not of inhabitants, taxpayers, electors or any other class of persons, and might exist in contemplation of law, after all these had become extinct, it is not to be regarded as merely a geographical term. The County, in legal intendment, is precisely as the State is, a moral entity recognized by law for special governmental purposes, and not resolvable by any known process into any anterior elements. The County differs from the State only in being a part instead of the whole. The former is a civil division of the latter—a juridical entity discernable to judicial eyes as existing independently of persons or things for certain purposes designated and declared by law. This being true, the defendants must fail unless they can show by general reasoning founded on a just view of our governmental system, that whoever works such a mischief as is arraigned in this case is responsible, not to the State, but to that part of it, or that by some special law this *fruit* of vicious administration, to wit, the claim against these depredators, as a chose in action, has been put in charge of the Board of Supervisors, as a governmental agency, to be collected by it for some purpose legally delegated to it. That has not been shown, and it cannot be shown. The six millions, if recovered by a County board or officer, would remain in its or his hands totally inapplicable, in any legal way, to any purpose whatever.

The County is a civil division of the State for certain defined purposes ; a city, a village, a ward, a town, an assembly district, a senate district, a judicial district, or a congressional district, is in like manner a civil division of the State for other defined purposes. None of them are distinct, independent interests, like a trading company or corporation : none of them have, on principle, any distinctive interests, as the representative of a class or of any individuals. They are to the State as parts of the human frame are to the whole.

These general views are of universal recognition wherever impartial intelligence presides, and they are fatal to the defense.

C.

A precise view of the method of local administration adopted in this State may be useful. To that end it should be closely examined.

Counties and towns constituted the general system. Each had a local governing corps of officials. The town had its supervisor, assessor, collector, treasurer, and certain other officers not necessary to be noted in this connection. The town, as to its legislative government, was a pure democracy. The town meeting was its constituent assembly. Its few and limited powers may be perceived by the enumeration in 1 R. S., 340, § 5, First Ed. The county, as the larger local division, had its legislative assembly consisting of the town supervisors. (*Ib.* p. 366, § 1, First Ed.) The county board appointed its own chairman, clerk and treasurer. (1 R. S., 114, § 13, First Ed. *Ib.* 366, §§ 7, 9.) This common council of the county itself had but a limited range of authority. (*Ib.* p. 366, § 4.) These references to the Revised Statutes will furnish an adequate illustration of the system for the present purpose. It can be traced back in the laws to the colonial period.

Cities were specially constituted, and with arrangements much more complex than those of the towns and counties. Each had a constitution made specially for itself; but, with the single exception of New York, they were, like towns, *portions* of the county, and stood in the same relation to the board of supervisors or general council of the county that the towns did. They were represented therein by their supervisors. (1 R. S., 366, § 1, First Ed.) At the period of our history to which we are referring in this exhibit of the system, they were few in number. (See List of Cities, 3 R. S., 547, First Ed.) At the revision in 1813 there were but four New York, Hudson, Albany and Schenectady ; but three of these required to be, or were, represented in any board of supervisors. But one had been added (Troy) at the revision of 1830. A slight glance at precedent legislation will show the way in which these, except New York, were represented in a county board of supervisors.

The State always collected its taxes through the town and county officers ; and acts in relation to the assessment and collection of taxes, elections, summoning of jurors, jails, court-houses, prosecutions of criminals, including payment of district attorney, etc., were usually in a general form, and charged these duties to a limited extent on town officers, the great mass devolving on what were called county officers. The counties held the titles to the jails, court-houses, clerks' offices, etc. This will suffice to show the general system of local government and administration.

"The City and County of New York," as it is called in the first Constitution, Article IV., always constituted one distinct civil division of the State ; but it formed from the beginning a marked and, indeed, a necessary exception to the plan or method of local government by a Board of Supervisors. This geographical district has been called by statutes indifferently the County of New York, the City and County of New York, and the City of New York. It had a chartered municipal corporation exercising the powers of local government over its whole territory from provincial times. There never was, in fact, any county distinct from the city. It is divided into wards, and never had within it any town or like civil division.

3 R. S., p. 2, subd. 5, and p. 121, § 1, First Edition.
See Kent's Charter, § 2, pp. 64 to 66.
See Colonial Act confirming same, passed October 14, 1732. Kent's Charter, p. 161.

⎧By the ancient Dougan and Montgomerie Charter a long list of royalties were granted, together with the fee simple in "all the waste, vacant, unpatented and unappropriated lands lying and being within the said city." *Kent's Charter, pp.* 16, 17.

In terms the most intensely sweeping that any conveyancer could have devised, the Charter also conferred upon the City Corporation all the powers of local government.⎫ In every subsequent Act of the Legislature, designed as a *new* charter or as a reorganization, this ancient Charter is excepted out of the usual repealing clause. *Laws of* 1857, *p.* 895, § 54. The last of these is the reorganizing *Act of* 1873, *page* 522, § 119.

How New York came to have Supervisors.

The system of local government in towns by the election of a Supervisor, Assessor, Collector, &c., in each town, and in counties through a Board composed of these town Supervisors, that aptly enough in this connection might be called the Common Council of the County, existed in this Colony and State from the earliest period. A County Treasurer was part of the arrangement. (See *Const'n of* 1777, § 29. 1 *Jones & Varick's Laws, p.* 343, § 5.)

The State taxes were collected in the counties through these officers, the Supervisors being required to levy the tax; the County Treasurer being required to pay the County's quota to the State Treasurer. (2 *Jones & Varick's Laws, p.* 343.) But, of course, this arrangement did not in terms include the City of New York, because it had no *town* Assessor or Collector, no Supervisors and no County Treasurer. This mere distinction in *names* rendered a separate Act necessary. And the duty of raising the State taxes as well as all the other taxes within the City and County was by such a distinct Act imposed upon the Mayor, Recorder and Aldermen, as such, but without denominating them a Board of Supervisors. The duties of assess-

ing and collecting were imposed upon the Ward
Assessors and Collectors, and the duty of paying over
the City and County's quota to the State Treasurer
was imposed on the *Chamberlain* or City Treasurer.
(See this Act, 2, *Jones & Varick's Laws, p.* 347.) This
was the renewal in substance of a previous Act which
was precisely like it in the particulars referred to.
Evidently it was discovered by those who drew up the
State Tax Laws, that an amendment of the legislative
nomenclature in respect to the City and County of New
York would make applicable to New York the General
State Tax Laws, thus avoiding double legislation or
repetitious explanatory circumlocutions in each Gene-
ral Tax Act. So, in 1787, there was passed "An Act for
the more easy assessment and collection of taxes in the
City and County of New York," which accomplished
the object. It may be found in 2 Jones & Varick's
Laws, 125, and the New York Supervisors' proceedings,
Vol. 1. *p.* 6. The Third Section is in these words:

"That the Mayor, Recorder, and Aldermen for the
time being, of the City of New York, or the major part
of them, of whom the Mayor or Recorder are always to
be one, shall be, and hereby are declared to be the *Supervisors* of the City and County of New York, and
shall be so considered in all laws already made, and
hereafter to be made, except in such cases where in
and by this Act, or any other of the laws aforesaid, it
is or hereafter shall be otherwise expressly directed."

Messrs. Jones and Varick, the revisors of 1788, failed
to avail themselves of this Nomenclature Act, as it may
be called; but their successors employed it.

See 2 Kent & Rad. R. L. of 1801, p. 144, §§ 1 and 2.
2 R. L. of 1813, p. 399, §§ 151, 152.

Section 151 of the latter Act expressly provides that
"in respect to all moneys to be levied and collected
in said City for the use of this State" the Chamberlain
shall perform the like duties as "County Treasurers;"

and by Section 152, ALL other moneys coming to his hands are directed to "be paid by him to such persons and in such manner as the Mayor, Alderman and Commonalty of the said City in Common Council convened * * shall from time to time direct." In these sections there is no mention of any County expenses or County fund. Indeed, the existence of any such expenses or fund is impliedly negatived.

The earliest organic act instituting and regulating the County Boards of Supervisors, printed in Jones and Varick's Revised Laws of 1788, vol. 2, p. 346, provides, in § 12, "that this Act shall not extend to the City and County of New York." In the revisions of 1801 and 1813, this exclusion of New York from the scheme of local government by Supervisors adopted for the rural counties, is not thus a separate section. But, in both, it is interposed as an exception in the section creating the County boards. The words are, "the Supervisors of the several cities and towns in this State, other than the City and County of New York." (1 Kent and Radcliff's R. L. of 1801, p. 558, § 1–2; 2 Van Ness and Woodworth's R. L. of 1813, p. 137, § 1.) This course of legislation was in admirable consistency with the sound conservatism of the common law. Ever studious of public convenience and hostile alike to uncertainty and to all practices which tend to a confusion of rights or duties, it holds as a rule that "there cannot be, at the same time, two Corporations in the same place, having the same or *similar* powers, privileges, and jurisdictions."

> Willcock on Municipal Corporations, § 16.
> Rex *vs.* Amery, 2 Term Rep., 569.
> King *vs.* Pasmore, 3 T. R., 240.

The inconvenience of such a thing is well portrayed by a learned Judge in 2 Robertson's N. Y. Supr. C. Rep., 255 to 257. Of course this rule does not prove that the supreme legislative power *could not* create two jostling governmental corporations within and completely covering the same territorial limits : but, appealing to judicial wisdom, it demands the rejection of any supposal that so inconvenient and unwise a thing could ever have been intended, unless there can be found clear expressions to that effect, or an implication so necessary as to be irresistible. No latitude of construction can be admitted in its favor.

We have shown that as late as 1813 our law-givers had no notion of erecting any such second governmental organization in the sphere already occupied and completely filled up by the City corporation with its complete official corps. If there shall appear any thing imperfect, dubious, or equivocal in the subsequent legislation on which a pretense of this kind has been founded, the Court will reject the pretense. Such an idea was not broached until a period forty years later ; the revisors of 1830 had no conception of it.

The chartered City of New York had from the beginning, as we have seen, an imperial status. Like the State itself, in other portions of our territory, her corporation owned all lands lying within her territorial limits not granted to private persons. This ownership extended four hundred feet into the bed of the navigable waters, from (say) the foot of Grand street, on the East River, to the foot of Canal street on the Hudson. Subsequent Acts of the Legislature were passed, from time to time, extending this riparian right, in favor of the City Corporation, further outwards, and all around Manhattan Island, subject only to the courtesy of a pre-emption unto adjacent proprietors, such as is ordinarily accorded by the sovereign power. All jails, court-houses and public edifices, of every description, belonged to the City Corporation ; all the ordinary and incidental powers of the local government were vested in that Corporation, and all expenses connected with the local government were defrayed by it out of its corporate treasury.

With the single exception of not having a Board of Supervisors, the City Charter, from the very first, embraced all the official machinery needful for the local services necessary to the State administration. It had no *towns*, but it had wards ; these wards had no supervisor, but each of them had an alderman ; and, like the towns, each ward had assessors and a collector. To make this machinery fit all State purposes, it was only needed that these aldermen should be denominated supervisors, and that was done by the Act of 1787. The Mayor and Recorder being old charter officers of high grade, and generally of superior capacity, were included. The assistants, the schepens of more ancient times, were left out ; and that single circumstance, in addition to the new name of supervisors, constituted the only difference between the Common Council of the Charter and the Board of Supervisors created by the Nomenclature Statute. The main duty that at first devolved upon this Board of Supervisors was to fill up the fifth column in the tax rolls prepared by the ward assessors, with the amount of each tax-payer's quota, and to deliver each roll to the proper ward collector, with their warrant annexed, authorizing him to collect the tax. (1 R. S., p. 395, §§ 33, 37.) These acts constitute what is meant by all statutes directing a board of supervisors to levy money or to cause it to be levied or raised by taxation.

It will be seen that this New York Board of Supervisors was merely a tax-levying commission, and not a board, body, or corporation, exercising powers of local government within the district. It had not in any just sense any resemblance to the Board of Supervisors in any of the other counties.

Notwithstanding its apparently lofty *status* the City Corporation was, in one respect, less gifted in point of power than the Boards of Supervisors in the rural counties. It had to depend upon its own corporate fund : it had not, like the rural boards, authority to impose taxes, or, as it is expressed in the English books, to levy a rate. As the Boards of Supervisors in the rural counties had such a power, the City Corporation officers could not comprehend why they could not, without annual express grants, "levy the taxes necessary to carry on and support the *City* Government." So, in 1862, the Board of Councilmen referred the Hon. Greene C. Bronson, then Corporation Counsel, to the statutes which, according to their reading, made the Supervisors much the same thing as the rural Supervisors, and solicited his opinion. (*Warren*, *pp.* 66, 67.) This is inserted as an able exposition by a learned jurist, given under official sanction.

CITY OF NEW YORK—LAW DEPARTMENT,
OFFICE OF COUNSEL TO THE CORPORATION,
February 25, 1862.

To the Board of Councilmen :

Having recently expressed the opinion, in answer to your inquiry, that taxes could not be levied, for any purpose, without legislative authority, you now inquire, in effect, whether such authority, so far as relates to this City, has not already been given.

You cite parts of the 150th and four following sections of the Long Act of 1813, in relation to this city (2 *R. L.*, 399), and request my opinion whether that "is not sufficient to enable the Supervisors of this County, without additional authority, to levy the taxes necessary to carry on and support the City Government." I had occasion to consider that question soon after coming into office, and then came to the conclusion that it would not be safe for the Supervisors to levy taxes without further legislative authority. (77 *Proceed. Ald.*, 328.) On such re-examination as I have now been able to give the question, I am confirmed in that opinion. What was then said, and is now repeated, must be understood of such taxes as have not been authorized by any law, subsequent to the Act of 1813. There are statutes, beside the annual tax laws, which authorize or direct the Supervisors to raise moneys, annually or otherwise, for certain specified purposes, and, of course, the power need not be repeated in the annual tax laws. But on the practical construction which has been given to the Act of 1813, it is not sufficient of itself to authorize taxation.

The Legislature has made a distinction between this and the other counties in this State, by giving a discretionary power to the Boards of Supervisors in other counties, which has not been conferred upon the Supervisors of New York. Without going further back than 1813, it will be found that an Act was passed on the 2d day of April in that year, "for defraying the public and necessary charges in the respective counties of this State" (2 *R. L.*, 137), which provides in its first section "that the Supervisors in the several cities and towns in each of the counties of this State, *other than the City and County of New York*, shall annually meet," "and examine, settle and allow all accounts chargeable against such county, and ascertain what sum *ought* to be raised for the payment thereof, and for defraying the public and contingent charges of such county;" and by the second section they are authorized to cause all such sums to be raised and levied. The 150th section of the Long Act, already cited, provides that the Supervisors of this County shall meet, "examine and ascertain what *sums of money are by law* imposed on said city *in that year*," "and shall cause the same to be raised, levied and collected in the said city, in the same manner as the contingent charges of the several counties of this State are directed to be levied and collected by the Act" of April 2, already cited. It will be seen that these two statutes, enacted at the same session of the Legislature, make a plain distinction between this and the other counties, not only in excepting New York from the operation of the general law applicable to the other counties, but by authorizing the Supervisors of other counties to determine what sum *ought* to be raised; in other words, to exercise their discretion or judgment on the subject, while the Supervisors of New York have no such discretion, but are only empowered to ascertain and levy such sums of money as are *by law* imposed on the county *in that year.*

Another Act, passed in the same session of the Legislature, prescribes the manner of assessing and levying taxes generally throughout the State. (2 *R. L.*, 509.) In 1816 the Legislature, for the purpose of resolving a doubt on the subject, declared that the third section of the last mentioned Act should not be considered to apply to the assessment of real estate in this County, "but that such assessment shall be made yearly, under the *annual tax laws* for the said City and County." (*Stat.* 1816, *p.* 75, § 5.) It will be seen from this enactment that the Legislature did not consider the Act of 1813 as conferring sufficient authority upon the Supervisors of the County to levy taxes, but that annual tax laws were necessary for that purpose ; and such laws have been passed, from year to year, for nearly half a century. The Act of 1816, to which I have referred, may be taken as a sample. It is entitled "An Act to *enable* the Mayor, Recorder and Aldermen of the City of New York to raise money by tax," and authorizes the Supervisors to raise two several sums for the purposes, among others, of supporting the poor and defraying the other contingent expenses of the City and County. This enabling statute was wholly unnecessary if the Supervisors already had the power to levy taxes "to carry on and support the City Government."

The statute to which you refer, in view of the construction which it has constantly received, cannot be regarded as giving the Supervisors power to levy taxes in their discretion, but only as a general provision, prescribing the manner in which taxes may be levied when they are authorized by law.

If your other inquiries have not been sufficiently answered in what has already been said, a brief notice of them is all that is required.

The Act of 1813, to which you refer, has not been abrogated ; but that fact is not important in the present inquiry, for the reason that it never conferred the authority of which you speak.

No law has been enacted since 1813 " which requires this city and county, more than any other city and county in the State, to ask special legislative authority " for levying necessary taxes to support the City Government. But the absence of a prohibition against taxing proves nothing. Affirmative authority to tax must be shown, or it does not exist. There is no difference in that respect between this and other counties. But a power to tax, in the discretion of the Supervisors, may have been conferred upon other counties, while our Supervisors can only levy such sums as have been authorized by law.

So far as relates to the necessity for legislative authority, there is no difference between "what is known as the City Tax Levy" and taxes which relate to the County.

In addition to examining the statute of 1813, to which you refer, I have also considered the effect of the Revised Statutes of 1830, by which the Act of April 2, 1813, is repealed in terms (1 *R. S.*, 1*st ed.*, 134), and which give some color of placing New York on the same footing as the other counties of the State. (1 *R. S.*, 365, *Art.* ii.) But even in the Revised Statutes of 1830, the provisions of the article relating to the duties of Boards of Supervisors are not extended to the Supervisors of the City and County of New York, when special provisions inconsistent therewith were then, or should thereafter be made by law. (1 *R. S.*, 368.) And we find in the same year, when this statute took effect, and

in every year since that time, the Legislature has passed
an *enabling* Act in relation to this County, just as had
been done before. This practical construction given by
the Legislature to the statute, seems to show that it was
not intended by the Revised Statutes to dispense with
the former usage, which required annual tax laws, or
some other special provision, to warrant the Supervisors
in levying taxes in this County "to carry on and support the City Government."

Respectfully submitted,

GREENE C. BRONSON.

It will be noted that the inquiry was not whether the
Board of Supervisors of the County was a corporation.
Neither did such a question suggest itself to Judge
Bronson. The questions, however, may have been
based on the idea that the Supervisors were a local governing body of the City in like manner as the Supervisors were in the rural counties. The distinctions
stated by Judge Bronson would, doubtless, have induced him to deny that the County of New York was
incorporated, had that question been presented to him.

The standing title of the tax levy annually passed by
the Legislature was as follows : "An Act to enable the
Mayor, Aldermen and Commonalty of the City of New
York to raise money by tax." (See specimens Laws
1831, p. 167 ; Laws of 1832, p. 75 ; Laws of 1840, p. 8.)
The details of these Acts, like their titles, show how
little place the idea of two local incorporated governments had in the minds of the city lawyers who framed
them or the legislatures that adopted them.

We are now, however, approaching the time when this
mere Commission or Committee for levying taxes grew
into a pretended additional governing body. The methods by which this condition was attained are quite
singular. The actors were different, as, from time to
time, these methods were employed. No very serious
evil was aimed at or attained until Tweed appeared

prominently upon the stage of political life. This was not earlier than 1857 ; but to prepare for a view of his achievements we must notice previous events.

Until that year, 1857, the Supervisors had no separate clerk, the Clerk of the Common Council acting as their clerk, and keeping their minutes. From 1787, when the Board was created with that name, until 1809, it had no separate minutes. Its minutes were mingled with those of the Common Council.

These facts appear in *the Supervisors' proceedings*, *Vol.* 1, *p.* 5. This book was printed by Tweed's new Elective Board of Supervisors in 1865. It contains the minutes of the Supervisors from 1809 to 1839. One of the People's Counsel has read over the first 500 pages of this book, which reach a period subsequent to the Amended Charter of 1830. He has carefully examined the rest of the volume. It contains an interesting history.

The City Corporation, as we have observed, owned all public lands in the City and County. It had from the commencement the control and government of all jails and court-houses. Its charter officers, as such, were the Justices of Oyer and Terminer, and the power to hold all local courts, and all judicial magistracies, civil and criminal, were portions of its corporate privileges. The Sheriff, Clerk, &c., &c., were officers of the Corporation, and subject to its authority. Of course all expenses connected with any of these establishments or officers devolved upon the City Corporation, were audited by its authority, and paid out of its treasury. As the State and City became more enlarged and populous, Acts were passed from time to time, which by some incautious phrase, or some misconstruction in practice, more or less varied the intercourse between the City Corporation and some local officers ; but it was a long time before any idea of a right to look anywhere else than to the City Corporation for any payments or allowances for services to the Cit or Count   arose in an   mind.

The general laws of the State, however, referring to Clerks, Sheriffs, Coroners, &c., as *County officers*, were thought by some persons to make it proper that the *Supervisors* should AUDIT some claims of these officers. Down to the Amended Charter of 1830, and for some time after that date, all acts of this kind were on their face simply in aid of the Common Council, the audited accounts were submitted to it by the Supervisors for consideration or for payment, as if the Supervisors were a Committee of the Corporation. (See Proceedings of the Board of Supervisors, Vol. 1, *pages* 75, 85, 95, 98, 100, 106, 111, 122, 124, 178, 186, 190, 194, *and especially p.* 320, 220.)

This Act of 1830 was the first Amended Charter. It was framed by an elected City Convention which sat in 1829. This was a very respectable body ; and among its members there were several eminent persons. (*Laws of* 1830, p. 127, § 15.) The Recorder of that day was too able a man to be an universal favorite. He alone, of all the ancient charter officers, was not elected, mediately or immediately, by the local constituency ; and this circumstance was seized upon as a ground of exclusion. By the Amended Charter he ceased to be an officer of the corporation ; but he remained, of course, a member of the Statutory Board of Supervisors. The annual tax levy of the same year expressly recognized this fact. (*Laws of* 1830, p. 162.)

After this Amended Charter of 1830, though not attempting to enlarge their auditing power, the Supervisors, for the first time, *direct* the Comptroller to issue a warrant for a Coroner's account. This form was usually adopted thenceforth. This may seem odd, as the Supervisors had no shadow of power over that Charter officer. The Recorder had long been a ruling power in the civic councils. He was originally *ex officio* law adviser to the Corporation. The Mayor, who formerly sat in the Civil County Court, had ten years previously given way to the first Judge of the

new Court of Common Pleas. (Laws of 1821, p. 64.
See Daly's History prefixed to 1 E. D. Smith's Reports,
page lxxviii.) Laymen now occupied the Mayoralty ;
and the Recorder, then, as, now Presiding Judge of the
General Sessions of the Peace and chief of the criminal
department of the local government, was the only
lawyer having a prominent place in any connection
with city affairs. And it was only in the Board of
Supervisors that any administrative power was left to
him. This *directing* the Comptroller *to pay* seems to
have been merely a little display of power by that
officer to make up for the absence of the reality. This
class of claims gradually increased, and doubts as to
which Board should *audit* them arose, pp. 495, 567,
650. In the latter page their number is spoken of as
resulting from "gradual encroachments."

General statutes relative to canvassing votes at elections, selecting jurors, &c., were deemed to devolve
some duties on the New York Supervisors ; and these
duties were performed, but they were slight. Some
involved no expenditure, and the others involved but
little, so that as yet there was no visible inroad upon
the system which made the City Corporation not only
sole receiver and sole paymaster in all the local business, but substantially sole auditor of local accounts.
Though this little change in form by the Recorder
may be looked upon as *the* grain of mustard seed, it
did not soon germinate so as to produce results of any
immediate importance.

Certain other events occurred contributing in slight
and unperceived degrees to vary the condition of this
Board of Supervisors.

Under a law of 1840, page 258, excluding the Aldermen from the bench of the Court of Sessions, two new
Judges were appointed to sit with the Recorder ; and
by § 5 the Common Council of the City was directed to
pay their salaries. This method of paying local charges
was in precise conformity with all previous practice.

The creation of these associate justiceships seems to have been a political measure, and it gave rise to litigation. Its opponents contended that one branch of the Act was unconstitutional. And they relied on an argument which, if sustained and carried to its legitimate results, would have invalidated the direction that the City Corporation *pay* the salaries. Saving an erroneous opinion of Judge Bronson's, since thorougly exploded, all the Judges as well as the Chancellor voted against the exceptants ; but the ultimate judgment of thirteen Senators went with them on grounds not relevant to any question now before this Court. That judgment may be said to have no other support than that *quasi* majority. (*See The People* vs. *Purdy*, 2 *Hill*, 31 ; *Purdy* vs. *The People*, 4 *Hill*, 384.)

This controversy compelled or induced the friends of the new Justices to throw the *auditing* of the salaries upon the Supervisors. (See Act of 1841, p. 267, § 4.) It declared that these salaries "shall be deemed County charges of the City and County of New York, and [that] the Mayor or Recorder and Aldermen of the City of New York, as the Supervisors of the City and County of New York, shall audit and allow" the same. These words about County charges were quite new in the legislation for New York. They may have helped *the thing* along. This was the fourth section of the usual annual tax levy. It was probably with some view to the salaries that the title took a new form. It was "An Act to enable the Supervisors of the City and County of New York to raise money by tax," p. 265. But so strong was the practice of the City Corporation in receiving every local *income*, and defraying every local *outgo*, that even now the Supervisors were not directed to *pay*. They were only directed to *allow*. The City Corporation still, in fact, received and paid everything.

The new title, thus for a slight purpose introduced in 1841, thenceforth attached to the annual tax levy,

and in the next year some one seems to have apprehended confusion from this cause; for it was then
guarded against. The *Laws of* 1842, p. 56, §2, expressly provide for the continuance of pre-existing
regulations, and enact that every person's tax shall be
collected in one payment, and that the money "shall
be paid into the hands of the Treasurer or Chamberlain of said City," a corporate officer, "at such times
and in such manner as directed by law." But progress in change had commenced.

In the *Laws of* 1851, p. 822, § 3, the Supervisors of
said City and County were authorized to fix *and pay*
the District Attorney's annual salary. In *Laws of*
1852, p. 592, §§ 6 and 7, they were directed to raise
and pay the expenses of Judges assigned to hold
Circuit Court in the City, and an additional compensation to Judges resident therein. This latter provision
gave rise to the case of *People* vs. *Edmonds*, 15 *Bar-*
bour, 529.

In this case, Judge Robert H. Morris, after obtaining from the Supervisors an allowance of his extra
compensation, and a resolution of the Board of Supervisors ordering the City Chamberlain or County Treasurer to pay it, moved for a mandamus requiring Mr.
Edmonds, who held that office, to pay him. This
motion was made in July, 1853. The Act had directed
the Supervisors to *pay;* but there seemed no little
difficulty in finding the money. There was still no
separate account of any things that could be called
County matters; there was not even, according to the
fiction-charged art of book-keeping, any County Treasury. The Act of 1842, p. 56, § 2, before referred to, had
positively perpetuated the ancient financial method.
Even though levied by Supervisors, every tax was required to be collected in one payment and "paid into
the hands of the Treasurer or Chamberlain of said
city." The Amended Charter of 1849, p. 281, § 11,
made one of the Comptroller's bureaux the re-

ceiver of all taxes. Besides, not only this Act, but the further amendment of 1853, by all their provisions, placed the whole of the local finances in the hands of charter officers and directed their management by the City Corporation. See especially the check on contracts or jobs in the latter, by requiring public proposals and an award to the lowest bidder. (Laws of April 12, 1853, page 412, § 12.) And, some guardian of the common weal having " smelt a rat" in the Board of Supervisors, the 15th section runs as follows: " No contract by the Supervisors shall be valid *unless expressly authorized by statute*; and such as are authorized shall be made in the manner provided by the twelfth section." It was under these circumstances that Judge Morris's motion came before a Special Term held by Judge Strong. The second branch of the opinion, 15 *Barb.*, 536 to 548, contains an industrious elaboration of the matter; and asserts, at p. 539, that "the inhabitants, in effect, constitute two corporations—one as a County under the general laws of the State (1 R. S., 364, §1), and the other as a city under their charter" (p. 539).

This was certainly a discovery. Such a thing had never before been thought of, although " the general laws of the State" which are relied upon were pretty old, as we have seen. Even the fourth revision, *i. e.* that of 1830, which is the "general law" actually cited by the Judge, had been a dozen years in operation. The prior "general laws," as we have shown by reference to the revisions of 1788, 1801 and 1813, expressly negatived this idea. What color the revision of 1830 afforded for it we shall presently inquire.

Probably the swell-mob of politicians by trade, who, with diamond pins in their shirt fronts and diamond rings on their fingers, for some years prior to Tweed's fall in 1871, hung around the City Hall of New York in steadily increasing numbers, took a hint from Judge Strong's opinion; but it would seem that for a time they had no great confidence in it. Until the year 1857, they continued to evince their distrust.

The example of giving the Supervisors, bit by bit, some administrative functions in fixing and *paying* salaries was followed up. Resolutions of that sort, made, it is to be presumed, without authority, were subsequently legalized. (*Laws of* 1855, *pp.* 200 and 202. *Laws of* 1857, *Vol. I, p.* 197.)

Perhaps there should be added to these a few other instances of similar legislation. But we have now reached a period somewhat fruitful. In 1857, for the first time, the year's legislation occupied two large volumes ; and among the improvements then introduced was the establishment of a new *Elective* Board of Supervisors. (*Laws of* 1857, *Vol.* 2, *p.* 285.) It was not declared to be a Corporation ; but its machinery contemplated that it should make appropriations, &c. That it was to be a Corporation and have lawsuits, is rather negatived by § 9, which gives it only a "legal adviser." It had not, nor has any New York Board of Supervisors, ever had either a Counsellor or an Attorney. (*See Laws of* 1870, *p.* 482, § 9.)

The intermediate stage of New York City and County Supervisorship, inaugurated by this Act of 1857, and now brought to view, lasted until 1870, when the grand separate elective board was abolished, and a new one of the most feeble and insignificant kind, consisting of the same officers as those who formed the Board of Supervisors at its origin, 1787, was created. (*Laws of* 1870, *p.* 481, §§ 1 *and* 11.) But during the thirteen years of its notable existence, the medieval board, as we may call it, was "the rallying point of fraud and anarchy." The six million swindle at its obsequies, by this §4 of 1870, *p.* 878, was a characteristic sacrifice.

It was a necessary part of the scheme for establishing the power of the quartette in 1870 that the grand

and glorious medieval elective Board should be abolished ; and it was abolished accordingly. (*Laws of* 1870, *p.* 481.) This manœuvre took from the Board of Supervisors all color of claim to any considerable powers of an administrative nature which it had been thus gradually assuming, sometimes with and sometimes without legislative authority. At a single stroke this *name*, the Board of Supervisors, was relegated, save in one diminishing particular, to the condition which it had occupied when the very same officers formed it during the period from its original creation in 1787, until, say 1857, or later. The only appendage of that power which shone as a city on a hill during the period of its medieval glory from 1857 to 1870, not then abolished, was its salaried clerk. This was permitted to remain, for it was no part of the quartette's policy to diminish offices or salaries. The comparative impotency of the Board of Supervisors, as thus newly constituted, is best illustrated by the requirement in its organic Act, that the Mayor's concurrence "shall always be necessary to the passage of any resolution, ordinance or act." (§ 2.) It would be an insult to the primeval Board to say this new *thing* was its equal. Yet THIS is the Board of Supervisors which existed when the present action against Tweed, Ingersoll & Co. was instituted. THIS is the rival which sets up its *ownership of the County* in opposition to the supreme power of the State in that behalf. But we must look back for a moment. Judge Strong's decision in *The People* v. *Edmonds*, 15 *Barb.*, 529, before alluded to, was pronounced in 1853 ; the volume containing it was published in 1854. It was in the year 1855 that the Supervisors began to *grant* salaries by resolution, and to procure subsequent Acts confirming the resolutions. Some of these are above recited. The new Board was elected under the Act of 1857. It commenced operations on the 1st January, 1858 ; the year's proceedings occupy a huge volume of

about 1,400 printed pages ; and—name of evil omen to
tax-payers !—WILLIAM M. TWEED appears at the head
of the list as foremost among the elected Supervisors.
A clerk was then appointed, who in 1873 still held the
office. This was Joseph B. Young. His deputy, Elbert A. Woodward, is the renowned distributing agent
of the conspirators Watson, Tweed, Connolly and
others.

The peculiar stage in the existence by New York City
or County Supervisors, inaugurated by the Act of 1857,
and now brought to view, lasted until 1870, when the
elective board was abolished ; and the new one, consisting of the same officers as those who formed the Board of
Supervisors at its origin, 1787, was created. (*Laws of*
1870, *p.* 481, §§ 1 *and* 11.)

The Statutes, in respect to the Supervisors during
this intermediate period, as it may be called, are interesting.

The tax levy of 1858, *p.* 487, was limited to $8,621,-
091 $\frac{81}{100}$. The tax levy of 1859, *p.* 1123, was limited to
$9,860,926 $\frac{8}{100}$. But each of these contained *unlimited*
powers as to judgments recovered against the City
Corporation.

The tax levy of 1860, *p.* 1017, by its title and enactments, authorized, for the first time, as that of 1859 did

by its enactments, a discrimination between city and county *purposes*, devolving on the City Corporation the power of regulating the expenditure of the former, and on the Board of Supervisors that power as to the latter. The City Corporation's part was limited to $6,085,448$\frac{40}{100}$; the Supervisors' part was limited to $2,740,478$\frac{18}{100}$; but under each head there were unlimited powers of extension, and in § 8 the Supervisors were authorized to borrow on *County bonds* in anticipation of revenue. Strangely enough these bonds were to be signed by the Mayor and Comptroller, neither of whom were officers of the Board of Supervisors, as well as by its Clerk.

The next change was the introduction of *two* distinct annual tax levies. This began in 1861, and ended with 1870. These double annual tax levies are full of singular provisions, leading to unlimited taxation, and the unlimited creation of debt through issues of *County* bonds and *City* bonds. The chief features worthy of notice in this connection, are the total amounts of each *nominal* limitation.

1861—County Tax Levy, p. 564	$2,675,057 00	
" City Tax Levy, p. 666	6,533,822 04	
		$9,209,879 04
1862—County Tax Levy, p. 817	$2,442,652 00	
" City Tax Levy, p. 860	4,662,226 38	
		$7,404,888 38
1862—County Tax Levy, p. 166	$2,954,019 29	
" City Tax Levy, p. 407	6,062,095 74	
		$9,016,115 03
1864—County Tax Levy, p. 937	$3,226,957 84	
" City Tax Levy, p. 940	7,351,664 78	
		$10,578,622 62
1865—County Tax Levy, p. 1552	$4,726,300 53	
" City Tax Levy, p. 1826	9,923,509 10	
		$14,649,899 63
1866—County Tax Levy, p. 1893	$5,271,405 50	
" City Tax Levy, p. 2056	8,457,257 39	
		$13,728,662 89
1867—County Tax Levy, p. 1998	$7,071,077 85	
" City Tax Levy, p. 1596	10,599,359 03	
		$17,670,436 38

1868—County Tax Levy, p. 2025.........	$7,062,785 61	
" City Tax Levy, p. 2007............	10,878,046 56	
		$17,955,832 17
1869—County Tax Levy, p. 2113.........	$7,713,607 63	
" City Tax Levy, p. 2119............	10,928,108 53	
		$18,686,716 16
1870—County Tax Levy, p. 875..........	$7,050,390 12	
" City Tax Levy, p. 881.............	13,187,665 13	
		$20,238,055 25

In round numbers, the annual tax was thus expanded
within the space of six years, from ten to twenty millions. The indefinite appropriations not being included
in this statement, nor any notice being taken of the
debt created under these indefinite appropriations, it
will readily be seen that this period in our history
marked by the existence of Tweed's elective Board of
Supervisors, was rogue's holiday in the Metropolis.
Though the specified amounts of the tax levies for 1870
exceeded twenty millions, a single little provision
among the *indefinites* of that very year was the 4th
section now in hand. Under it $6,000,000 were *audited
away* by Hall, Connolly and Tweed, as shown by the
complaint now before the Court.

There was, of course, during this remarkable period,
a competition between these two bodies, the Common
Council and the Board of Supervisors, as bidders at
Albany for the privilege of controlling expenditure.
A steady increase of taxation and of debt, as just exhibited, was the natural fruit. Murmurs arose among
the suffering tax-payers, besides which rivalries between the two bodies and some opposing sets of politicians became very active. From these causes, with,
according to common report, the aid of a vast expenditure in secret ways at the legislative capital, there
sprang, in 1870, the new, so-called, Charter, for the
City Corporation, with a new Board of Supervisors in
place of the elective Board. These enactments were
framed by some very subtle penman. The full scope
of his devices cannot be perceived without reading, in

connection, several Acts of 1870 and 1871 ; nor indeed can any one of these devices be well understood without keeping in view the entire range of New York local legislation during those two years.

From an early period it had been a common practice to create, from time to time, distinct official agencies in the metropolis for purposes of local government, more or less connected with, or independent of the City Corporation. The 315 sections contained in the Act entitled "An Act to reduce several laws relating particularly to the City of New York into one Act," 2 *R. L. of* 1813, *p.* 342, contain a series of these gathered together from preceding statutes. They are very various in their nature. Some of them, as will be seen at a glance, have little relation to the City Corporation, and some have none ; yet here they are found all mingled together under one head. It would not be difficult to argue that many of the local boards thus existing had, within certain very narrow limits, the functions of a distinct corporate body or of a *quasi* corporation. See *as to Commissioners of Alms House*, 2 *R. L. of* 1813, *p.* 439, §§ 246, 248—as to *Master and Wardens of the Port*, *Ib. p.* 440, § 281.

Subsequently to that period, *i. e.*, 1813, and prior to 1870, many other local legal organisms of the like character grew up. It would be tedious to enumerate them all. Most of them are drawn into the new, so-called, Charter of the City Corporation (*Laws of* 1870, *p.* 366) ; and their nature can be discovered from a perusal of that Act and its subsequent amendments.

The scheme of those who projected and brought into active existence the local government of 1870 and 1871, to which attention is now being called, involved a general, if not universal, absorption of these various local statutory creations within the municipal government as known and recognized in the so-called City Charter ; or in other words, it made them functionaries of the City Corporation. (See remarks of Daly, F. J., in Gildersleeve v. Board of Education, 17 Abbott's Rep., 212.) Though but slightly relevant to the precise point of technical law, which is under investigation, it may not be amiss to observe that the scheme had a most extensive scope.

It was designed that the four officers, who have been called the quartette, should absorb all the powers before vested in the various branches of local government, or, at least, all their patronage. Not only was the before potent Board of Supervisors to fall beneath this sentence, but even the ancient Common Council was doomed to surrender all substantial authority. (*See the New Charter, Laws of 1870, pp. 367 to 397, as amended by the Tax Levy of same year, pp. 881 to 917; and, as further amended, Laws of 1871, p. 1231 to 1353. Laws of 1870 p. 391, § 102; and p. 905, § 30.*)

Here may be seen a most ludicrously prolix and repetitious enumeration of the insignificant powers reserved to the Common Council. (*Laws of* 1870, *p.* 370.) On a slight scrutiny it will be perceived that the newly organized departments named in the same volume at p. 373, actually possessed, in effect and substance, all the local authority. The quartette, as Board of Apportionment, (*Laws of* 1871, *p.* 1268, § 2,) held the purse, and was supreme over all. Only one of the quartette was to be elected. That was the Mayor; he was to appoint his three associates. The Board of Apportionment seems not to have been found necessary until 1871. In 1870, the departmental functions were thought sufficient.

These departments, now being *in* or *under* the City Corporation, were so contrived as to exercise all the control over expenditure which had been gradually growing up in the Board of Supervisors; and so, of course, it was a necessary part of the scheme to abolish the greatness of that Board, and, as before stated, it was abolished accordingly. (*Laws of* 1870, *p.* 481.)

It may be well here to re-state our position. It is that the Board of Supervisors never was, even in its palmiest days, a governing body with general administrative powers, to which corporate existence was necessary, and that no statute ever declared it to be a corporation.

Manifestly, the New York Board of Supervisors was originally created as a Tax-levying Commission, and received that name simply to render the State tax laws, as they might be from time to time enacted, applicable to the New York local machinery. This object demanded no corporate powers. As one duty or other was by statutes unadvisedly added, or by misapplication of some general law assumed, the Supervisors became, either *de jure* or *de facto*, public officers charged with the performance of those duties; but they did not thereby become *ex-necessitate* a body corporate. When these duties were most numerous, *i. e.*, from Tweed's elective Board of 1857 to its extinction in 1870, their mere increase did not change the nature of the duties, or the character in which they were performed; nor did they convert, by construction of law, the elective Board into a *quasi* Corporation. And if, by any construction, such an effect could be deduced from this multiplication of special duties, the common law principle before referred to would not give the Board of Supervisors any more than a very special and limited corporate existence, confined to the particular purpose of enabling it to execute those special duties.

Besides, if the multiplication of those powers rendered Tweed's medieval Board of Supervisors a governing body, it descended from that high estate in 1870, on being remanded to a less grade of power than it originally possessed.

But Judge Strong says, in People v. Edmonds, 15 Barb., that the County or the Board of Supervisors was declared to be a corporation by statute. Judge

Parker so held at the General Term in this case. See paper marked D., pp. 184 to 188.

In his "*laws relating to the City and County of New York*," Vol. 1, p. 30, Mr. Hoffman quotes, with apparent acceptance, the remark of a Judge at Special Term, that "two separate and distinct *organizations* exist in this County for the purpose of civil government, embracing the same territory, and each possessing its appropriate functions." The Judge may have meant, as the author evidently thinks he did, that these organizations were both *incorporated bodies ;* but it may not be amiss to observe that the Judge does not, in terms, say so ; neither does the Judge in *People* vs. *Stout*, 23 *Barb.*, 341. The language of each Judge, taken literally, is true ; and it would be equally true, if he had said that there were *twenty* separate and distinct *organizations* instead of only *two*. Mr. Hoffman's work is not authority.

The question, corporation or not, was not before any of these Judges, except Judge Parker, even incidentally ; and any suggestion or inference by them on this question is *obiter*. Judge Parker did not look as closely into this complex question as was requisite to avoid misunderstanding ; and none of the others adverted to prior revisions or to the peculiar arrangement and phraseology of the Revised Statutes on this point.

We have already shown that in the first three revisions New York was industriously and expressly excluded from the "general laws" organizing county governments by Supervisors, and giving the County Boards corporate powers.

The revision of 1830 was prepared by jurists of great ability. They aimed at what may be called codification, within that limited measure which their judgment commended as safe, and they dealt with this subject accordingly. They declared in the towns and in the counties a corporate existence, gave to them corporate

names, and regulated the methods of suit by and
against them. They also provided appropriate means
of paying judgments in the latter case. (See R. S.,
Part First, Chapters XI. and XII.)

The revisors were quite aware that although New
York had a Board of Supervisors, there were not, in
law or in fact, two local governments therein. They
did not see any propriety in, much less any necessity
for, a second municipal or governmental corporation.
Chapter XII. of the First Part, is devoted to organizing the county governments. In that chapter, after
the provisions as to counties generally, which are in
several particulars quite inappropriate to New York,
comes *Article I., of Title* 2, containing provisions relative to the *meetings* of Boards of Supervisors. Its last
section is in these words :

"The Mayor, Recorder and Aldermen of the City of
New York, shall be the Supervisors of the City and
County of New York ; and all the provisions of this
Article shall be construed to extend to them respec-
tively, except where special provisions inconsistent
therewith, are or shall be made by law, in relation to
the City and County of New York."—1 *R. S.*, 368, § 17,
First Ed.

The next Article, being *Part I., Ch. XII., Title* 2, *Art.*
2, relates to County Treasurers, and its last section is
similar. It is as follows :

"The Chamberlain of the City and County of New
York shall be *considered* the County Treasurer thereof; and all the provisions of this *article* shall be construed to apply to him, except where special provisions inconsistent therewith, are or shall be made by
law, in relation to the City and County of New York."

It will be observed, that in these parts of their systematic revision, the editors, by using in each instance
the word *article* instead of the word *Chapter*, indicated
their conception that it was these *articles* alone that

should have any operation within the City and County of New York. The *articles* which declare counties or their Boards of Supervisors to be corporate bodies, and as such capable of suing or being sued were not thus made applicable. *Main* v. *Prosser*, 1 *Johns., Cas.* 131, *and case cited.*

This shows the intelligent perception of our legislative history possessed by these learned gentlemen. It shows their knowledge that there never would have been any propriety in judicial ingenuity stretching its powers to invent a second local governing Corporation in the same territory which was adequately governed by "The Mayor, Aldermen and Commonalty, &c," It also shows that they did not intend to legislate into existence such an *inutility* as, at best, such a separate Corporation would have been. It performs a still further office: it gives a key to the mistaken conception of Mr. Hoffman and Judge Strong that there were two local Governments or Corporations. Both of these eminent gentlemen inadvertently read the word "*article*" in 1 *R. S.*, 368, § 17, *First Ed.*, as if it had been the word "*Chapter*." See STRONG, J., *in* 15 *Barbour*, 536, and *Mr. Hoffman, in his Treatise, Vol.* 1, *p.* 33.

It is in the first title (1 R. S., p. 366, § 4,) that the revisors inserted all the powers in respect to *County charges* on which the New York Supervisors ground their usurpations. That article is not declared to be generally applicable to New York, or at all except in a very limited and partial way. (1 R. S., p. 368, § 17.)

It is a familiar rule of law that mere changes in phraseology or arrangement in statutory revisions are not to be construed as changing the previous law, unless the intent be manifest. (See Taylor *v.* Delancy, 2 Caine's Cases in Error, 151; 20 Johns, 722; 2 Hill, 381, note *b* ; and Wait's Table of cases.) The previous revisions had all studiously excluded the City and County of New York, and its Board of Supervisors, from the general system, but in methods varying according to the taste of the respective revisors. In 1830, the whole order and arrangement of the Statutes was remodelled. The revisors of that year sought by this means to attain symmetry, and avoid exceptions, circumlocutions and prolixity, generally. They attained their object in this instance by giving to the detailed regulations about meetings and County Treasurers a narrow and limited application to the City and County of New York, just as in the revision of 1813, and by making no mention of New York in the organic title. 1 R. S. p. 364, being Chap. XII., Title 1. That title is headed, "of the powers and rights of Counties as bodies corporate."

It is submitted with confidence that the provisions of the "general laws," as Judge Strong denominates that part of the Revised Statutes, did not alter the pre-existing law, or bring the City and County of New York, or its Board of Supervisors, within the operation of the incorporating and power-granting clauses of that Code. These were suitable to the rural Counties, and were designed for those Counties only. They were wholly inapplicable to New York, and could only work confusion and mischief there.

Several scraps of recent legislation may be cited tending to show that the Legislature, or, more properly speaking, the fraudulent lobbyists who drew their Acts, had adopted or fallen into Judge Strong's mistake, and supposed the Board of Supervisors or the County of New York to be within the general system of the rural Counties, and, by consequence, *incorporated.* Here also a well settled and most beneficial rule of Constitutional law stands in the defendants' way. The Legislature has no judicial power; and when it gives, either directly or by inference, an erroneous opinion on a point of law, that opinion is not authoritative and does not control the Courts. (Reiser *v.* Tell Association, 39 Penna. R., 144; State *v.* Baltimore and

Ohio R. R. Co., 12 Gill & Johns, 433; Terret *v.* Taylor 9 Cranch, 51.)

Even the omnipotent Legislature of England is not deemed to create law by ventilating a mistaken opinion on a legal question. (Per Ld. Cranworth, Mersey Docks *v.* Cameron, 11 House of Lords Cases, p. 522.)

Perhaps the most striking of these left-handed legislative recognitions is in the Laws of 1870, page 878. The second section of that Act is in these words :

" No action shall be maintained against the County of New York, unless the claims on which the action is brought shall have been presented to the Board of Supervisors of said County, and passed on by them, or they have unreasonably refused or omitted to take action on the same. Before any execution shall be issued on any judgment recovered upon such claim, a notice of the recovery thereof shall be given to the Comptroller, and he shall be allowed ten days to provide for its payment, by the issue of revenue bonds in the usual manner according to law." (*Laws of* 1870, *p.* 878, § 2.)

The absurdity of this section is most striking. Doubtless it was penned by that member of the quartette who was their general draftsman. He evidently thought that the Board of Supervisors was a full Corporation like " the Mayor, Aldermen and Commonalty, &c.;" that it had property which might be seized and sold upon an execution against it; and so he invented these provisions for *its* convenience ! ! Thus to craft and thievish acquisitiveness we find added the grossest ignorance. Even the actually incorporated County Boards of the rural districts needed no such *protection.* Yet the section is now cited as a legislative recognition that the Supervisors' Board was suable.

If a blunder of this sort could be held to make law, it would only operate to the extent of its precise words. Thus interpreted, this section, though subjecting the

County to suit, and its goods and chattels to sale on execution, like those of an individual debtor, would go no further. It would not confer a *power to sue.*

The express incorporation of the Counties in the Revised Statutes, together with the precise and elaborate provisions facilitating suits against them contained in the same Code, seems to have produced in rural County cases some difficulty. The Judges could not suppose an intent to change the long settled practice of generally exempting local governing bodies from suit for ordinary charges. So the principle enunciated and settled in the leading cases among this class would seem to be that these bodies could not be sued for *debt* or on *contract.* (Hill *v.* Supervisors, 2 Kern., 62 ; Boyce *v.* Supervisors of Cayuga, 20 Barb., 295 ; Chase *v.* Saratoga, 33 Barb., 607; Martin *v.* Greene Co., 29 N. Y. R., 647.) From these cases a jurist might naturally deduce the conclusion that a County, or its governing Board, could only be sued for a *tort.* And, in truth, this does not vary much, if at all, from the true principle. Yet, perhaps, this is not the best mode of expressing or stating it. Thus putting it on a distinction in the forms of proceeding could alone have created a necessity for the able and elaborate opinion of FOLGER, J., in Newman *v.* The Supervisors of Livingston Co., 45 N. Y. R., 676.

That suit looked like the old action of assumpsit for money had and received and *seemed* to sound in contract. But it was essentially a claim in tort. Though the officers representing the County acted honestly, and with the best of motives, they had no warrant of law, and their exaction of money from the plaintiff was illegal and tortious It was, however, a purely official act.

The Revisors of 1830 adjusted this whole matter most judiciously. They declared the governing boards corporate bodies, thus rendering them, *prima facie,* suable in all cases and for all claims. But they created in the same law a specific remedy, by application to the County ¦Board, for the allowance of all county or town charges—that is to say, for all claims arising in the due, lawful and regular exercise of the powers of local government. By consequence, no suit could be brought for *any* of these, except a mandamus. Other claims could only be for departures from regular and legal action. For some of these suit might lie only against the individuals offending ; for others the just and appropriate remedy was against the corporate body in its official capacity. The case in 45 N. Y. R. was an instance of the latter.

It is plain that the Revisors codified the doctrines and policy of the common law with admirable skill.

The Government is not suable. It followed that Government officials were not suable for duly exercising their offices. (Whitfield *v.* Ld. Ledespencer, Cowper 765, 766, and see other cases of this class cited by Blackburn J., in Law Rep. 1, English and Irish appeals, H. L. p. 111 and p. 124, 128.) It was perceived that this might often produce injustice. In many cases of administering office for the government, local or general, there ought to be a remedy *against the fund.* To meet this exigency governmental commissions were, by being incorporated, or in some other way *made suable.* · In all these cases, where a special remedy by appraisement or the like was not given, the corporate or official entity was held to be suable, as such, thus giving a remedy against the official fund for wrongs to individuals arising from defective or irregular administration. (Southampton and *al. v.* Local Board, 8 Ellis and Bl., 812 ; The Mersey Dock Trustees *v.* Gibbs, Law Rep. 1, Eng. and Ir. Appeals, H. L., p. 107 to 109.) See this principle clearly stated by Denio, Ch. J., in Darlington *v.* Mayor, 31 N. Y. R., 200.

Practice shows a general understanding of public officers and the bar, that the New York Board of Supervisors is not and never was a corporation.

On the question whether an action at law can be maintained by or against the New York Supervisors, practice and decisions have been carefully looked into in this connection with the following results :

1. It is not known to the Corporation Counsel, nor can it be otherwise ascertained, that any action was ever brought *by* the Supervisors except the three which were brought by the Mayor's *direction* against Mayor Hall himself, Comptroller Connolly and Commissioner Tweed, on October 19, 1871, and which are alleged by The People to have been collusive and fraudulent. In addition to being unjustifiable in motive, they were unprecedented.

2. Actions or proceedings have been had *against* the Supervisors.

They are of three classes.

First.—Applications for the writ of mandamus have been frequent. These cases require no notice in this connection. They do not involve a supposal that the Board was a Corporation. Such writs lie against any and every public officer.

Secondly.—Actions in equity to restrain the collection of a tax. In all of these the point might have been made that the Board was not a legal entity *thus* suable ; but jurisdiction was denied *in toto*, and without any notice being taken of this precise question, the plaintiffs' actions were dismissed.

> Sandford *vs.* Supervisors, 15 How. Pr. R., 172.
> Mut. Ben. Ins. Co. *vs.* Supervisors, 2 Abbott N. S., 233.
> Mut. Ben. Ins. Co. *vs.* Supervisors, 8 Bosw., 683.
> Same *vs.* Same, 38 Barb., 322.
> N. Y. Life Ins. Co. *vs.* Same, 4 Duer, 192.
> Mut. Ben. Ins. Co. *vs.* Same, 8 Keyes, 182.

Thirdly.—There is a small class, consisting, as far as known, of only two or three cases, in which ordinary actions at law were brought against The Board of Supervisors, as a Corporation. The plaintiffs failed in each of them ; but a more full statement of them may be satisfactory. This class alone has any relevancy to the point before the Court.

Thomas Phœnix, Ex-District Attorney, presented a claim for fees to the Board of Supervisors, which they declined to allow. (See *Vol.* 1 of *Supervisors' Minutes, pp.* 673 to 675.) Mr. Phœnix sued the . Board in the Superior Court of New York. The action was referred to Daniel Lord, J. Prescott Hall, and another. They reported that no such action was maintainable, and the Court, per Jones, Oakley and Talmadge, J.J., confirmed the report. Mr. Phœnix acquiesced, and resorted to a mandamus. (1 *Hill*, 362). This was in 1839–'40. The case not being reported, is stated from his minutes by the only participant in the decision who is now living.

Brady v. *The Board of Supervisors of N. Y.*, 2 *Sandford's N. Y. Superior Court Reports, p.* 460. *And On Appeal*, 10 *N. Y. R.*, 260.

This case was brought in the same Court as that of Mr. Phœnix, and was very like it. The plaintiff had been legal adviser to the Supervisors, and sued for services.

Mr. Chief-Justice Oakley gave a long and very able opinion against the maintenance of the action. His attention seems not to have been drawn to the distinction under R. S., between the Boards of Supervisors in other counties and that body in New York ; but even as to these very provisions, treating them as applicable to New York, he expressed the opinion that they only codify the pre-existing judge-made law.

" Looking at these provisions of the Revised Statutes, it will be perceived that every County is a Corporation, with defined and restricted powers, to be exercised in a particular manner, viz., by the Board of Supervisors itself, or by some person in pursuance of a resolution by them adopted. *There is no grant of corporate power to be used by or in behalf of a County in any other mode,"* pp. 469, 470.

The report in the Court of Appeals is not accompanied by any opinion. Hon. Henry R. Selden was the reporter. He states that the affirmance was for the reasons given below, and the third point in his head-note states that "Supervisors of a County, as such are not a body corporate." (10 N. Y. R., 260.)

The last of this short list is McGarry *vs.* The Supervisors, 7 Robertson's Superior Court Reports, 464.

This was a very singular case. By consent of some unascertained person, the Supervisors were slipped into the record, by an amendment at the trial, as defendants, in lieu of the City Corporation, which had been regularly sued. Judgment was given for the plaintiff at the Special Term, but it was reversed at the General Term as grossly irregular. A full search through the dockets was made, and this is the only judgment that could be found in any action against the Supervisors of New York. It stands reversed.

We have seen that the Board of Supervisors of New York never was sued, except in the two instances of ex-District Attorney Phœnix and ex-Corporation Counsel Brady. In these cases it was held that the Board *could not* be sued for County charges or on contract; and the latter judgment was affirmed by the Court of last resort.

It is proper, however, not to pass this question by without bringing before the Court a line of action adopted by the Tweed Medieval Board of Supervisors and sanctioned by the Legislature, which, we must concede, whilst it did not make that Board a local governing body, did make it, by an unavoidable necessity, a corporate entity. This character, however, we conceive, was given it only by implication, and for the special and limited purposes indicated by the legislation now in this connection to be brought under notice.

The Tweed Board of Supervisors, organized under the Law of 1857, had considerable difficulty in making jobs, because they owned no lands in the City and County; but after awhile they obviated this difficulty. Some delay had occurred in the working of a special Court-House Commission created in the famous legislative year 1857; so, in 1861, the Supervisors obtained an Act enabling them to acquire lands under their name as the Board, etc., "for the building of a court-house." (Laws of 1861, p. 451.) It was to be paid for by County stock, to be issued and sold by the Comptroller. The history of this manœuvre is told with great simplicity and directness by Mr. Justice Leonard in the People vs. Opdyke, 40 Barb. R., 308. He says: "There are certain duties imposed by law upon the Board of Supervisors in respect to the Courts, and the furnishing of court-rooms suitable and sufficient, which it would not be in their power to perform, except by the consent of the Common Council, if the title to, and exclusive control of, the buildings where the Courts of the State were to be held were not vested in them." This notion of their *duties* was taken from that part of the Revised Statutes which did not apply to them.

The Act for this purpose passed through the Legislature very readily, because the rural Supervisors held precisely this relation to the public buildings within their Counties. And then Tweed's Supervisors accordingly applied to the Supreme Court and procured to be condemned to the use of the County of New York, a piece of the Park, which belonged to the Mayor, Aldermen and Commonalty of the City of New York, thereby creating a debt from the County of New York to the City Corporation of New York. This debt is represented by bonds from the County Corporation to the City Corporation. And ever since, as a mere sham or book-keeping formality, the County has been paying interest to the City ! ! ;Nothing can be imagined more extraordinary or ridiculous than what

was thus done. The governing body of New York that
had always governed it, and always supplied it with
court-houses and with jails, had land as sites for any
additional court-houses or jails that might be needed,
yet a piece of its land was taken out of its hands and
condemned to the use of the *County*, in order that the
County, forsooth, might have the fun of building a new
court-house or a new jail for itself ! ! !

In the same year, 1861, page 65, an Act was passed
authorizing the Supervisors to hire court-rooms. By
other like Acts, they acquired power to hire a jail and
armories. By these operations, all essentially similar,
the Supervisors got themselves into the condition of
being freeholders, and thus they do now own some
land in New York. But let us not overlook one circumstance. Not one single foot of that land can be
sold on execution. It is all held in trust under the
laws of the State for such public purposes as an
armory, a court-house, or a jail. Such lands cannot be
sold under an execution. The Supervisors cannot sell it.
They cannot obtain a rent for it. It could not be levied
on for the payment of any of these bonds. In *Darlington agt. the Mayor*, reported in 31 *New York Reports, page* 193, Ch J. Denio says :

"I am far from supposing, however, that such
" estate, real or personal, as may by law, or by author-
"ized acts * * * be devoted to public use, such
"as the public edifices, or their furniture or orna-
" ments, or the public parks or grounds * * * can
" be seized to satisfy a judgment. Such, clearly, can-
" not be the case, for these structures are public prop-
" erty, devoted to specific public uses, in the same
" sense as similar subjects in the use of the State Gov-
"ernment."

From the very nature and constitution of the trust
such property cannot be thus levied on. It is believed
that except in the wholly inapplicable provisions of
the Revised Statutes, the Supervisors have now no

color of statutory authority for superintending, furnishing or repairing these pieces of property, or incurring any expenditure in that way.

That these grants of power to take the fee of lands or to take a lease constituted the Board of Supervisors a legal person or corporate entity *to that extent,* may be admitted. But it went no further. (Per Ld. Kanyon, in 2 Term Rep., 672, citing Dyer, 100.)

D.

It may be thought scarcely respectful to the Court to argue in support of a proposition so plain as that, all public interests not placed in the special charge of some particular board or officer, and which may require vindication by judicial proceedings, are represented by the State in its sovereign capacity.

Indictments for crimes and misdemeanors constitute one large class of illustrations.

Bills to restrain and prevent public nuisances afford another.

Actions against public officers and public corporations for breach of trust or neglect of duty present another.

Instances might be adduced *ad infinitum.*

But this plain proposition is denied ; and even if the right of action be in the State, it is contended that the phraseology adopted by the Revision of 1830, in codifying the common law, as to the duties of the Attorney-General, has so restricted the powers of that officer that he cannot prosecute for such grievances as are mentioned in the complaint.

A very able answer to the defendants on both grounds may be found in the opinion of DUER, J., in Davis *v. The Mayor, &c., 2 Duer's R.,* 666.

"The powers of the Attorney-General in England were derived from the common law, and he was unwilling [at first] to say that any such powers be-

longed to the Attorney-General of this State; he was
unwilling to say that the latter possessed any powers
beyond those which either expressly, or by a necessary implication, are given to him by Statute. But
an examination of the Revised Statute, which defined
the powers and duties of the Attorney-General, had
removed the difficulty. By the rule of the common
law, the Attorney-General is a necessary party in all
suits in which the Crown is interested, and by the
first section of our Statute (1 R. S., 179,) it is made
the duty of the Attorney-General to "prosecute and
defend all actions, in the event of which the people of
the State shall be interested;" in other words, in all
such actions he is made a necessary party. In England, a corporate act affecting injuriously a whole community, is deemed a *public* wrong, which, as such,
the sovereign is bound to redress, and it is for this
reason that in all suits in which this redress is
sought, the Crown is held to be interested. The
doctrine and the reasoning, it seemed to him, were
just as applicable here, where fortunately the sovereignty resides, not in any individual, but in the
People, nor could he doubt that the People, as the sovereign power, ought to be considered as interested in
the event of every suit in which the illegal act which is
sought to be restrained or annulled, may, from its
nature, be justly treated as a public wrong. The
English decisions, therefore, in his opinion, were not
only proper to be consulted, but, unless it could be
shown that they had been contradicted and overruled
in our own courts, he held himself bound to follow
them."

The very peculiar practice-order made in this case
was reversed on appeal (see 4th Kern, 526); but all
Judge Duer's doctrines and principles were approved.

The State admits that all governmental action,
whether by any Executive department or in the judicial administration, must be conducted in proper

and convenient order, and through the agencies by law for the purpose appointed. And, therefore, this action might fail if it could be shown that any particular person or entity, other than the State itself, had been put in charge of the interest sought to be protected by this action. This is precisely the point, and the only point, ruled or indicated in *People* v. *Booth*, 32 *N. Y. R.*, 398.

As appears by the Report itself, and also by the printed case in the State Library (Court of Appeals Cases, Vol. 165, No. 20), the complaint expressly averred that the property in question belonged to the Corporation ; the forcible wrong or trespass complained of was also expressly stated to have been committed against the will of the Corporation. In such a case, no one could doubt but regular practice required the action to be brought by the faithful, honest, non-collusive corporate body. The interference of the Attorney-General was needless and, indeed, was utterly absurd. The People's counsel, or the Court of Appeals, had no thought of a case like the present. The casual remark about the State not being " called upon to incite the City Corporation to activity" was altogether irrelevant.

Court of Appeals.

The People of the State of New York

against

James H. Ingersoll, Impleaded with William M. Tweed, and others.

Points and Brief for the Defendant and Respondent Inger-soll, upon the RE-ARGUMENT *of the Plaintiffs' Appeal to the Court of Appeals, from the Judgment sustaining the Demurrer to the Complaint.*

FIRST QUESTION.

" *Was the title to the money the subject of the controversy in the county of New York?* "

The respondent maintains that it was.

2

First.—The money, the subject of the controversy, was taken from the treasury of the county of New York by the defendants.

At the time it was taken, it was on deposit in the National Broadway Bank, to the credit of an account kept by the county treasurer of said, county in his official character.

(Case, folio 9.)

It was paid out by the said bank for and on behalf of the said county treasurer, and to the debit of his said account 'upon warrants signed and countersigned, as warrants for the payment of county moneys are required by law to be.

(Case, folios 17–18.)

Such payments were (it is alleged) received by and divided among the defendants.

(Case, folio 33.)

No matter how it got into the treasury, so long as it came there in formal compliance with law, it was in the *possession* of the county.

Newman v. *Supervisors of Livingston County*, 45 *N. Y.*, 676, 687, 688.

Second.—Unless it is clear, from the circumstances through which this money came into the county treasury, that some person other than the county had title to it, the first question must evidently be answered in the affirmative.

Does any such legal effect follow from the circumstances under which the money came into the county treasury? We think not.

In the many oral and written discussions of the circumstances referred to, there has been some confusion and failure to distinguish between the different acts authorized by the Act of April 26, 1870, between the different acts done, and between the different actors in the transactions in question.

The 4th section of the Act of April 26, 1870, directs:

> 1st. The audit and certification of the liabilities of the county by the three officers designated.

> 2d. Provision for payment of the amounts found to be due by the issue of revenue bonds of the county.

> 3d. Provision for payment of such revenue bonds from the taxes of the following year by the Board of Supervisors.

> 4th. Payment of such liabilities by the comptroller.

It is only the first two of these provisions that have any bearing whatever on the circumstances under which the money in question found its way into the county treasury.

The others were not to be acted on, and were not acted on, if at all, until after the money was there, and title to it vested either in the county or in some one else.

(1.) As to the first provision, it is alleged in the complaint that the three officers designated, certified that large amounts had been audited and were found to be due, when, in fact, they had not been audited and were not due.

(Case, folios 7, 17, 31, 32.)

4

(2.) As to the second provision, it is alleged :

" That from time to time, as such certifications were
" respectively made known to him or his subordinates,
" the said comptroller caused to be issued bonds *as*
" *prescribed by the said act, in order to provide funds to*
" *pay the amounts so certified*, and obtain from *bona fide*
" purchasers thereof   *   *   *   * $6,312,000, which
" last mentioned sum was, in formal compliance with
" the statutes and usual modes of official proceeding
" in said city, deposited in the National Broadway
" Bank of the city of New York, as county treasurer
" of the said county, by virtue of his said official
" character as such chamberlain."

(Case, folios 8, 9.)

(3.) As this is the proceeding through which the
money in question came into the county treasury, it is
important to ascertain its precise character and effect.

What are revenue bonds of the county of New York,
and what is the process of providing funds by the issue
thereof ?

(4.) It should be particularly noticed that this act
of 1870 itself gives us no answer to this question, except in a sort of negative way, and this negative is
very important.

While the person to do every other act required or
authorized by section 4 is particularly designated, this
is simply directed *to be done*—the manner and the
agents being left absolutely to the existing provisions
of law and the exercise of ordinary corporate or county
official functions. It is not to be done by the officers
designated by the act. Their functions cease with the
signing of the certificate.

(5.) It should also be noticed that as matter of fact
it does not appear by the complaint, either by direct
allegation or by inference, that any of the defendants

or any one charged with being in confederation or combination with them, had anything whatever to do with either the issuing of the bonds or obtaining the money on them, or getting that money into the treasury, or with any single step of the proceeding by which the money in question came into the Broadway Bank ; or that there was any fraud or willful wrong on the part of any person acting in such preceedings, or anything special or peculiar about it, except that the certificates, by which it appeared to the officials by whom the money was provided, that it was their duty to provide it, were false.

(6.) The proceeding referred to in this provision by which this money did come into the treasury is described and regulated by *Chapter* 37, *Laws of* 1862, by which it appears that under the allegations of the complaint, and in fact, the Board of Supervisors of the county of New York borrowed the money in question on the faith and credit of the county of New York (§ 1).

And that the money was paid directly by the lenders into the treasury of the county of New York (§ 2).

And that upon presentation of receipts for such payments the comptroller caused to be issued to the lenders bonds of the county of New York, called " County Revenue Bonds " (§ 3).

And that these bonds were signed by the comptroller, countersigned by the mayor, sealed with the common seal of the Board of Supervisors, attested by the clerk of the board (§ 4).

(*See also Supervisor's Ordinance of March*
28, 1862, *Sups. Doc., No.* 4, 1863.)
1 *Hoff.*, 413.

Third.—This provision of money was a very simple

and ordinary proceeding, and it seems to us quite obvious that the money so borrowed and received by the county belonged to it ; but we proceed to consider the relations assumed by the lender and the borrower—the county—as bearing on the title to the money.

(1.) These relations are, of course, to be tested by facts as they were, and not simply as they may have been at the time supposed to be. It may, therefore, assist our conception of the case, if we suppose that immediately after the issue of the bonds, and while the money was still in the county treasury, the fraud which induced the county to borrow the money was discovered; the Board of Supervisors learned that they had in fact no legal authority to borrow it and the lender learned that the issue of the bond which he held was not authorized by law. In what relation did they find themselves ?

(2.) It is evident that there had arisen a right on the part of the lender, and a correlative obligation on the part of the county, for the return of the money loaned either *upon* the bond, because it was binding on the county, or irrespective of it, because it was not binding.

(3.) If the first theory of the case was the true one and the principles of *N. Y. and N. H. R. R. Co.* v. *Schuyler* (34 N. Y., 30) could be applied to the case, then the lender was entitled to have his bond treated precisely in all respects as if it had been legally and properly issued under the Act of 1870 ; and he was entitled to have put in force for his benefit, as a bondholder, all the provisions of that act, and of the previous legislation applicable to such bonds, which would have been obligatory in providing for payment of such legally and properly issued bonds. And as a part of this right, he was entitled to have the amount of his bond included in the tax levy of 1871 as a valid bond under the Act of 1870.

Nothing short of this would be upholding the obligation *as a contract.* No relegation to the general and discretionary taxing power of the State would satisfy the condition. The law under which the bond is by this theory assumed to be issued, is a part of the contract, and if it be upheld as a contract under the law, the provisions of the law must go with it.

Fourth.—The practical effect of this view of the case, if this money had remained in the county treasury, is very plain. The county had borrowed money, which it had agreed to repay in the following year. It had the money. The county was entitled to apply it in payment of the ordinary debts and expenses which would have otherwise been paid out of proceeds of taxation in 1871, precisely as if it had been raised on ordinary revenue bonds of that year, and while this amount would have been added to taxation to pay the bonds, the same amount would have been deducted from taxation through the payment of other debts, just as the amount of the regular income of the county from sources other than taxation, is applied in payment of debts, and deducted from the amount raised by taxation in each year.

It is altogether a mistake to suppose, as has been supposed, that the county is restricted in the payment of particular debts, to moneys raised or provided for the special purpose of paying those particular debts. It can pay any debt which it is authorized by law to pay out of any money not specially appropriated to some other purpose.

Its regular revenues are so applied, and the aggregate amount thereof deducted from the aggregate amount of taxes each year.

1 Hoff. Laws, 500.
2 R. S., Marg. page 474, § 104.

There is, therefore, no color for the idea that the money so borrowed did not belong to the county to be found in any practical or technical legal obstacle to its use by the county.

Fifth.—How can it be seriously claimed that money which the county had in its possession, which it had borrowed, which it was to repay, for which it had given consideration, and which it had power to use, did not belong to it?

If the county of New York did not own it, it owns no money that it borrows, and no county in the State owns any money that it borrows.

Sixth.—The case is still more simple if the bonds given be regarded as invalid by reason of the want of actual authority in the Board of Supervisors to issue them, or, what is equivalent, if it be deemed that there was no authority to levy taxes in 1871, under the Act of 1870, for their payment.

(1.) In this case, the lender either as having been deprived of his money illegally and wrongfully, or as having paid it under mistake of fact, or for a consideration which had failed, would be entitled to recover it from the county by action, and to have this very money paid in satisfaction of his judgment.

> 2 R. S., pp. 474, 475.
>
> Chapman *v.* City of Brooklyn, 40 N. Y., 372.
>
> Newman *v.* Supervisors of Livingston Co., 45 N. Y., 686.

(2.) Under this view of the case, the title to the money in question lay somewhere between the county that had it and the injured bondholder who was entitled to get it. It seems equally clear that the former had title to it as against every one but the latter. That is quite sufficient to answer the *First* question proposed affirmatively for all purposes of this action.

Seventh.—Before leaving this *First* question, we notice two positions which have been taken by the plaintiffs on former arguments of this cause.

1st. They say that these moneys were obtained and received by agents of the State, designated in the Act of 1870, and therefore they infer that the State has title to them.

We answer that the moneys were not obtained or received by agents of the State.

(1.) The officers mentioned in section 4 of that act were officers of the county of New York.

> 1 *Hoff. Laws*, 370.

If the Legislature had intended to appoint the persons designated State officers, the section would have been unconstitutional and void.

> *N. Y. Constitution, Art. 10, Sec. 2.*
> *N. Y. Constitution, Art. 3, Sec. 7.*
> *The People ex rel. Bolton v. Albertson, Court of Appeals,* 1873.
> *The People v. Tweed, N. Y. Oyer and Terminer,* 1873.

The construction which will uphold the statute must be adopted and the duties imposed be regarded as imposed upon county officers; otherwise the section being void, they were not agents of any one, or officers at all, for the purposes of the act.

(2.) The money was not obtained or received by the persons who it is claimed were made State agents. It was borrowed by the county, paid by the lenders directly into the county treasury, and the consideration for it given by the Board of Supervisors in the bonds of the county. It stands on precisely the same footing in this behalf as every ordinary exercise of corporate and municipal power under the authority of law.

The cases of *Lorrillard* vs. *The Town of Monroe* (1 Kern., 394), and *Sheboygan Co.* v. *Parker* (3 Wallace, 96), relied on by the plaintiffs, illustrate excellently what was *not* the character of either the actors or the acts done in this transaction.

2d. They say that the parties injured by the issue of the bonds and the obtaining of the money in question were future taxpayers of the county, *cestui que trusts* of the State, and, therefore, title to the money was in the State.

We answer, that at the time when this money was in the county treasury, and the time to which this question of title relates, no injury had been done to any tax-payers, for the money was there either to refund in extinction of the bonds, or it was there to pay debts of the county, thereby reducing the taxation of 1871 to just the amount by which it was to be increased to pay the bonds.

Second Question.

If the money was the money of the county, can the Board of Supervisors maintain an action for the cause stated in the complaint in behalf and for the benefit of the county?

The respondent maintains that it can.

First.—The power of the Board of Supervisors to maintain actions in general is as follows :

The county of New York is one of the original counties of the State, and was such when the Revised Statutes were adopted.

> *People* v. *Edmonds,* 15 *Barb.,* 529.
> 1 *R. S.,* 83 (*1st Ed.*), § 1
> *Constitution,* Art. 3, *Sec.* 3.

"Each county, as a body corporate, has capacity to sue and be sued in the manner prescribed by law."

> 1 *R. S.,* 364 (*1st Ed.*), § 1.

"All acts and proceedings by and against a county in its corporate capacity shall be in the name of the Board of Supervisors of such county."

> 1 *R. S.,* 364 (*1st Ed.*), § 3.

"Actions may be brought by the supervisors of a "county * * * * * to enforce any liability or any "duty enjoned by law to such officers or the body "which they represent * * * * * and to recover dam-"ages for any injuries ¨done to the property or rights of "such officers, or the bodies represented by them."

> 2 *R. S.,* 473 (*1st Ed.*), § 92.

No repeal of these provisions as to the county of New York is shown.

That they apply to that county is shown very clearly and conclusively (if it needs to be shown) in the dissenting opinion of Judge Parker in the General Term, Third Department in this case reported *sub. nom.* *People* v. *Tweed,* 13 *Abb. Pr., N. S., p.* 25, and in the *pamphlet of General Term opinion,* handed to this court on the former argument, pp. 73 to 77, Judge Parker says :

"I see no reason to doubt that these provisions apply as well to the county of New York as to all the other counties of the State, and if they do, that county has capacity to own money, and to bring suit to recover it from one having wrongful possession of it.

The learned counsel for the plaintiff endeavors to separate the county of New York from the other counties of the State, in respect to these powers, and to show that it was not intended by the revisers, nor the Legislature, to invest it with the corporate powers and capacity which Article 1, above referred to, gives, in terms, to " each county."

" This is argued from the fact that, in the first article of Title 2 of Chap. 12 above referred to, which is entitled " Of the Boards of Supervisors," the last section (§ 17) has this provision:

" The mayor, recorder and aldermen of the City of New York, shall be supervisors of the city and county of New York, and all the provisions of this *article* shall be construed to extend to them respectively, except when special provisions, inconsistent therewith, are or shall be made, by law, in relation to the city and county of New York" (1 *R. S.*, 368, § 17, 1*st Ed.*), and also that in Article 2 of the same title and chapter, entitled " Of the county treasurer." it is provided that " The chamberlain of the city and county of New York shall be considered the county treasurer thereof: and all the provisions of this *article* shall be construed to apply to him except," &c., as in section 17, above (1 *R. S.*, 370, § 29, 1*st Ed.*).

Based upon these sections, the learned counsel for the plaintiff says: " It will be observed that, in these parts of their systematic revision, the editors, by using in each instance the word *article* instead of the word *chapter*, indicated their conception that it was these articles alone that should have any operation within the city and county of New York.

The articles which declare counties, or their boards of supervisors, to be corporate bodies, and as such capable of sueing and being sued, were not thus made applicable.

The learned counsel for the plaintiff can scarcely be supposed, from this view of the scope and object of the provisions of the two sections quoted from Articles 1, and 2, to have examined them and the other parts of the chapter with due care. When in § 17 of Article 1 it is provided that all the provisions of *this* article shall be construed to extend to the mayor, &c., as super-visors, nothing more was done than is common, when an officer already in existence, is, by statute, invested with the character of another officer, viz., to go further, and invest him with the powers and duties of such other officer. The same may be said as to the pro-vision in § 29, of Article 2. The application of the pro-visions of the *chapter*, in these cases, instead of the *article*, would have been quite inappropriate and im-possible. The provisions of the *chapter* extend far beyond the scope of the powers and duties of boards of supervisors, or county treasurers. It includes pro-visions entirely inapplicable to those officers—treating for example, in its different articles, "Of the powers and rights of counties as bodies corporate"—"of the effects of a division of a county on its corporate rights and liabilities"—"of loan officers and commissioners of loans"—"of the clerks of counties"—"of sheriffs and coroners"—"of surrogates"—"of district attorneys," and of various other matters having no relation to boards of supervisors, or county treasurers.

The application of the provisions of the *chapter* to the mayor, &c., as supervisors, or to the chamberlain as county treasurer, would extend to them provisions relating to those other officers and subjects, and would be unmeaning and absurd. It is evident from an examination of the chapter, that the use of the word *article* instead of the word *chapter* in the sections above referred to, carries with it no implication of an inten-tion of the Legislature, that it was those two articles alone that were to have application within the city and county of New York. The article giving counties, as corporate bodies, capacity to hold property and to sue, is not, by the effect of the provision in section 17 and 29, respectively, expressly, or by implication, limited in its application, so as not to include the county of New York—and there is nowhere manifested, in this chapter, or anywhere in the Revised Statutes, an intention to except the county of New York from the operation of that article.

Neither is there anything in the circumstance that the territory and the inhabitants of the city and county are identical, as plaintiffs' counsel claims there is, which at all detracts from the right of the county to claim a separate corporate existence, notwithstanding the city charter confers upon the municipal corporation all the powers of local government. * * * *

Mr. Justice Strong, in *The People* vs. *Edmonds* (15 *Barb.*, 539), says : " Manhattan island, with the adjacent islands, was constituted a county by a law of the first Legislature ever held in the colony of New York on the first of November, 1683. It has been designated as a county in all the subsequent acts dividing this State into counties. It takes its organization as a county under the general laws of the colony and of the State and not under its charter as a city. The inhabitants, in effect, constitute two corporations—one as a county under the general laws of the State (1 *R. S.*, 364), and the other as a city under their charter."

Although the history of legislation, in respect to the county of New York, and the practice under it, has been invoked to prove that the county has been treated as excepted from the provision of law making it a body corporate, with capacity to sue, &c., we have been pointed to no act or acts of the Legislature passed since the Revised Statutes came into operation, whereby that provision has been repealed or abrogated—nor to any law doing away the effect upon the county of New York, of the provision contained in section 92 of art. 4, title 4, chap. 8, of part 3 of the Revised Statutes (2 *R. S.*, 473, 1st ed.), to the effect that "actions may be brought by the supervisors of the county * * * to enforce any liability, or any duty enjoined by law, to such officers, or the body which they represent * * * to recover damages for any injuries done to the property or rights of such officers, or the bodies represented by them."

For aught that I have been able to discover, these statutes remain in full force, not superseded by the various statutes passed with reference to the city and county of New York, but in most of these statutes the existence of the county of New York, and until 1857, of the board of supervisors of the county, as established by the Revised Statutes, as above stated, have been recognized. In 1857, an act was passed for the election of twelve supervisors to constitute the board of supervisors of county (*chap.* 590, *Laws of* 1857). This organization of the board continued until 1870, when an act was passed (*chap.* 190, *Laws of* 1870), making the mayor, recorder and aldermen of the city again the board of supervisors of the county of New York, and providing that " all the powers and duties conferred by *general* or special laws upon the board of supervisors of the city and county of New York, or upon any supervisors thereof * * * shall respectively belong to, be devolved upon, and be thereafter fully possessed and exercised respectively by the board of supervisors constituted by this act, or by any supervisor thereof."

This capacity to sue, in the name of its. board of supervisors, expressly given by statute to the county of New York, is not affected by the circumstance that the board of supervisors of that county has been, by special provisions of law, in relation to the city and county of New York, inconsistent with some of the general powers conferred upon boards of supervisors of counties restricted in its powers and duties. Nor is it necessary to the preservation of such capacity, that it should be " the sole general legal representative of all public or common interests of the county's inhabitants or tax-payers." The board of supervisors of the county of New York is still the representative of the inhabitants of the county in reference to the property and finances of the county, and still authorized

Second.—The cause of action stated in the complaint is one of those which the supervisors are empowered to maintain by virtue of the provisions above cited.

(1.) The cause of action is simply *that the defendants got the money*; and that they got it under such circumstances that it was their duty to return it, or under such circumstances that their getting it was a wrong and a damage to some one.

The circumstances are stated and the amount of money demanded. Further than this the complaint does not undertake to go.

One defendant is alleged to have certified the bills without audit; but the others are not charged to have had connection with this, and that is not what they are sued for.

Other of the defendants are alleged to have prepared and presented fictitious bills, upon which the money was afterwards paid, but Tweed is not charged with having any knowledge of or connection with this, and is not sued for it.

No wrong or liability is charged against any one having to do with the provision of the money by the issue of bonds.

All these are but circumstances—not injurious in and of themselves—not constituting any substantive part of the cause of action—but showing the character of, and the liability created by the act of taking and dividing the money. This act is the cause of action, whatever the action may be called.

(2.) If the money thus taken belonged to the county, then the *liability* to return it was a liability to the county, and the *damage* done by taking it was a damage to the county. This is certainly true, as a general proposition, and whoever asserts that it is not true in this case, should give some satisfactory reason for the exception.

(3.) It is said on the part of the plaintiff, as a reason why this general proposition is not true in this case:

1st. That the county is not injured by the taking of the money, because the payment of the bonds is not charged on the county treasury, or on county property, but the State has secured their payment by imposing the duty upon a class of its taxpayers selected by itself.

2d. That the taxpayers are only injured, and the county does not represent them.

We answer that these assertions are equally true of all county and municipal property.

All such property, if destroyed or removed, must be replaced directly or indirectly by taxation.

Every injury to the property of a body politic is an injury in the same ultimate sense to the taxpayers of that body, and to them only.

Every suit by a Board of Supervisors to enforce a liability to their county, or recover damages for injury to its property or rights, must involve just the elements of injury to taxpayers which are claimed to exist here, and if they are reasons why the Supervisors cannot sue in this case, there are no cases in which the provision of the Revised Statutes last cited applies. The State must, henceforth, redress all injuries to county and to municipal property.

A suit upon this cause of action, by the Board of Supervisors, does involve a representation of taxpayers, to just the extent of all suits by Board of Supervisors, by virtue of the statute. To that extent, and for that purpose, they are specially constituted and empowered representatives " of that undefined, unknown " and unascertainable class of individuals."

The answer to each question upon which reargument has been ordered, should be affirmative.

WILLIAM FULLERTON,
ELIHU ROOT,
Of Counsel.

Court of Appeals.

The People of the State of New York

against

James H. Ingersoll, impleaded with William M. Tweed, Elbert A. Woodward and Andrew J. Garvey.

ADDITIONAL POINTS FOR DEFENDANT, UPON THE ARGUMENT OF THE PLAINTIFF'S APPEAL FROM THE JUDGMENT SUSTAINING THE DEMURRER TO THE COMPLAINT.

It is the object of this argument to meet certain objections which are made by the Attorney-General to an affirmative answer to the questions proposed by the Court, and certain suggestions which the Attorney-General makes by way of avoidance of such questions.

These objections and suggestions are :

First.—That the money, which is the subject of this controversy, never was lawfully in the Treasury of the County of New York.

Second.—That the County of New York had not the power of disposition of this money.

Third.—That only an " undefined, unknown and unascertainable class of individuals," who will be the taxpayers of New York at some distant future time, are the

parties injured by the acts complained of, and that they
are represented only by the State.

Fourth.—That there is an independent right in the
Attorney-General to bring this action, whether the County
bring it or not.

FIRST.

It is said by the Attorney-General that the money in
question was illegally and improperly paid into the
treasury of the County by the Comptroller.

To this we answer:

I.—The complaint alleges, "*That the money in
"question was in formal compliance with the
"statutes and usual modes of official proceeding
"in said city, deposited in the National Broad-
"way Bank, in the City of New York, to the
"credit of an account therein kept by the
"Chamberlain of the City of New York, as
"County Treasurer of the said County, by
"virtue of his said official character as such
"Chamberlain.*"

This being an allegation of a fact in the complaint, it must be taken as true on the argument of this demurrer.

II.—The law *required* the money in question to be
paid into the treasury of the County as it was
paid.

The following statutes contain the provisions of
law under which this money was paid into the
County Treasury, and under which it was to be
paid out by the Comptroller, as directed by the
law of 1870.

I. Chapter 37 of the laws of 1862, section 2, pro-

vides: "That moneys borrowed upon the re-
"venue bonds of the County of New York shall
"be deposited by the parties lending the same
"in the County Treasury."

II. Chapter 623 of the laws of 1865, section I.,
provides: "That all revenue of the City and
"County, of every kind, shall be deposited in
"certain banks in the City of New York to be
"designated by the Chamberlain."

III. Chapter 137 of the laws of 1870, article 5,
section 37, provides (under the head of "Finance
Department"): "For a bureau, the chief officer
"of which shall be called the Chamberlain, for
"the reception of all moneys paid into the.
"treasury of the city, and for the payment of
"money on warrants drawn by the Comptroller,
"and countersigned by the Mayor."

IV. Chapter 590 of the laws of 1857, section 6,
provides: "That the Finance Department, the
"Mayor, Aldermen and Commonalty of the
"City of New York, and its officers, shall have
"the like powers and perform the like duties in
"regard to the fiscal concerns of the Board of
"Supervisors, as they possess in regard to the
"fiscal concerns of the Mayor, Aldermen and
"Commonalty, and that *no moneys shall be*
"*drawn from the Treasury of the County, ex-*
"*cept on a warrant drawn by the Comptroller,*
"*and countersigned by the Clerk of the Board*
"*of Supervisors.*"

V. The Revised Statutes, vol. 1, page 370, 1 Ed.,
sec. 29, provides: "That the Chamberlain of the
"City and County of New York shall be con-
"sidered the County Treasurer thereof."

Section 22 of the same article provides:
"That it shall be the duty of the County
"Treasurer to receive all moneys belonging to
"the County, from whatever sources they may
"be derived."

It follows, from the statute above cited, that it was the duty of the Chamberlain, as County Treasurer, to receive the money in question in his official capacity, and that the only manner in which this money could be paid out of the Treasury was by the Comptroller, as directed in section 4 of chapter 382 of the laws of 1870 ; and, also, that the only way in which the Comptroller could pay the amounts found to be due, as he was directed to do by this section of the Act of 1870, was by a warrant drawn on the County Treasurer. The Comptroller had no power to fulfill the injunction of the statute of 1870, cited by the Attorney-General as showing that he had the money in question, in any other manner than by drawing a warrant upon the County Treasurer.

The County Treasurer, therefore, must have had the money, and not the Comptroller.

SECOND.

It is said that the County had no power to use the money in question when it had it, and would have none if it recovered it again.

The first section of this very chapter 382 of the laws of 1870 provides : " That from the amounts " which the Board of Supervisors are authorized to " raise by taxation, *shall be deducted the aggregate* " *amount of the estimated revenues of the County,* " for the year 1870, not otherwise specifically appro- " priated by law."

So that it appears by this section, that there were to be in the treasury of the County for the payment of the amounts authorized to be paid by the Act, two classes of moneys.

First : Those received from the revenues of the County.

Second : Those raised by taxation.

The money so received from the regular revenues of the County were applicable to the payment, and were intended to be applied to the payment of any of the debts authorized to be paid, without any distinction between the different moneys in the treasury arising from different sources.

This is conclusive in favor of the position of the defendants that the county can pay any debts which it is authorized to pay out of any moneys which it has, not otherwise specifically appropriated, and that all moneys paid into the treasury lose their identity and become merged in the common account.

If a valid claim had been audited and certified under this Act of 1780, and presented to the Comptroller for payment he could have paid it, and it would have been his duty to pay it; if there had been funds in the County Treasury derived from any source whatever, not otherwise specifically appropriated, whether the amount had been "*provided for*" by the issue of revenue bonds, or remained to be thereafter "provided for" by the issue of such bonds. The Statute does not say that the moneys to be paid shall be "provided," but it is that the amounts found to be due shall be "*provided for*" by the issue of revenue bonds.

This would be satisfied, as well by the issue of bonds after payment by the Comptroller, out of the unappropriated moneys in the Treasury, as by an issue of bonds before payment.

The funds raised by the issue of revenue bonds to provide for the amounts found to be due, became, whether such amounts had been paid, or were thereafter to be paid, but a part of the general fund in the County Treasury, not distinguished or distinguishable from any other moneys in the treasury, and under the control of the county for all lawful objects.

THIRD.

It is said that "the real and only injury, unless to the
"State, was to that undefined, unknown and unas-
"certainable class of individuals, who, at some un-
"known period, were to be assessed under the
"tax laws for the payment of these bonds;" and
that "when the wrong was perpetrated, and this ac-
"tion commenced, they may have been all foreign-
"ers or unborn," and therefore it is urged that the
Supervisors of the county of New York have no
right to recover the money in question.

The untenable character of this argument will
readily be perceived, when we consider the constitution of the body of citizens inhabiting the county,
or who are liable to pay the taxes assessed upon those
living within its limits.

It seldom or ever occurs, in the very nature of
things, that all of the tax-payers of a county derive
benefit from the taxes which they pay. Every year,
month and week witnesses a change in the body of
tax-payers. People move in the county of New York
to-day, and become liable to taxation for the payment of debts contracted years gone by, and from
which they derive no benefit.

Many who pay taxes to-day will cease to be inhabitants of the county before the money is expended
for any purpose from which they can derive any advantage.

The law takes no notice of these constant and
necessary changes.

The Board of Supervisors are organized as a body
corporate, and represent the county itself. They have
the capacity "to sue and be sued;" "to purchase and
"hold lands for the use of its inhabitants;" "to
"make such contracts, and to purchase and hold
"such personal property as may be necessary to the
"exercise of its corporate and administrative powers;"

" to make such orders for the disposition, regulation,
" or use of its corporate property as may be deemed
" conducive to the interests of its inhabitants."

No one would think of questioning the power of
the Supervisors of a county, because their acts in
effecting any one of these objects would affect the
class of persons who might be inhabitants of the
county at some future period, and therefore were
" undefined, unknown and unascertainable."

The powers of the Supervisors, within the limits
prescribed by the Statute, are exercised for the benefit of those who may be the inhabitants or tax-payers of the county at any period in the future.

The present debt of the city of New York, irrespective of the bonds in question, is not payable
until years to come, and is then to be paid by that
"undefined, unknown and unascertainable" class
who, at the maturity of the bonds, may reside within
the limits of the county.

From the very nature of things and the constitution of society, the recovery of this money by the
Board of Supervisors, and the payment of it to its
County Treasurer, must be regarded in law, whether
it results so in point of fact·or not, for the benefit of
those who, in the end, may be taxed to pay the
bonds in question.

If this objection should obtain in this and all other
cases where it is equally applicable, the practical
results would be that the wheels of government
would be stopped.

When a person becomes a citizen of the county of
New York, *eo instanta*, he is liable, as a tax-payer,
to contribute to the payment of existing obligations,
from which he has derived no advantage, and also to
provide for future expenditures when he may have
ceased to be an inhabitant.

FOURTH.

The answers to Mr. Tilden's argument as to the independent and paramount powers of the Attorney-General of England, are as follows:

1. This action differs radically and entirely from those in which the power of the Attorney-General has been exercised. Those were without exception either to enforce the performance of a trust, or to compel the return of trust funds to the custodian from whom they had been diverted. No such relief as is asked here has ever been given by any Court to the Attorney-General of England.

2. The power of the English Crown, through its Attorney-General, over public officers, was based upon the peculiar character of English municipal corporations. On the other hand, our corporations are entirely different in their character, and are controlled directly by the State, without the intervention of any Attorney-General, through the agency of local officers, who are themselves, in the exercise of their statutory duties, agents of the State in the same sense, and to the same effect, that the Attorney-General is.

The reason of the power of the Crown to exercise control in actions by its Attorney-General over the administration of trusts by the officers of its municipal corporations is, that those corporations are in England similar in their nature to our private corporations. Their officers are not the creatures or the agents of the Crown. The Crown does not act through them, and, therefore, the only means by which the Crown can protect the citizens affected by their acts, is through bill or information by the Attorney-General. That jurisdiction exists here as to private corporations, for the same reason that it exists in England both as to private and as to municipal corporations. But the reason does not exist here as to the political subdivisions of the State, or the quasi-corporations created by the state for the purpose of carrying out its will, or administering trusts for the benefit of the citizens resident in their respective localities.

These political sub-divisions and quasi-corporations are the creatures of the State. The acts of their officers, are the acts of the State. Actions brought by the officers mentioned in the 92d Section of Chapter 8 of Part 3 of the Revised Statutes above cited, are as truly in the exercise of the power of the State to protect its citizens, or redress injuries to their interests, as actions brought by the Attorney-General of England to enforce the performance of duties by the officers of English municipal corporations. This remedy being substituted by our statute for that which exists in England, there is no reason as well as no authority for assuming the continuance of the English rule.

FIFTH.

The duty of protecting the rights of citizens of particular localities within this State by appeal to the Courts in cases where, if in England, the Attorney-General might interpose, has been provided and specially assigned by statute in this State, in part to designated officers of the localities themselves, and in part to the Attorney-General, each acting by virtue of the statute *quoad hoc*, as the agent of the State. By Title 4, Part 3, Chap. 8, Section 105 of the Revised Statutes (Vol. 2, page 472, 1st Ed., it is provided that " actions may be brought by the Super-" visors of a County, by the loan officers and Com-"missioners of Loans of a County; by County "Superintendents of the Poor ; by Supervisors of "Towns; by Overseers of the Poor of the several "towns; by School Commissioners and Commis-"sioners of Highways of the several towns; by

" Trustees of School Districts, and by Trustees of
" Gospel and school lots * * * * to enforce
" any liability or any duty enjoined by law to such
" officers and the body which they represent
" * * * * and to recover damages for any in-
" juries done to the property or rights of such officers
" and the bodies represented by them ; " and it is pro-
" vided (1 R. S., page 179, first Ed., sec. 1,) that " it
" shall be the duty of the Attorney-General to pros-
" secute and defend all actions, in the event of which
" the People of this State shall be interested ; " and
it is provided by the Code (Sec. 111), " every action
" must be prosecuted in the name of the real party
" in interest, except as otherwise provided by Section
" 113," which does not apply in this case. It cannot be maintained that the People of the State have
such an *interest* in the event of the action which
may be brought by the Board of Supervisors of a
County as to empower the Attorney-General to bring
such action in the name of the people, because, if it
were so, it would be the *duty* of the Attorney-General
to bring the action under the foregoing provision of
the Revised Statutes, which the Supervisors are
directed to bring by the same statute. No such
action as this has ever been brought by the Attorney-
General for this State, and nothing can be clearer
than that no such action was ever contemplated in
any of the legislation of the State.

No provision has ever been made among the clearly defined powers of the Treasurer of the State,
authorizing him to receive the money. No provision
has ever been made by which any officer has any authority in law in any manner whatsover to apply the
moneys, if so recovered and paid into the Treasury
of the State, to the use or for the benefit of the class
of citizens alleged to have been injured by the acts
complained of. If such an action as this had been
contemplated for the redress of injuries to the citizens or tax-payers of counties, the law certainly
would have provided means by which the injuries
could be redressed in the action.

The sovereign power of the State is not necessarily exerted through the Attorney-General. It may adopt different forms and modes to accomplish its purposes, and when the Legislature determines that certain actions shall be commenced and rights enforced, in the name of officers known to the law in the political divisions of the State, it is as much an exercise of State sovereignty as if the action had been commenced in the name of the People of the State by its Attorney-General, because they are commenced by and under its authority, and according to its mandate.

The power that enables it to designate the names of persons or officers in whom certain actions shall be commenced also enables it to disqualify itself from bringing such actions in the name of the People. Such disqualification, when established by an act of the People through its Legislature, must continue until it is removed, and the power resumed by legislative action.

It matters not in whose name the law requires an action to be commenced on behalf of a municipal corporation, provided the proper object can be effected.

The Legislature creates municipal corporations, and possesses the power to determine how their rights shall be prosecuted and their wrongs redressed, and when it determines that a County shall be represented by a Board of Supervisors, and all actions affecting its property brought in the name of such Supervisors, it not only determines the party plaintiff to any action for that purpose, but also deprives the People of the right to bring it in their own name.

This new and revolutionary doctrine, that there is a concurrent and paramount right in the State to bring actions in behalf of a county, notwithstanding the Act of Legislature providing that such actions shall be brought by the Board of Supervisors of a county, is heard of for the first time in this State, or in this country, in the prosecution of this action, and is not be received with favor. The proposition is wholly unsustained by the authority, and entirely at war with the manner in which the law has been heretofore administered in this State. The political divisions of the State, and the officers who govern them, are provided for by statute. The duties which they are to perform, and the manner of prosecuting rights and redressing wrongs, are defined by the same authority: There is no *casus omissus* which makes it necessary for us to seek for extraordinary remedies, or look to the common law of England for precedents. The argument that the sovereign powers of the State is exerted through local municipal officers as well as through its Attorney-General, does not belittle the State or circumscribe its authority.

The argument of Mr. Tilden seems to be predicated of the belief that we are attacking in some way the jurisdiction of the Court to maintain this action.

Such a question has never been raised or even suggested in this case on behalf of the defendant. The distinction between the jurisdiction of the Court and the right of the People to maintain an action in the Court is too apparent.

Mr. Tilden, in reviewing the cases of Doolitle *vs.* The Board of Supervisors of Broome County, Roosevelt *vs.* Draper, and Wetmore *vs.* Story, where the right to maintain an action was denied the individual tax-holder, asserts that the denial of such right of action in the tax-payer is equivalent to an assertion of a right of action in the People by the Attorney-General. He says, that the tax-payer, stripped of a right of action in his own name, on behalf of himself and associates, relegated to a condition of helplessness which calls for the interposition of the sovereign as *parens patriæ.*

This proves nothing so far as this case is concerned. Because a tax-payer has no authority, either by statute or common law, to bring an action to redress a wrong to a whole community, of which he forms but a small part, and where he sustains no injury which is not common to all, falls far short of proving that the Board of Supervisors of a County, who are authorized by statute to maintain an action, cannot redress a wrong against the County. The question here is not whether there is no one to sue because tax-payers cannot, but it is whether the officers of a county shall exercise the power conferred upon them by law.

It will hardly be contended that should the Legislature now pass an act authorizing the tax-payer to maintain the action (which was denied to him in the cases referred to), that still the exercise of such authority would be regarded as concurrent with the People of this State.

4. Mr. Tilden's argument proves too much or nothing. If it be true, then the Attorney-General has a supervisory power over the administration of all local offices in all counties and municipal corporations throughout the State. If the Treasurer of the County of Erie, or Oneida, or Columbia, pays out money in excess of his authority, the Attorney-General may recover it into the Treasury of the State. If he refuses to pay out money in the performance of his duty, the Attorney-General can compel him to do so. Nor is it easy to see why the commission of a wrong is essential, as a condition, under this theory, to the State obtaining the money hitherto supposed to belong to its Counties, or why all moneys in all Counties throughout the State may not upon the same reasoning be gathered into the State Treasury, and managed and disbursed under the parental direction of the Attorney-General.

WILLIAM FULLERTON,
ELIHU ROOT,

COURT OF APPEALS.

THE PEOPLE OF THE STATE OF NEW
YORK,
Plaintiffs and Appellants,

against

JAMES H. INGERSOLL, impleaded
with WILLIAM M. TWEED, ELBERT
A. WOODWARD and ANDREW J.
GARVEY,
Defendant and Respondent.

REPLY *of Appellants
to* INGERSOLL'S
Additional Points.

I.—The Legislature of 1870 (p. 878, § 2), assuming
that there may have then existed some claims which
it designated "liabilities against the County of New
York," authorized Hall, Tweed and Connolly to audit
them ; directed provision for them be made by the issue of revenue bonds in anticipation of the tax-levy of
1871, and also directed that the Comptroller should
pay the claims on the said Auditors' certificate.
Claims wholly false and fraudulent were in due form
—but without examination—certified by the Auditors,
and payment was made accordingly. Pursuant to
a fraudulent conspiracy between Tweed, the only
Auditor who is made a party, and the other defendants, the money thus obtained was divided between
them. The Act directed the Supervisors of New
York to levy a tax in 1871 sufficient to reimburse the
bond-holders.

This action was commenced *after* the money had
been borrowed and paid to the conspirators. The
bonds matured December 31, 1871. The action was
commenced *before* that date, and, of course, whilst
the bond-holders yet remained unpaid. In its primary
aspect, it is an ordinary common-law action of *tort.*
(*Union Bank* v. *Mott,* 27 *N. Y. R.,* 633.) It is

brought by the State against one of its Auditors and his confederates to recover damages to the extent of the wrong for these mischievous and oppressive acts. The wrong done was setting in motion (16 *Wallace, p.* 13), by an abuse and perversion of powers granted, a process which must ultimately injure some unknown and unascertainable class of the State's future tax-payers. (See *First and Fourth Points in Pltff.'s Brief on Re-argument, pp.* 17 *and* 26.)

In such an action the injured prosecutor selects, at his free will and pleasure, of his grace and mercy, or in his capricious ill-will, as many or as few of the *tort feasors* as he thinks fit. No exception can therefore be taken to the omission of Hall and Connolly as defendants. They might have been simpletons who were misled by their ignorance, thus being in some sense morally innocent. If they were otherwise, policy or expediency might justify the Executive in declining to prosecute them. Guilt or negligence in the Auditors is not necessary to the maintenance of the action ; nor is the *status* of public officer a necessary qualification to becoming a prosecutable swindler in such a case. Had the three Auditors been honest and diligent in the highest degree, and also accurate to a hair in the observance of all legal forms, still the private persons who contrived the deception upon them, and thereby generated or worked into existence this legally valid and effectual nest-egg for the inevitable oppression of future unknown tax-payers, would be liable—that is, if any one would be liable. (*See Mr. Curtis' argument ; paper marked A, page* 10. *Also a like doubt hinted at in Mr. Justice Parker's dissent; paper marked D,* 183.)

These propositions are so plain, so obviously correct, that an extended argument in their favor might well be pronounced indecorous.

It is indeed a useful maxim, and must ever be observed by attorneys in bringing actions, and Courts in sustaining or dismissing them, that where the law has appointed a prosecutor, that very prosecutor must bring the action (*Plff.'s Brief on Re-argument, pp.* 120, 121), and it is not to be denied that such an appointment may be implied from circumstances.

We have shown in our Brief on re-argument (*pp.* 116 *to* 119), that *perhaps* a legal title to some land was, by a singular artifice, vested in "the Board of Supervisors of the County of New York." (*Laws of* 1861, *p.* 452.) Now, it may be that, under the second head just referred to, *i. e.*, as a matter of inference or judicial construction, ejectment or trespass to recover possession of these lands, or for an injury to them, should be brought in the name of this body, as, *quoad hoc*, a corporation. And so of like things.

In this single aspect a sort of relevancy may be conceded to the inquiry, did this money which was raised upon the bonds *belong* in any way, at any time, or under any circumstances, to any officer or entity other than the State, who or which might, in the due order and harmony of judicial proceedings, come into Court, and on the ground of *title* maintain an action for it? We will, by and by, look more fully into this point of actual or constructive ownership, and this right of action in some other than the State to be *thence* inferred. But, at this stage, we would draw special attention to the inquiry, was the New York Board of Supervisors expressly, or by implication, *appointed* to the office of prosecutor in respect of such wrongs as the present?

The affirmative of this point, if maintainable, would constitute a complete defense to the action, in that primary aspect of it now under consideration.

Not a word or a line of authority for this proposition has been cited. *Expressio unius exclusio est alterius* is a maxim. After that recent period, when the practice of authorizing the Supervisors to *pay*, or to direct payments, was introduced, it became necessary, of course, to keep a County Treasury, and taxation was

authorized to the extent of these authorized payments.
Neither "the County" nor "the Supervisors" ever
had, or could have had, any other funds or resources;
yet a right of action for these very taxes being necessary, as to personal property, it was not given to the
Supervisors, though they were the very body by whose
order all taxes were levied. It was expressly given to
the Receiver of Taxes. (*Laws of* 1867, *p.* 752, § 11.)

More impressive still—the Surrogate is a County
officer. In the tax levies for Tweed's Medieval
Board it will be found that the Supervisors took upon
themselves the duty of paying his salary and clerk
hire and other office expenses. He, of course, was to
account for and deduct the fees received. In 1870 the
late Surrogate was suspected of being a delinquent.
In the very Act containing the Auditors' Section 4,
now in question, the Board of Supervisors were expressly authorized "to investigate the alleged deficiency in the accounts of the late Surrogate, * * and to
institute the proper legal proceedings to recover the
amount of such deficiency." (*Laws of* 1870, *p.* 880,
§ 10.)

II.—The main ground of the defense, however, is the
unsound postulate that something called *the County*
owned the money and was the injured party. This
was put forth boldly, but was a pure assumption in
the argument of Mr. Curtis. (*Paper marked A.*) The
same assumption is the basis of Mr. Justice Parker's
dissent, and of his rather lugubrious "trust" that the
manifest scoundrelism of the conspirators will not
"control the application of [the supposed] rules of
law" on which, as their only subterfuge, they rely.
(*Paper marked D, page* 180.) These supposed rules
are merely of a technical nature, such as no just man
need weep to find are broken reeds. This "very com-

mendable regard for the law itself'' (14 *N. Y.*, *p.* 210)
is much more frequently affected by a professional
champion when striving to defeat justice by a technical
objection, than felt by Judges when dealing with it.

The claim of ownership by the Supervisors has been,
in part at least, placed upon the simple ground of possession. This was adverted to by the defendant's counsel at the hearing ; and, agreeably to a promise then
made, the FIRST head of their Additional Points is now
devoted to it.

Better and more distinctly stated on the oral argument than now in these Additional Points, this branch
of their argument is, that the money in question duly
and lawfully passed into the County Treasurer's bank
account, and there rested for a moment before the conspirators got possession of it. On this fact, supposing
it to be a fact, it is contended that the money belonged
to the County during that moment, and that, by consequence, the County Board of Supervisors acquired the
legal title to it, and the right to recover it from the conspirators who obtained it by means of the certificates
of audit held by them.

If the facts were all as alleged, we deny the conclusion attempted to be deduced.

This money was never granted or given to the County,
or to the Supervisors, in any way whatever. If the
County Treasurer, as is not the fact, had been the
legally authorized custodian of it for this brief space,
this fact would not have given, either to him or to the
County, any beneficial ownership of it. Its possession,
if authorized at all, was only for safe-keeping until the
certificate holders should demand it.

Possession is title enough in trespass against a wrong-
doer who, without right, divests or interferes with
that possession. He who, on the cry '' stop thief,''
knocks down the fugitive and wrests the stolen goods
from him, has a perfect title as against all the world
except the owner. But surely this is not the kind of

title which would bar or impede an action by the really injured party against the thief, whether for the specific goods or for damages. Again, if, whilst the money remained in the hands of the bank, the County Treasurer or the Comptroller during the interval referred to, the conspirators' villainy had been made public, it must be admitted that the possessor, whether his possession was technically rightful or not, could, as a matter of pure fact, safely have refused payment to the conspirators, and retained the money. But this would not prove that such possessor had a beneficial ownership of the money. Such a lawless possession and contempt of the law's own express command, in refusing to recognize the certificate-holder's title, could no doubt be defended. Before the Code of Procedure it might have been impossible to resist, *at law*, the swindler's action. Perhaps a bill in Equity and an injunction might then have been necessary. A mandamus is a proceeding at law, but the writ issues or not in discretion, and, of course, it would not have been granted in such a case. Under the Code, it is presumed that the possessor's liability to the State would be a perfect answer to the swindler's action. These circumstances neither show a title to the money in such temporary possessor, nor any defect in the State's right of action.

Whilst admitting that the Comptroller used the County Treasurer's bank account as a temporary place of deposit for this money, it has been asserted that the act was unauthorized and did not, in point of law, transfer the money to the County Treasury.

Frivolous and immaterial as this issue is, it has been made; and the State's counsel choose to stand by it.

The complaint, in terms, concedes that this act was done "in formal compliance with the Statutes." That, however, is not the admission of a *fact;* and we have shown that *the law* cannot be *admitted*. The Court knows and must declare it. (*See Plaintiff's Brief on Re-argument, pp.* 14 *to* 16.)

It may be convenient here to re-produce *verbatim* (*Laws* 1870, *p.* 878, § 4), so much of the section as bears on this precise point: "The amounts found to be due shall be provided for by the issue of revenue bonds of the County of New York, payable during the year 1871, and the Board of Supervisors shall include in the ordinance levying the taxes for the year 1871, an amount sufficient to pay said bonds and the interest thereon. Such claims shall be paid by the Comptroller to the party or parties entitled to receive the same, upon the certificate of the officers named herein."

That the Comptroller was to be sole actor in this proceeding is shown in *Plaintiff's Brief on Re-argument,* *p.* 12. That the Comptroller, *in fact,* proceeded precisely as this argument suggests is alleged. (*See Complaint, fols.* 8, 9.) He, himself, "obtained" the money from the *bona fide* holders of the bonds.

To show that the Comptroller did not receive and could not lawfully have received the money on those bonds, the defendant, at the argument, referred to the Laws of 1862, page 132. (*See his Brief on Re-argument,* *p.* 5.) It was then contended, and is now re-asserted, that Section 2 of that Act required the money to be "paid directly into the Treasury of the County of New York." This Act of 1862 is wholly inapplicable to the bonds in question. It refers exclusively to moneys borrowed "in anticipation of the collection of the annual taxes of the County"—* * "to pay the ordinary charges and expenses under appropriations made by the said Board of Supervisors for the support of the County Government, including the Metropolitan Police within said County." And it expressly provides, "that the amount so borrowed shall at no time exceed the sum which the said Board may, by then existing laws, be authorized to impose and raise by taxation during the year in which such moneys may be borrowed."

The moneys derived from the bonds in question were

not to be paid under "appropriations by the Board of Supervisors," or for ordinary current expenses or charges. They were to pay od claims against a former "superseded" and "abolished" Board. Neither the moneys nor the bonds could have any reference to the sum authorized to be raised "by taxation *during the year* in which such moneys may be borrowed," for these moneys were to be borrowed on bonds issued in 1870, in anticipation of a tax to be levied not in that year, but in 1871. Neither were the bonds, nor lawfully could they be, "made payable within one year from the date" when the lenders deposited their money, as required by the cited Act of 1862 (*page* 132, § 3). The bonds in question were all, properly of course, issued prior to September 2, 1870 ; and they were made payable December 31, 1871. (*See Complaint and Schedules annexed to it.*) The Comptroller's authority for issuing such bonds as are mentioned in the cited Act of 1862, was, first, a resolution of the Board of Supervisors authorizing the loan to be taken up ; and, secondly, the County Treasurer's certificate that the proposed lenders had deposited the money with him. (§§ 2 and 3). The Comptroller's sole authority for issuing the bonds now in question, was the three Auditors' certificate of allowance. In a word, the Act of 1862 regulates the practice of issuing County bonds during the year, in anticipation of that same year's taxes, for moneys lent and deposited with the County Treasurer, to be paid out on the resolutions and audits of the Board of Supervisors for the same identical current expenses, then already authorized to be defrayed by taxation in that same year. The bonds in question may be denominated eccentrics. They were specially authorized to discharge old claims on the allowance of a Special Board of Audit, and the lenders were to be reimbursed in a future year. The Act in question was itself the County tax-levy of the current year ; the taxes authorized to be levied were all for other purposes; none of them were to be levied for the payment of these bonds. (*Laws of* 1870, *p.* 875, §§ 1, 3). We have not found any actual repeal of the cited Act of 1862; but § 7 of the same Act of 1870 (*page* 879) seems to be a complete substitute therefor. It authorized His Majesty the Comptroller to borrow without bonds in any way he might please; but, like the Act of 1862, it limited him to "expenditures under the appropriations for each current year."

The plaintiffs have asserted that after putting this money into the County Treasury, had he been able to do so, in the legal sense of these words, the Comptroller could never have gotten it out again coercively by any lawful authority of his own, unless through an action at law.

This is easily shown. The Act of April 12, 1870 (*p.* 481), which "superseded" and "abolished" the great Tweed Elective Board and created a wretched little starveling in its place, enacts in § 5 that "no money shall be drawn from the Treasury except the same shall have been previously appropriated to the purpose for which it was drawn." This word, appropriated, in the organic and regulative Act creating this new Board, must be understood to mean appropriated *by the Board.* And § 6 enacts that "all moneys drawn from the Treasury by authority of the Board of Supervisors shall be upon vouchers for the expenditure thereof, examined and allowed by the Auditor and approved by the Comptroller; and no such moneys shall be drawn therefrom except upon a warrant drawn by the Comptroller, and countersigned by the Mayor and Clerk of the Board." It thus seems quite clear that, before the Comptroller could repossess himself of the money so improvidently deposited by him in the County Treasury, and thus become enabled to pay as directed by the Act in question, he would be obliged to coax the Board into passing a resolution, and also to obtain counter-signatures upon his check from the Mayor and the Supervisors' Clerk.

In the *Additional Points* of the defendant to which we are replying, reference is made to § 6 of the original organic Act of Tweed's Elective Board. (Laws of 1857, vol 2, p. 286.) We presume this Act is repealed, or that it is obsolete, being wholly superseded by the Act of 1870 (*page* 481), which abolished that Board. But let it for the present purpose be considered in force, as far as it can possibly be so. Its §§ 2 and 6 are a little more explicitly expressed ; and being read in connection with the corresponding sections, 2 and 6, of the Act of 1870 (*p.* 481), they strengthen the views here expressed. They all relate to moneys brought into the County Treasury for the purpose of being appropriated by resolutions of the Board of Supervisors. They relate exclusively to moneys paid out on such appropriations through a Supervisors' audit, and a check countersigned by the Mayor and the Supervisors' Clerk—not by the Comptroller's sole action, as the money in question was to be paid.

This will be seen by perusing these sections. But we must request the Judges not to accept as accurate the matter within quotation marks on the Defendant's *Additional Points*, *p.* 3, purporting to be a copy of Section 6 in the Elective Supervisors Act, Laws of 1857. It is not a copy, but a paraphrase, and it leaves out the vitally important distinctive portion which shows that the italicized part refers to moneys paid by the resolution and audit of the Supervisors' Board, and that it does not in any way refer to such moneys as those obtained from the lenders on these bonds of 1870. This same defect in point of accuracy occurs on *pages 2–3 of the Defendant's Additional Points*, as it respects the Act of 1862, above examined. It purports to give, in quotation marks, the very words of § 2. (*Laws of* 1862, *p.* 132.) Such is not the fact. The matter is a *very* misleading paraphrase.

The § 22 of the County Treasurer Article in R. S., cited at the foot of the Defendant's Additional Points,

p. 3, if it could be supposed to refer to New York, proves nothing in this connection. It speaks of "moneys belonging to the County."

So much for the effort to prove a title in the County by mere momentary possession.

The claim of actual or beneficial ownership in the County was sufficiently repelled in the Brief and Points submitted on the Re-argument.

III.—The defendant, orally and on paper, lays great stress on the alleged fact that the money in controversy was raised on the bonds of the County. *Ergo*, it is said the money belongs to the County.

The defendant totally misapprehends the office of the County bond mentioned in the Statute.

The bond creates no liability against the County.

The County cannot be sued on the bond in any such manner as to involve the County in a loss.

The sole remedy of a bondholder, in case of non-payment of the bond, is by mandamus, to put in motion the machinery provided by the Statute for the levying of a tax and the payment to him of his proportionate part thereof, evidenced by his possession of the bond.

Even if the County could be sued on the bond, it would not alter the legal *status*. After judgment obtained, resort would be necessary to the same process of mandamus, because the County owns no property subject to levy on an execution. (*Riggs* v. *Johnson County*, 6 *Wallace's U. S. R.*, 166.)

The Statute, in effect, provides for *discounting the tax*. The persons who discount the tax, or any portion of it, are furnished with County bonds to designate what amount of the tax they have discounted, and what amount of the tax when collected is to be paid to them.

The security for the contract of discount or loan is the levying of the tax.

The law providing for that levy cannot be repealed, and even should the Legislature pass a statute repealing it, its provisions would be enforced by mandamus. (*See case last cited.*)

A precise legal similitude to the County Board may be seen in the English mortgage of rates.

In England local improvements are effected under Acts of Parliament, giving the power to "Commissioners" corporate, or individuals named in the Act, and who are empowered to levy rates and to raise money by mortgaging the rates. A form of mortgage is provided, which is a mere assignment of the rates or of a certain amount of them. (*Commissioners' Clauses Act*, 1st *Chitty's Stat., p.* 625.)

The County bond in th.s case has precisely the same effect as the mortgage of rates under the English Statutes.

The so-called mortgage does not *purport* to create an obligation ; our bond does. In that matter of form lies the only difference.

The thing really discounted in both cases is the same —*i.e.*, the tax directed by the Legislature to be levied. The office performed by the mortgage in the one case is the same as that performed by the bond in the other —*i.e.*, to indicate that the person holding it has discounted a certain portion of the tax or rate, and is entitled to repayment according *to the terms of the law*.

Were Parliament, like our Legislature, restricted by a constitution, its levy of a rate could not be repealed. Were our Legislature, like Parliament, unrestricted by a constitution, its repeal *of the law* would take away all remedy on the bond.

Thus, if any inference as to ownership of the money is to be drawn from the form or nature of the instrument on which the money was raised, it must be in favor of the State ; for, as we have seen, it was raised under the State's law, on the State's credit, and by the State's contract. The County bond was nothing but a mere form, the use of which was prescribed by the State.

This argument would not apply to all cases of public corporate acts in incurring liabilities pursuant to State laws. The Legislature may act on local districts in two ways. First, directly. Second, indirectly, by the creation of municipal corporations or *quasi* corporations, giving them certain discretionary powers.

In the first case, which is the case at bar, the remedies must be pursued by the State. In the second case, where the local governing corporation has had a discretion, has been an *actor*, it may be entitled to remedies.

In this case, had the Legislature appointed the Auditors, and made them responsible to an incorporated Board of Supervisors, having power in its discretion to levy a tax or not, and in the former event to discount the tax by issuing bonds, the money raised on such bonds might then have been County money—not because raised on *County* bonds, but because raised on a County tax ordered by a County *legislature*, to be disbursed in its discretion by itself.

In the case at bar, the Board of Supervisors was but a ministerial agent of the State to levy the tax which the State law *directed*.

The distinction has been made by this Court in *People* vs. *Flagg*, 46 *New York*, 405.

IV.—The defendant attempts to show that the County had power to use these funds when first raised, and would have, again, if the County recovered them.

That the authority to raise any money only existed after amounts were found due, and to the amount *found* due, would seem to dispose of the first suggestion.

The section quoted by the defendant—in his *Additional Points, p.* 4—is in itself an appropriation by the Legislature, and over which the Supervisors had no control.

V.—Out of compliment to those who might doubt the right of the State to a remedy by action of the kind heretofore cognizable in Courts of law only, the State puts forward the proposition that the action is sustainable as a case IN EQUITY. This is to be regarded as its second aspect. It is like an inner work in fortifications to which, when driven from its first line of defense, the garrison retires.

Judge Parker's dissenting opinion (*Paper D, p.* 192) adopts the defendant's position, that in this, its second aspect, the action cannot be maintained. And this for the same reasons that are developed in one set of bungling procedures of the Supreme Court. (New York Ice Co. *v.* North-Western Transportation Co., 20 How. Pr. R., 424; and same Vol., p. 255.) That action was endowed with a ridiculous immortality by a criticism in this Court. (S. C. on Appeal, 23 N. Y. R., 357. See further, if needful, this same case in Wait's Table. Also, Lattin *v.* McCarty, 41 N. Y. R., 109.)

The defendant's counsel at bar argued that, under the old division of actions, a simple demand for money, or pecuniary compensation for a wrong or damages, could not be enforced in equity. This is utterly unsound. When the *title* was equitable only, the remedy had to be sought in a Court of Equity. The Code could not distinguish, *in any short way*, or even by the most tedious circumlocution, cases which, being in the old phrase at common-law, were constitutionally triable by jury only, from those which might, because equitable, be tried by a judge. As a consequence it was necessary to put into the jury-class many equity cases. This the Legislature could constitutionally do; the converse could not be done. (*Bradley v. Aldrich*, 40 *N. Y. R.*, 510 *to* 512.) But for the corrections administered by this Court in these decisions, the bench below and its barristers would have brought back, with ten-fold entanglement and obscurity, the abolished " distinction between law and equity."

By way of a final glance at this second or equitable aspect of the case, we observe :

1st. If this action had been brought against Tweed, Hall and Connolly alone, or with others, alleging misappropriation of the funds they or some of them were authorized to raise, and praying that the defendants be directed to replace the funds, the action would have been precisely like the English cases cited.

In those cases the relief asked was that the funds be replaced. And this was *because* there was a continuing trust. There was an unexecuted purpose to which they could be and were by law required to be applied.

Here there were no unpaid liabilities provided for by the Act. Either there never were any such or they had *all been paid*, consequently there was no unexecuted trust. There was no such continuing purpose.

There is left no legal purpose to which the funds could be applied; and yet, unless they actually belong in judgment of law to the certificate holders, they are *public* funds. If they are public funds they cannot be applied to any public purpose until the Legislature shall have appropriated them to some such purpose.

It being then impossible, for the want of any existing appropriation, for the Court to direct that these funds be replaced or restored ; if, nevertheless, they are public funds it follows, that the Executive branch of the Government, through its Attorney-General's appeal to the Courts, should recover the funds, "cover them into the State Treasury," there to await the action of the Legislature appropriating them to some proper purpose.

Were the appropriation already made, the Court could direct the recovered funds to be restored or replaced, so that they might be applied in accordance with the appropriation thus lawfully made and defined. This is what was done in the English cases. In the absence of an appropriation, a simple *quod recuperet* is all that any judicial Court can award, leaving the appropriation to be made by the proper department, the Legislature.

Whether the appropriation, when made, will accord with moral justice or the equity of the tax-payers of the suffering local district, is a matter that concerns the Legislature and not the Courts.

It may be well here to remark that since the English Municipal Corporations' Act, English and American Municipal Corporations are on precisely the same footing ; and the only cases in which it was held that the Attorney-General could not sue were those in respect to the original corporate property of those *old* English Municipal Corporations which, prior to the Municipal Reform Act, were held to be "similar in their nature to our private corporations," and, therefore, owners in their own right of their corporate property.

It was in such cases that the Attorney-General could not sue, and in such Municipal Corporations abuses as ours that he could.

Attorney-General vs. *Corporation of Carmarthen, Cooper's Eq. R.*, 30.

Attorney-General vs. *Belfast,* 4 *Irish Ch.*, 142, *and the other cases be ore cited.*

That such an action will lie against Ingersoll, the private co-conspirator, as well as against Tweed, the official delinquent, is shown by most of the English cases referred to.

Notably so is the case of *Attorney-General* vs. *Compton*, 1*st Younge and Collyer*, 417.

The persons who have received the money wrongfully paid to them by the public officers are joined in the actions ; and, as to them, the judgment is *quod recuperet.*

2ndly. It is alleged that the English cases cited are "either to enforce the performance of a trust or to "compel the return of trust funds to the custodian "from whom they have been diverted. No such relief "as is asked here has ever been given by any Court to "the Attorney-General of England."

In all those cases, the principle asserted is the right of the Court in England to deal with breaches of public trust by the same methods and by the same remedies which it applies to cases of private trust. Where the appropriate result can be effected by an order to the trustee, directing the disposition or application of the fund, that will be done.

In the present case such a remedy would be inappropriate. The Commission was appointed to perform a single function, and then dissolved. It had no succession. There is no remaining or existing trustee to hold the fund. The purposes of the trust are accomplished and the trust exhausted.

Money raised beyond any amount which could have been applied to the purposes of the trust is *outside of the law.* It was raised contrary to law, and in breach of the trust to fix how much was necessary to be raised. The law did not contemplate that any such money should ever come into existence ; and, consequently, it made no provision for its custody, or use, or application. It has no owner or *custodian*, except in the duty and right which may result to the sovereign in such cases of extraordina malversation,

Of course, a mere direction to a Trustee would be absurdly inapplicable.

But equity has other remedies which are appropriate. If the jurisdiction exists, the Court will apply these appropriate remedies.

The great Master of Equity practice, Lord Redesdale, in the Dublin case (1 Bligh, (N. S.) page 312) contemplated a similar remedy to the present. He says:

"It is expedient, in such cases, that there should be "a remedy, and highly important that persons in the "receipt of public money should know that they are "liable to account in a Court of Equity, as well for "the misapplication of, as for withholding the funds. "Suppose, even, the case of a public accountant, "clearly within the Act, who, having embezzled or "misemployed the public moneys, had rendered ac-"counts which were imperfect or fabricated, could not "the Attorney-General, upon discovery of the fact or "the fraud, proceed by information *to recover the* "*moneys* so fraudulently withheld or misappro-priated?" (P. 341.)

3rdly. The other objection urged by defendant's counsel to the applicability of the English cases is, that

"The power of the English Crown, through its At-"torney-General, over public officers, was based on "the peculiar character of English municipal corpora-"tions."   *   *   *   *

"That corporations are in England similar in their "nature to our private corporations."

"That jurisdiction exists here as to private corpora-"tions, for the same reason that it exists in England "both as to private and as to municipal corporations."

This reasoning involves a double error:

1. This jurisdiction did *not* exist as to municipal corporations whose funds were deemed to be private.

2. It *did* attach the moment their funds were made *public* funds, and for the reason that there then was a trust. The right to sue was accorded to the Crown

as the executive power, by its Attorney-General, because the trust was public.

The famous Municipal Corporations Reform Act of 1835 created no new jurisdiction. It simply changed the character of the corporate funds. It made them public funds, and the immemorial jurisdiction over such funds attached. (See Mr. Tilden's argument and citations at General Term. *Paper marked C, pp.* 65, 66, 71, 72, 76, 77.)

(See Mr. Tilden's Points on present argument, p. 8.)

GENERAL OBSERVATIONS TOUCHING THE EQUITY JURISDICTION.

1st. It should be noted, in this connection, that this jurisdiction exists not merely in the cases which, by a phrase borrowed from the Statute of Eliz., are denominated *charitable,* but in all cases of trusts which are *public.*

Mr. Tilden's argument at General Term and cases cited. Paper marked C, pp. 55, 56, 57 and 58.

See especially *Att'y-Gen'l.* v. *Eastlake,* 11 Hare, 205, in which Sir William Page Wood, afterwards Lord Chancellor Hatherly, elaborately discusses this subject.

2d. It should likewise be noted, in this connection, that in some of the principal English cases the funds misapplied were those in respect to which a much wider discretion for the use and application existed in the Municipal Councils than the Annual Tax Levy of the City of New York ever gave to any of the Municipal officers.

See Mr. Tilden's Argument at General Term, Paper marked C, p. 67.

Lord Campbell said, in *Parr* v. *Attorney-General,* in the House of Lords (8 Clark & Finelly, page 409):

"The Municipal Corporation Act creates a trust for "corporation purposes : first, for certain specified "purposes, and then, when these are answered, *for*

"*other general purposes, for the benefit of the town.*
"Then this being trust property, there is nothing in
"the Act of Parliament to take away the jurisdiction
"which the Court of Chancery would otherwise have
"over it, or to take away the right which the subject
"would otherwise have to relief in a Court of
"Equity, in case of any misapplication of the trust
"property." (Pp. 431-'2.)

As to the FIFTH head in defendant's *Additional
Points, page* 9, it should be observed :

1st. The counsel for the defendant seem to assume
in this part of their argument that the decree in
all imaginable cases of action by the People to redress
breaches of public trust, must be for the payment of
moneys into the State treasury. They put their argument thus :

"If the Treasurer of the County of Erie, or Oneida,
"or Columbia, pays out money in excess of his au-
"thority, the Attorney-General may recover it into
"the Treasury of the State. If he refuses to pay out
"money in the performance of his duty, the Attorney-
"General can compel him to do so. Nor is it easy to
"see why the commission of a wrong is essential, as a
"condition, under this theory, to the State obtaining
"the money hitherto supposed to belong to its Coun-
"ties, or why all moneys in all counties throughout
"the State may not upon the same reasoning be gath-
"ered into the State treasury, and managed and dis-
"bursed under the parental direction of the Attorney-
"General."

No such idea has been advanced by the counsel for
the State. No such results are deducible from the
principles maintained by them, or found in the cases
cited.

The contingency in which the decree would be for

the payment of the money received, is, as in the present case, where the law has provided no other authority having the power of disposition or custody.

If the law has, in a particular case, provided a primary right of action in a local authority, the right of the People would arise only on the default of that authority, and the decree would be for the restoration of the fund, not to the delinquent officers—that would be a practical absurdity—but to some proper custodian; and, if necessary, the Court could direct a proper Receiver and the application of the fund.

If the law has, in a particular case, given a concurrent right of action, the decree would be as in the last instance.

2d. It is, of course, possible for the imagination to expand a chimera in respect to any general jurisdiction of the Court, or general right to sue of the People, or general duty of the Attorney-General. Nothing would be easier than to do so in respect to the acknowledged powers of that officer, as applied to the myriad of private corporations which exist in this State.

But all such reasoning answers itself. Experience shows that the interposition of that officer is made with at least sufficient reserve. In one of the early English cases similar apprehensions were indulged in by counsel, but the Court did not think them worthy of discussion or even of notice.

The practical evil of the present time is the want of efficient responsibility on the part of the hosts of public officers who pervade our State and country. It is not well to strike out of our jurisprudence any of the auxiliary remedies sanctioned by the English Courts, merely because we have not had occasion to invoke it until recently.

No officer in the land is less to be feared *as an actor* in such matters than the Attorney-General. He can do nothing, of his own motion or authority, except to invoke, in a public manner, the justice of the Courts. Evil can never flow from such a course, until the Courts themselves become feeble or corrupt. Should such a day ever arrive, the mob rule of the atheistic communist or the despotism of a Nimrod will be preferable to flimsy constitutions never regarded, or statutory enactments made only to facilitate the official plunderer.

VI.—Reply to defendant's SECOND head on page 4 of his *Additional Points :*

1st. In the second and third subdivisions of the Ninth Point submitted by Mr. Tilden, it was alleged that the Supervisors possessed no legal power of disposing of any moneys raised by the Commissioners of Audit, beyond what was necessary for the purposes of this very 4th section ; that they have no power of appropriating any excess under said Sec. 4 ; that under the general law they have no power of appropriating this or any other moneys, but are expressly denied any such power. And it was contended that, without making out some power of disposition, or some right of possession as to the fund, they could not maintain an action to recover it.

The only attempt to break the overwhelming force of this position, is by claiming for the Supervisors, in 1870, a right of indirect use as to this fund by deducting it out of the sum to be raised by taxation for the year 1870.

The statement of defendants' point is as follows :

The first section of this very chapter 382 of the laws of 1870, provides : "That from the amounts which "the Board of Supervisors are authorized to raise by "taxation, *shall be deducted the aggregate amount of* "*the estimated revenues of the County,* for the year "1870, not otherwise specifically appropriated by "law."

Correctly quoted the law runs as follows (Laws of 1870, § 1, p. 875) : "In addition to the several amounts "authorized and required by existing laws to be raised " by tax in the city and county of New York, for the "use of the State, and for defraying a portion of the con- "tingent and other charges and expenses of said city "and county, for the year eighteen hundred and seventy, "the Board of Supervisors of said county are hereby "empowered and required, as soon as conveniently may "be after the passage of this Act, to order and cause to "be raised by tax, on the estates subject to taxation "according to law, within the said county, and to be "collected according to law, the following sums of " money, for the several purposes hereinafter specified, "*deducting from the aggregate amount thereof the* "ESTIMATED *revenues of the county* FOR THE SAID "YEAR, not *otherwise specifically appropriated by* "*law*, that is to say : For advertising, forty-five "thousand dollars, &c., &c."

The deduction from the aggregate amount of the taxes authorized to be levied for 1870 is, "the *estimated* revenues of the county for the said year not otherwise specifically appropriated by law."

The moneys raised on bonds issued under Section 4 were no part of the "*estimated* revenues of the county for the said year." There was not in these official *estimates*, any such item as this, "To be won from Tweed's gang of swindlers, $6,300,000." Nor were the moneys raised on these bonds of a class "*not* specifically appropriated."

On the contrary, they are expressly devoted to such "liabilities against the County" as were "incurred previous to the passage of the Act," as "audited" by the commission created by this fourth section ; and the payment of the entire fund to the holders of such claims, "on the certificate of the officers named" in the Act was peremptorily and unqualifiedly ordered.

So it appears that in 1870, no power existed in the

Supervisors to appropriate or apply this fund, or any part of it, to any purpose, or to exercise over it any power of disposition whatever. The purposes were absolutely fixed by this Section 4 ; and an agency to make the application to that purpose was created who *quoad hoc* was wholly independent of the Supervisors. They had no vestige of authority in the matter. The intent to exclude them is most apparent. Tweed, the "present President," was to be one of the auditors throughout. When his office of President or Supervisor wholly ceased, he still continued an Auditor.

2nd : The argument on page 5 of defendant's additional points, that the moneys received from revenues in 1870, and the moneys received from taxes, and the moneys to be received on these bonds, were capable of being applied interchangeably has no foundation.

On the contrary, every dollar claimed from the revenues and taxes of 1870 (p. 875), was appropriated, specifically and in detail, to objects enumerated in Section 1, which contains more than three pages.

So also every dollar raised by bonds under Section 4 was applicable to the purposes specified in *that* section, and to nothing else.

The conclusion that all these moneys were "under the control of this County for all lawful objects," has no foundation. Every dollar of it was appropriated by law, and there was no "control" to divert it or to make any disposition of it independently of that made in this same fourth section.

3rd : There is a monstrous suggestion in this part of the defendant's argument. It is that county bonds might lawfully have been issued *in anticipation* of audits under this fourth section. If so, the amount so to be issued was unlimited. Instead of being in anticipation of a nice, *little* swindle of $6,000,000, which, in the vastness of metropolitan financial operations, might escape notice, it might have been to countless millions. If the Comptroller could have foreseen the necessity of flight, he would probably have acted on this idea. It is a wholly inadmissible construction of the Act. Duly certified audits to the amount were indispensable conditions precedent to the issue of a single bond under that Section 4.

4thly: Though it may seem to be needlessly returning on our footsteps, we will, as auxiliary to this reply now tendered to the SECOND head in page 4 of the defendant's *Additional Points*, recall attention to the squelching process by which Tweed, in 1870 and 1871, before this action was commenced, reduced "the County," or the Board of Supervisors, below even the measure of its original power, when, as a mere committee of the chartered Municipal Corporation, it was appointed to perform the merely clerical function of filling up a column in the assessment-rolls and attaching the Tax Collector's warrant. (*See Plaintiffs' Points on Re-argument.* p. 87, also *Laws* of 1871, p. 1230, § 3.)

The full history of the New York Supervisorship, given in the *Plaintiffs' Points on Re-argument*, pp. 83 to 99, need not be here repeated; but in this connection we refer to it as a proper preliminary to what here follows.

One can hardly turn to a statute concerning expenditures in New York, without finding a direction to the Supervisors to raise by taxation the amount prescribed as necessary, but this only proves that that body was, as we have asserted and shown, the tax-levying commission. Its duties, as such, were essentially clerical; before this action was brought they had become so, absolutely and to all intents and purposes. (*Laws of* 1870, *p.* 879, §§ 8 *and* 11.)

Long prior to what is called the New City Charter of 1870 (Laws of 1870, p. 366 to 397,   ), New York had many official bodies, corporate, *quasi* corporate, or neither, acting as auxiliaries to the actual local governing municipal corporation, called "The Mayor, Aldermen and Commonalty, &c." As to several of these, whether or not they were corporations, suable and entitled to sue, as such, was often debated.

See as illustrations of this:

Gardiner *v.* Board of Health, 4 Sandf. Superior Court Law Reports, 153, affirmed 6 Selden, 409.

Appleton *v.* Water Commissioners, 2 Hill, p. 432.

In Gildersleeve *v.* The Board of Education, 17 Abbott, 212, Daly, F. J., delivering the opinion of the Court, says that when they form "integral parts" of the governing corporation they are not suable. He instances the New York Board of Supervisors as a specimen of this sort of thing. And certainly he is fully sustained by Brady *v.* The Board of Supervisors, 2 Sandf. N. Y. Superior Court Law R., 460; affirmed on appeal, 10 N. Y. R., 260.

We have shown that the New York Supervisors never sued at all save by the six collusive suits in these cases, and never were successfully sued. (*Plaintiffs' Points on Re-argument, pages* 114 *to* 116.)

It has been said that a multitude of the minor auxiliaries of local government in the rural counties have the faculty of suing and being sued (2 *R. S., p.* 473, 1*st Ed*). We ask, then, are they, too, independent, *imperia in imperio,* each vested with sole authority, to the exclusion of the State, of defending from oppressive taxation, *under any head resembling their duties,* the local tax-payers? Infinite confusion would result from such a doctrine.

But our present purpose in referring to these local agencies in New York is to show that before the commencement of this action Tweed's legislative friends wrapped them all up in the newly constituted or amended *City* Charter of 1870, reducing the Board of Supervisors to the lowest grade of power at the same time.

Dates are here to be kept in view.

A.—New or amended Charter, April 5, 1870 ; pages 366 to 397.

B.—Elective Supervisors "abol-
ished," and new, present Board ⎬ " 12, " page 481.
created.

C.—LAST *County* tax-levy, " 26, " page 875.

D.—*City* Consolidation Debt Act, " 6, 1871, page 629.

E.—County Consolidation Debt Act, " 6, " page 631.

F.—Act investing quartette with
all power of directing taxation, and
distributing proceeds, commonly ⎬ " 19, " page 1268.
called the two per cent. Act.

By *A*, the new Charter, *all* the departments of local administration are absorbed, as integral parts thereof, into the Municipal Corporation called "The Mayor, Aldermen and Commonalty, &c." (*Laws of* 1870, *p.* 373, § 30.) By *C*, the last County tax-levy, *all* existing liabilities of the Supervisors, not funded, are delivered over to the auditing trio, Hall, Tweed and Connolly, for adjustment, and for payment on their audit by the latter. (*Laws of* 1870, *p.* 878, § 4.) By *D* and *E*, power to postpone all existing City and County funded debts for 20 to 50 years, is conferred upon Connolly alone, and exclusively of any action by any one else. (*Laws of* 1871, *pp.* 629 *to* 633.) By *F*, the entire power of ordering local taxation and dividing or apportioning its proceeds is vested in the quartette, but by *unanimous* vote only. (*Laws of* 1871, *p.* 1269.)

This serves to show in a general way the complete absorption of power by the quartette ; but certain special features require to be noted ; *first*, the elaborate and expansive enumeration of Common Council powers exhibits their insignificancy (*Laws of* 1870, *pp.* 369 *to* 371, § 21); *secondly*, the Supervisors were reduced to a non entity by the requisite of Hall's concurrence in every act of theirs (*Laws of* 1870, *p.* 481, § 2) ; *thirdly*, their latest tax-levy shows that nearly every power over money or appointments which had been in their hands was taken away (*Laws of* 1870, *p.* 875 *to* 878, § 1); *fourthly*, the power they once had of remitting or reducing taxes was taken away from them and vested in the Commissioners of Taxes appointed by Connolly (*Laws of* 1870, *p.* 879, §§ 8 *and* 12); *fifthly*, all borrowing for the County is exclusively delegated to Connolly (*Laws of* 1870, *p.* 879, § 7); *sixthly*, even the little patronage of appointing doorkeepers to the Courts is taken away and conferred upon Connolly (*Laws of* 1870, *p.* 880, § 9); and *seventhly*, to cap the climax of their miseries, the great Court-House job, specially described in *Plaintiffs' Points on Re-argument, pp.* 116 *to* 119, which, certainly made them landholders, and probably, *ex necesitate*, gave them a limited corporate existence, was now ruthlessly wrenched from their grasp and vested in four Commissioners appointed by Hall. (*Laws of* 1870, *p.* 880, § 11.) The whole thing, issuing bonds, keeping and paying the money, &c., &c., are turned over to Hall's Commissioners or to Connolly. The prior Court-House laws are here erroneously referred to. (See them in Laws of 1864, p. 497; of 1862, p. 335; of 1861, p. 451.) Without going further into these diminishing details, as might be done, it will be seen that scarcely any portion of the power held by Tweed's Medieval Board was permitted to descend to the present one. For a list of the Mayor's powers of appointment see Index to Laws of 1870, p. 2293. The last *County* tax-levy contains, as all previous ones are believed to have contained, the most explicit prohibition against the Supervisors' using for one purpose any money granted for another. (*Laws of* 1870, *p.* 878, § 3.)

Thus, before this action was brought, the notion of a County Treasury had become a mere matter of bookkeeping. The notion of a *County Government*, as early as April 19, 1871, page 1,269 § 3, was cut down to the inferences derivable from the use of a single letter. "Purposes of the City and County Governments," says that section. This was long before the commencement of this action.

The repayment of these borrowed moneys stands deferred for twenty or more years. *Plaintiffs' Points on Re-argument, pp.* 10, 11. Aside from the fact that positive statute directs the payment of the bonds from future taxation, neither Connolly, if he could recover this money, as the sixth special ground of demurrer suggests (*see case, fo.* 98), nor the Supervisors, if they had it, could lawfully apply it to reimbursing the lenders. The lenders would not accept it, if tendered to them, for the investment is preferable. What, then, is to become of it during those twenty or more years ? Is it to lie idle whilst the lenders are receiving interest ? Has any Board or officer power to invest it ? Surely not.

An error in the computation of time occurred on page 98 of the *Plaintiffs' Points on Re-argument.* In commenting on the Special Term decision (*People v. Edmonds*, 15 Barb., p. 539) we said that "a dozen" years elapsed after their work was published before any one imagined that the Revisors of 1830, in rearranging the Laws relative to the Rural Boards, had, by some slip or inadvertence, created a second governing corporate body in the City and County of New York. The actual lapse of time was *twenty-three years.* Had the question been then submitted to a Court of Appeal, whether the Revisors had generated such a legal monster as twin local governments exercising similar powers in respect to the same rteritory and people, the decision would certainly have been in the negative. Had there been then presented in like manner the kindred question, whether authorizing the New York Supervisors to fix and pay two or three salaries had converted them intoa constructive *quasi* corporation, the answer would also have been in the negative. The subsequent expansion of this latter abuse could not rightfully vary the result. And if it could, the shrinkage which occurred before the commencement of this action, in 1870 and 1871, must carry the question back to the position it previously occupied.

If the communal idea on which this whole claim for *Supervisorial* authority is founded could be accepted at all, surely "The Mayor, Aldermen and Commonalty," &c., the ancient Municipal Corporation, is the local lord paramount to be clothed by construction with this power of representing the interests of the local public. Yet the defendant's counsel have never ventured to suggest such a thing, although the attorney who drew Ingersoll's demurrer did, indeed, tuck in the city corporation as a possible *owner* of the fund, admitting also Dick Connolly as a rival claimant to that honor. (Third and sixth causes of demurrer, case, fol. 97–99.)

VII.— To conclude:

1. We have no idea that there is any need for a resort to *Equity* jurisdiction. There never was, by positive law or reasonable implication, any *trust* whatever, public or private, impressed upon this money. Nevertheless, the general principles of the English Equity cases are very apposite.

2. In point of fact, the very money itself never belonged to the Comptroller, or to the Supervisors, or to the County Treasurer, or to the County, or to the Bank. It is equally manifest that it did not in strictness belong to the State.

3. Just as, by physical confusion, one may, without right, acquire a title, in law, to the chattels of another, or, by ouster, may become wrongfully seized of another's lands; so, by the extraordinary and unparalleled

malversation perpetrated in this case, the certificate-holders acquired a perfect and unimpeachable title to and ownership of the specific moneys borrowed. But the abuse of State power having worked a certain future mischief to the State's tax-payers, the State, both as employer and as representative of the whole People, is entitled to a remedy by action of tort for damages against all who took any part in the wrong committed.

Ch. O'Conor,
Wm. M. Evarts,
W. H. Peckham,
James Emott.

S. J. Tilden,

Associate Counsel.

Court of Appeals.

THE PEOPLE OF THE STATE OF NEW
    YORK,

                      Appellants,

           vs.

JAMES H. INGERSOLL, impleaded,
    WM. M. TWEED, &c., and others,

                Respondents.

CHARLES O'CONOR and WHEELER H. PECKHAM, for
Appellants.

DAVID DUDLEY FIELD and ELIHU ROOT
                    for Respondents.

ALLEN, *J.* :

The history of this action, a fragment only of which
is presented by the record before us, has been peculiar, and if the practice adopted is to ripen into a precedent may be regarded as unfortunate. Ordinarily
a judgment deliberately given upon a question directly
in issue has been, and should be, regarded as the law
of the particular case by other judges in subsequent
stages of the litigation until reversed upon appeal. In no
other way can justice be duly administered or the decisions of the courts command the respect of suitors and
the public. Conflicting decisions by different judges,

resulting in final judgments in the same action, each
carried out to its legitimate results, necessarily lead to
confusion, and, indulged in to any great extent, will
bring reproach upon the judicial system.

The principal question, and indeed the only question
of importance that has as yet been presented to the
courts, is as to the status of the plaintiffs and their
right to maintain the action. That was first presented
by the demurrer of the defendant first served with
process, and the decision was for the plaintiffs, overruling the demurrer at Special Term, affirmed at General Term, the three Justices sustaining their respective
views in well considered and elaborate written opinions. This result was acquiesced in by that defendant
who answered over, and the action stands for trial
upon the issues of fact joined therein. Thereafter,
upon the motion of the present defendant, about one-
third of the complaint was, by order of another Judge,
stricken out as "irrelevant and redundant," the allegations being claimed by the defendant, and held by
the Court not essential either to the right of the plaintiffs or the liability of the defendants, in respect to the
cause of action stated. To the complaint thus expurgated and pruned of what was regarded by the Court
below as superfluous and redundant statements, the
present defendant demurred, and had judgment
both at Special and General Terms, upon the
ground that the plaintiffs had no standing in Court
or right to maintain the action in respect to the matters
and causes alleged. Thus two conflicting decisions
have been given and are now operative, under one of
which the plaintiffs, having a judgment affirming their
right to maintain the action, the parties have put themselves upon the country ; from the other the present
appeal has been taken. The precise question presented
by this appeal may—if the matter stricken out by the
Court upon the application of the present defendant
was, in fact, "irrelevant and redundant," in no way

affecting the cause of action or the status of the plaintiffs, in case of a recovery by the plaintiffs—be presented upon an appeal from the judgment upon the
issues of fact now ready for trial, and thus, if the practice is tolerated, several successive appeals from judgments and decisions, in different forms, may be brought
in the same action by different parties, each presenting
but the one and the same question. It is true that the
complaint has only been expurgated of the supposed
redundant matter as to the present respondent, and as
to the other defendants it stands as originally served,
and the cause must proceed against them upon the
facts alleged, so far as material to the right of the
plaintiffs to sue, and upon the theory upon which the
action was brought and the complaint framed by the
learned counsel for the plaintiffs, and this constitutes
another of the anomalies of this case. Whether the
allegations and statements stricken out as to this respondent were or were not material, and might or
might not be available to give the plaintiffs a right of
action, is not before us upon this appeal, and no opinion is therefore expressed upon the question. It may
be that if these allegations should be sustained by
proof, the case would be regarded as so essentially different from that presented by the demurrer before us
that the judgment in the one case would not control in
the other. All possibility of conflict or successive appeals
on the same question would have been obviated had the
part stricken out been regarded by the Courts as redundant, as it had been adjudged, and the decision of
the Court first made adopted as the law of the case,
irrespective of the individual opinions of the Judges.
In its present form a very doubtful question is involved
as to the right of the plaintiffs to appeal, there being
no final judgment as to all the parties defendant. But
in view of the magnitude of the amount and the novelty
and importance of the questions involved, and the
serious embarrassments and possible loss that migh

arise from a dismissal of the appeal, I incline to forego
the consideration of the question of practice and consider the appeal upon its merits, as if no question
existed as to its regularity. The action having been
severed as to this defendant in the manner and by the
proceedings before referred to, the demurrer of the
defendant and the present appeal must be considered
as if the present respondent were the sole defendant
and the action stood against him alone. The appeal
in the action as it comes before us does not involve the
right of the State to maintain an action against the
Auditors, or any of them, for malfeasance in office, or
any person occupying an official position and who
has been faithless to his trust.

The action is for the recovery of a sum certain
alleged to have been obtained by the respondent
and the other persons named in the complaint, his
associates and confederates, by false and fraudulent means and devices and by a corrupt and
fraudulent combination and conspiracy. The gist of
the action is the obtaining by the defendant and
others, and appropriating to their own use, a large
sum of money, to which they were not entitled, by
the false and fraudulent practices detailed, and the
demand is for judgment for the amount alleged to
have been thus obtained, with interest. It is not in
terms averred that the money, in any legal sense or in
equity and good conscience, belonged to the plaintiffs,
so that the defendants can be charged with the same as
received to their use, or that the wrong was perpetrated
directly against the State or the people of the State—
that is, the whole State as a legal entity and the whole
body of the people : but the want of such averment, it is
claimed, is supplied, and the necessity of such averment obviated, by allegations as to the source from
which the money came and the authority and agency
by and purposes for which it was procured.

The title to and ownership of the money sought to

be recovered must determine the right of action, and if the money did not belong to the State, but did belong to some other body having capacity to sue, this action cannot be maintained (People *vs.* Booth, 32 N. Y., 397).

The eminent senior counsel for the plaintiffs, in his argument in the Supreme Court of the demurrer of another defendant, with copies of which we have been furnished, in answer to a question put as to "who did own the money?" asserted that the State owned it, and in substance conceded that none but the true owner could have an action for its recovery. He says: "I believe I have answered the question, who owns the money? It is but another way of putting the question, Who can maintain the action? Of course, the action ought to be maintained by the party who is to be regarded as the technical owner of the money, and the party so regarded in the law is the party to maintain the action." I have quoted this paragraph as expressing accurately and tersely the precise point upon which the right of the plaintiffs to sustain the action hinges, and it is in strict conformity with People *vs.* Booth, *supra.* It may not be material whether the property in the money was absolute or qualified, general or special; but there must be an ownership of some kind to give an action. The party to maintain an action for a tort or wrong to property must be one whose property rights have been tortiously interfered with or invaded—one who, as trustee, special property man, bailee or general owner, has been pecuniarily damaged. The State cannot any more than an individual have a civil action for the recovery of money, whether by way of damages for fraud or other wrong, the wrongful conversion of chattels or for money received by and in the possession of others, except upon proof of title and ownership. A distinction is to be observed between actions by the people or the State, in right of the prerogative, incident to sovereignty and those founded on some pecuniary interest or proprietary right. The latter are governed by the ordinary rules of law by which rights are determined between individuals.

A class of cases referred to and examined at great length by counsel do not call for an extended consideration if the title to the money fraudulently taken was in the County of New York, and an action lies at the suit of the Board of Supervisors, in behalf of that county, for its recovery.

It is well settled in England that, in right of the prerogative of the Crown, the Attorney-General, in his name of office, may proceed, either by information or by bill in Equity, to establish and enforce the execution of trusts of property by public corporations to prevent the misappropriation or misapplication of funds or property raised or held for public use, and the abuse of power by the governors of corporations or public officers, or the exercise of powers not conferred by law, and generally to call upon the Courts to see that right is done to the subjects of the Crown who are incompetent to act for themselves. Ordinarily the remedies sought have been preventive, but in some cases, as incident to the preventive and prospective relief, a claim has been made for retrospective relief, especially when the misappropriated funds could be traced and reclaimed in specie. The jurisdiction has been sustained upon the general principles of the right and duty of the Court to grant preventive relief, and the relief actually granted, if any, in addition and as incident to that has depended upon circumstances. The right of the Attorney-General to intervene and the jurisdiction of the Court was at first referred to, the statute of Elizabeth concerning charitable uses and the trusts enforced as charities, later a public use, although not strictly charitable, was held within the equity of the statute; but a distinction was made as to the source from which the funds proceeded, and moneys, the avails of rates and taxes levied by Act of Parliament, were held not within the statute ; but this distinction was soon ignored, and respect was had to the purpose for which property and funds were held, rather than their source and origin, in determining whether they were held for a public and charitable use within the jurisdiction of the Court of Chancery. Still more recently courts have held that the statute of Elizabeth was not the source of the jurisdiction of the Court of Chancery, but that trustees of property for public use were also subject to the action of account, and that the Court of Chancery had concurrent jurisdiction in the courts of common law in compelling an accounting, and that by reason of the technicalities of the action of account proper in courts of law a court of equity afforded the better remedy of the two. The Municipal Corporation Act of 6 William, 4 ch., 76, has been referred to ; but I do not understand that it affects the question as to the general jurisdiction of the Court of Chancery over public trusts at the instance of the Attorney-General. It did make large classes of property held by boroughs and other municipal corporations trust property, and the corporations trustees of the same, which before had been held as the property of the corporations, unaffected by any trust and as private property, but in no other respect affected the jurisdiction of Courts of Equity. The same principle has been held applicable to Commissioners and other public officers clothed by Parliament with power over property for a public use. In all the cases the action of the Court was invoked against faithless trustees and to compel a proper execution of the trust and a right use of trust funds by those charged with their administration. A breach of duty or a violation of trust by the trustees, either actual or threatened and impending, is at the foundation of every action by the Attorney-General or the Crown or the people as sovereign, and essential to the right of either to maintain, as well as to the right of a Court of Equity to entertain jurisdiction of a suit by either touching property and funds held by public or municipal corporations for public use. If the property of a corporation be illegally interfered with by corporation officers and agents or others, the remedy is by action at the suit of the Corporation, and not of the Attorney-General. (Attorney-General *vs.* Brown, 1 Swanston's R., 265 ; Same *vs.* Hicks, 2 S. and S., 67 ; Same *vs.* Eastlake, 11 Hare, 205 ; Same *vs.* Mayor of Dublin, 1 Bligh, N. S., 312 ; Same *vs.* Mayor of Liverpool, 1 M. and C., 171 ; Same *vs.* Wilson, 1 Cr. and Ph., 1 ; Same *vs.* Corporation of Poole, 2 Keene, 190 ; S. C., *sub. nom.* ; Attorney-General *vs.* Aspinwall, 2 Keene, 513, and 2 M. and C., 613 ; S. C., 4 ; M. and C., 417, and 8 Cl. and Fin., 409.)

Decisions are cited from the reports of this country and of this State, entitled to consideration and respect, affirming to some extent the doctrine of the English Courts, and applying it to like cases, as they have arisen here. But in none has the doctrine been extended beyond the principles of the English cases, and aside from the jurisdiction of Courts of Equity over trusts of property for public uses, and over the trustees, either corporate or official, the Courts have only interfered at the instance of the Attorney-General, to prevent and prohibit some official wrong by municipal corporations of public officers and the exercise of usurped or the abuse of actual powers. A case is not made by the complaint within the doctrine contended for or the cases relied upon or within the reasons which lie at the foundation of the doctrine, and it is not necessary, therefore, to consider whether the doctrine to its full extent, or within what limits, if at all, it is a part of the common law of this State, or whether it has been superseded or modified by statute. Doubtless the prerogatives of the Crown, except as effected by constitutional limitations, exist in the people as sovereign, but to what extent the exercise of this prerogative is committed to the public officials, either by the Legislature or by the common law, is a question worthy of grave consideration and not to be lightly decided, and should only be determined when necessary to a judgment and decision. Whenever the Legislature by statutory enactment has conferred upon State officers or public bodies authority to represent the body of the people in the exercise of any prerogative right no question can arise, for in those matters, except as restrained by the constitution, the Legislature is supreme. If there were no other remedy for a great wrong and public justice, and individual rights were likely to suffer for want of a prosecutor capable of pursuing the wrong-doer and redressing the wrong, the Courts would struggle hard to find authority for the Attorney-General to intervene in the name of the people. But, in the absence of such a necessity, the exercise of high prerogative powers ought not by a species of judicial legislation to be committed to the discretion of any individual or body of men. Such a committal of power should be the act of the Legislature, who can hedge it about with all necessary safeguards. This action is not to establish or enforce a trust. The parties defendant are not, nor is either of them a trustee, charged with any duty or entrusted with the possession of funds or property to be administered by them for any public use. They are sought to be charged as tort feasors, for a consummated and completed tortious act.

The present respondent is not alleged to have occupied any official position or to have owed any allegiance to the State or any of its civil or political divisions except such as every citizen owes, and is not charged with having occupied any fiduciary relation to the City, County or State of New York, or to the funds of either. Unless the people of the State, or the

State as a body politic and corporate, owned and were
entitled to the money wrongfully abstracted, the defendant cannot be made a trustee for the State by reason of his tortious act—that is, he can only be charged
as an involuntary trustee of the true owner of the fund.
Only one of the other defendants had any official relation to the transaction detailed, and such relation was
not that of trustee, in any sense, of any funds or property or of the credit of the public. He, with others,
was charged with certain specific duties, which did not
include the possession, care or disposal of the public
funds or credit. These duties were concluded long before the commencement of this action, and the complaint
against him, so far as it touches his official action, is for
malversation in the administration of his office or agency, by means of which large sums of money have been
lost to the true owner and appropriated by himself and
others. Whatever other remedies the people may have
to redress or punish this wrong, no precedent has
been referred to for the maintenance of a civil action
by the people to recover either the money lost, or for
compensatory damages without proof of a right in the
State as a political and corporate entity to the money
as owner, and which would give it a place in the
treasury of the State when recovered, or of some
pecuniary damages sustained by the State, the
compensation for which would of right belong to
its treasury. The people, by the complaint, claim
as owners, and do not seek to reclaim the money
and compel its appropriation to any particular use or
purpose. The claim of counsel in their printed brief,
and upon argument, was that it must be assumed that
upon the recovery of the money by the State and its
reaching the State treasury the Legislature would
make such disposition of it as should be equitable and
just, not claiming that there was any valid trust which
could be established and enforced in equity. Such a
shadowy and unsubstantial equity depending upon

the will and future action of the Legislature for its recognition and establishment, is not the equivalent of or substitute for a trust of which the courts can take cognizance. In all the cases of public or charitable use established at the suit of the Attorney-General or the State, the particular use has been averred, and without such averments the bill or information would have shown no equity and the Court would have been without jurisdiction.

Attorney-General *vs.* Huber, Same *vs.* Eastlake, Same *vs.* Brown, *supra*, are illustrations of the principles controlling the jurisdiction of courts of equity over individuals and public bodies acting officially in respect to property interests of the public. In all the cases the parties proceeded against and whose action was sought to be controlled or restrained had the acting administration of property or the power to raise and control funds, dedicated or granted for public use, and their offices and duties were continuing, and respect was had in the relief sought to their future action. So the other cases referred to (*supra* of Attorney-General *vs.* Dublin, and Same *vs.* Liverpool), are instances of the application of the principle and the exercise of the jurisdiction against municipalities having control and direction of funds and property for the public use. The Attorney-General *vs.* Wilson, (1 Craig & Phil. 1,) differs from the others in this, that the Borough of Leeds appeared on the record as relator and as a co-plaintiff with the Attorney-General. The right of the corporation of Leeds to maintain the action was recognized and affirmed by the Court, and it was said that the right of action prior to the passage of the Municipal Corporation Act of VI. William, 4, was solely in that corporation, for the reason that the fund was the property of the corporation, and was only subjected to a trust, and the jurisdiction of the Court of Equity as a trust fund by that Act, and was held that the corporation was a proper party to the action, its right of action not being destroyed, because by the Act the Attorney-General had a right to complain of a violation of the trust. In that case, as in the others, the foundation of the jurisdiction was an existing and continuing trust, and the object and purpose of the action was to compel the due execution of the trust, and for relief against a fraudulent misappropriation of the trust fund by former governors of the corporation and managers of the trust.

But without further pursuing in this connection the consideration of the rights of the people of the State and the powers of the Attorney-General as their representative to call the parties to an account for their malfeasances, and to reclaim the money tortiously and fraudulently appropriated, the right of the County of New York to sue for and recover the money as owner and proprietor should be considered as the question primarily to be determined, for in the absence of any fraud or collusion on the part of the governing body of the county in the perpetration of the wrong and commission of the fraud, or any inability or disinclination of the proper officers of the county to prosecute, if the money was the property of the county, property belonging to its treasury, and the robbery and wrong was against the county, whether the money was held upon any paritcular trust or was applicable to the general purposes of the county, or was incapable of use for county purposes except by legislative permission, there would be no necessity or occasion for the intervention of the people or their Attorney-General, as there might be if the authorities of the county—the trustees, in fact—had been participants in the fradulent abstraction of the moneys or accessories to the frauds by refusing to prosecute. It is material to recall the fact that all the allegations of collusion on the part of the county officers in the perpetration of the fraud and wrong and in the illusory prosecution of the offenders, as well as of any unwillingness on the part of the county or its corporate authorities to prosecute for the recovery, have been expunged from the complaint as to this defendant.

It would not be claimed that if the county has a cause of action and can recover the money (and there are no obstacles to an action by the county and no omission of the officers of the county to bring an action) that the State can maintain an action for the same money. True, in some cases, as in the case of general owner and bailee, or principal and agent, either can, under certain circumstances, maintain an action for money or upon contracts ; but these are exceptional cases, and this case is not within the exception or the reasons for it. There is no such or analogous relation between the State Government and the counties of the State, and the general rule must apply that a right of action for the same thing cannot, in the absence of legislation or some peculiar reason giving duplicate actions, exist at the same time in two independent corporations or individuals. For the wrongful conversion of money or property belonging to a municipal corporation or for which it may have an action, these cannot be concurrent remedies by the State and the municipality prosecuted *pari passu.* If the State has a right of action it results from and as an incident of its sovereignty, and must necessarily be paramount to that of the subordinate body, and upon the exercise of the right by the State the right of the corporation must be suspended, and upon a recovery by the State the corporation be barred of its remedy. Otherwise a party may be vexed with two litigations, and possibly have two recoveries against him for the same cause of action. I find no authority or precedent for thus depriving a municipal corporation of a civil and corporate right of action, and of property, in the discretion of the law officer of the State. A county is not independent of the State, an *imperium in imperio*, but is in all things subject to the State and the Legislature of the State, as sovereign, and its boundaries, its rights, privileges and powers may be enlarged or curtailed, and its property and property rights controlled from time to time in the discretion of the Legislature; but when grants, whether of rights or of power, are conferred by the Legislature, they are held absolutely, and to be enjoyed and exercised independently, subject only to the general laws of the State, the terms and conditions annexed to the grant, until withdrawn or modified by the Legislature. This is consistent with the Town of Guilford *vs.* Supervisors of Chenango (3 Kern, 143), and Darlington *vs.* Mayor of New York (31 New York, 164). Chancellor Kent, in speaking of municipal corporations, says: "They may be empowered to take or hold private property for municipal uses, and such property is invested with the security of other private rights" (2 Kent's Comm., 275). As remarked by Judge Denio, in Darlington *vs.* Mayor, &c., *supra*: "This does not exempt such property from Legislative control, and in that respect property rights stand upon the same footing as other corporate rights, whether political or civil. Property owned by a city, county or other municipal or local government is held by it as a public corporation and subject to the law-making power, and the governing body, by whatever name called and known, are merely trustees for the public, who are the *cestui que trust* of the corporation. A municipal corporation is the trustee of the inhabitants of the territory embraced within its limits."

An effort has been made to distinguish the County of New York from the other counties of the State in respect to its powers, priviliges, obligations, and corporate capacity as one of the civil and political divisions of the State. But a brief consideration will serve to show, as was impliedly, if not expressly, conceded by counsel for the plaintiffs, that there is no substantial distinction—that is, no difference—between the organization and power of the County of New York and those of the other counties of the State, which in the least affects the question under consideration. From the first the State has been divided for governmental and political purposes into counties, and every part of the State has been incorporated into and embraced within the territorial limits of some county and subjected to county government. Every Constitution of the State has recognized this fact, and made provisions consistent with it and based upon it. New York was one of the twelve original counties into which the State was divided by a law of the first Legislature, held in the then colony of New York, on the first day of November, 1683—2 R. L., 44, 5, 6. The first charter of the City of New York, granted after the treaty of peace of 1674, by which the English were reinstated in the possession of the colony, was by Governor Dongan, in 1683, although the charter of Governor Nicolls, of 1664, had been recognized and corporate proceedings had under it from 1674 to the granting of the Dongan charter—Hoffman's Treatise, 20. From an early period, if not from the first, the boundaries of the City and County of New York have been the same. Perhaps at one period this was not so, but the fact is not material, and only of interest as a matter of local history. See Hoffman's Treatises on the Corporation, Appendix XIX., XX., XXI., Notes 17 and 18.

From 1683 to the present time the County of New York has existed, with substantially the same territorial limits as at present, at all times having and exercising more or less of the political and corporate rights that were held and exercised by the other counties of the State. By reason of the coincidence of the boundaries and the constituencies of the two distinct organizations, the City and County of New York, and their common interests and sources of revenue, the county organization has been of less political importance than in other sections of the State, and the governing body has been differently constituted, and has exercised less power. At times many of the powers exercised elsewhere by the Boards of Supervisors have been devolved upon the Common Council of the city, and duties ordinarily performed by county officers have been performed by city officials. It is not important to trace the changes that have been made from time to time, by some of which the distinction between the City and County Government has been to some extent ignored. At no time has the County ceased to exist, and at all times a body has existed known as the Board of Supervisors of the County, who were the governing body of the County, exercising such legislative, administrative, and corporate powers as the Legislature has seen fit to entrust to it. To the extent that other special provision has been made by law for the performance of the functions in other counties performed by the Boards of Supervisors, the County of New York has been excepted from and not subject to the general laws affecting counties and prescribing the powers and duties of Boards of Supervisors. But in all other respects the County has been subject to such general laws, and possessed all the powers corporate, as well as governmental, conferred by law upon the counties of the State.

In 1857 a most material change was effected in the constitution of the County Government, and from that time the functions of the governing body and the corporate powers of the County have been greatly enlarged, and the County Government has more nearly assimilated to that of other counties. In that year the controlling power in both branches of the Legislature and the Executive Department of the State was in antagonism with the party dominant in the City and County of New York, and either with a view to the better administration of the government of the County, or for the purpose of dividing the political power and the emoluments of office in the City and County of New York, provision was made for the government of the County by a hybrid body—that is, by a Board of Supervisors, so chosen as to secure an equal number from each of the two political parties. As a reform in government the project was doubtless a failure ; but as a means by which individual members of the two parties were enabled to combine and enjoy the luxuries of power, patronage and plunder, it has proved a perfect success. It is probably true that up to that time the County, as such, had but little, if any property, even that which was necessary for public use ; but that circumstance did not affect its political existence or corporate capacity. A county may be absolutely destitute of all property and pecuniary means, and yet the political and corporate existence be as perfect and the corporate rights as complete as under any other circumstances. Very few of the counties possess any property save the necessary lands and buildings for public use, and some, at an early day, may not have been the possessors of these, but their records may have been kept in the dwelling, store or office of the clerk charged with their custody, their courts held in a school-house, occupied by the suffrance and permission of the school trustees. But the county organization was none the less perfect by reason of the poverty of the county, or its imperfect preparation to perform all its functions. It suffices for all the purposes of the present argument that from 1857 until the passage of the law of 1870, the County, under the administration of a Board of Supervisors, did exercise many and large political, legislative and administrative powers, acquire property, incur pecuniary liabilities, and perform other corporate acts under the sanction of law. The Board of Supervisors of the County of New York were not certainly, during all that time, distinguished from the Boards of Supervisors of other counties by the want of power or the opportunities for its exercise, although the powers were not in all respects identical. The legislation which is the occasion of the present litigation, recognizes and affirms the corporate existence and capacity of the County of New York as distinct from and independent of the City Government, and as possessing all the essential powers conferred upon other counties; and if there were no other foundation for the claim, that legislation would be sufficient to invest the County with all the attributes which pertain to a county organization and a municipal corporation, and bring New York within the province of the general statutes upon the subject of counties and their corporate rights and powers, except as otherwise specially provided by law.

The Act (Chapter 382 of the Laws of 1870) "to make further provisions for the government of the County of New York" distinctly recognizes the existence of the county, with every element of power and circumstance that can be claimed as necessarily incident to any other like organization. It directs the Board of Supervisors to cause to be raised by tax the sums of money necessary for the payment of the claims specified in certain sections thereof, after deducting from the aggregate amount of the claims the estimated revenues of the County, thus recognizing the existence of liabilities against the County, and the possession by it of property and sources of revenue other than the power of levying taxes. It also regulates the bringing of actions against the County, and Section 4 is based upon the acknowledged fact that the County had incurred obligations and contracted debts which were a County charge to an amount so large that it was inexpedient to levy a tax for the payment of them at that time, and hence provision was made for borrowing money for that purpose. By the special provisions made for the audit and payment of the claims referred to, the legal

rights and obligations of the County were not essentially
varied, or the relation between the State and County
affected, or any new relation created between the State
and the creditors of the County. A special process
was devised and put in execution to meet a present
necessity, somewhat different in detail from that provided by general laws for the adjustment and payment
of county charges, but the whole process was by and
in behalf of the County as a corporate body having
the power to act for itself, and there was no special or
general agency to act in behalf of the State. It was
merely a grant of corporate power modified and varied
from that ordinarily conferred upon this and other
counties, as made necessary by the peculiar circumstances, and to the limit of the power thus conferred
the County was an independent individual agent, and
the State, as such, was neither entitled to the fruits nor
responsible for the consequences of the exercise of such
power. The County was permitted to change the form
of its indebtedness, but the indebtedness remained, as
before, a County charge. The authority to borrow was
conferred upon the County, and to be executed by
County officers.

The special duty of auditing the claims was imposed
upon the individuals designated by the Act, but their
duty ended with certifying the amounts of the several
claims, and the county officials had no control of their
action. The Legislature might have fixed the sums
and adjusted the claims in the statute, or authorized
the amount to be determined in any other way or by
any other tribunal. To this extent the county, in respect to this class of claims, was taken out of the general statutory provisions authorizing claims and charges
against counties to be audited by the Board of Supervisors. (1 R. S., 366 § 4 ; Id., 368, Section 17.) Those individuals were not strictly County officers, neither were
they State officers, but constituted a special commission for performing a service for and binding upon the

county, which is ordinarily performed by a county
board, and which would seem to have been before
then performed by the Comptroller of the city, pursuant to the provisions of Chapter 854 of the Laws of
1868. Precedent was found for a special Board of
Audit, for the adjustment of claims against the County
of New York, in Chapter 806 of the Laws of 1867, constituting Chauncey M. Depew, Benjamin W. Bonney,
Lewis B. Woodruff and John H. Martindale such
Board. Every other act, save the audit of the claims,
was to be performed and was performed by the county
officials and in behalf of the county. The money was
to be and was borrowed upon the bonds of the county,
executed and attested by the proper officers and paid
by the Comptroller to the proper claimants. The
Chamberlain of the city is by law made County Treasurer, and all moneys belonging to the county, from
whatever source derived, of right are received by him
and disbursed upon proper warrants. (1 R. S., 370,
Sec. 29.)

By the act substituting the non-partisan Board of
Supervisors for the former organization (Laws of 1857,
Chap. 590, Sec. 6) the Finance Department of the City
and its officers (of whom the Comptroller is chief), are
to have the like powers and perform the like duties in
regard to the fiscal concerns of the Board of Supervisors as in regard to the local concerns of the city, and
it is directed that no money shall be drawn from the
treasury of the county except on the warrant of the
Comptroller, countersigned by the Mayor and Clerk of
the Board, thus making the Comptroller and Mayor
ex officio county officers. The complaint, therefore,
is strictly accurate in the averment that the moneys obtained from *bone fide* purchasers of the bonds issued
by the Comptroller as prescribed by the Act were, "in
formal compliance with the statutes and usual modes
of official proceeding in said city, deposited in the National Broadway Bank of the City of New York, to the

credit of an account therein kept by the Chamberlain of the City of New York as County Treasurer of the said County, by virtue of his said official character as such Chamberlain."

The Comptroller was not a depositary or disburser of the public funds, and the Act did not contemplate that he should receive and disburse the money. The brief direction in the Act that he should pay the claims audited must be read in connection with the general laws defining his powers and prescribing his duties in respect to county matters and as a county officer, or an officer charged with duties affecting the county. It was merely an authority, and a direction to draw a warrant upon the County Treasurer in the usual form, as was done in this case. It was not intended to take these funds without the protection of the safeguards provided by law for all public funds. Thus the funds were, as averred in the complaint, legally and properly paid into the county treasury as county moneys, to be drawn out only in the manner and upon the warrants authorized by law. In the withdrawal of these funds all the forms of law were complied with. The relation of the County of New York to these moneys, and its right as a municipal corporation to and over them, was precisely the same as would have been that of any and every other county in the State to moneys raised upon its credit or in virtue of power conferred upon it for county purposes. The question then is as to the rights of a county, as a public corporation, in respect to funds raised by authority of law upon its credit, and in the hands of its treasurer, and whether an action could be maintained by the county in any form for the recovery of the money, if tortiously or fraudulently taken from the county depositary or embezzled by him.

Corporate capacity is conferred upon each county in the State—and New York is not excepted—to sue and be sued, to purchase and hold lands within

its limits, for the use of its inhabitants; to make contracts and possess personal property, and to dispose
and regulate the use of its corporate property; and
all suits and proceedings by and against a county in
its corporate capacity are directed.to be in the name of
the Board of Supervisors of such county, that serving
pro hac vice, as the corporate name. (1 R. S., 364,
Sec. 1-3.; Id., 384, Sec. 1, 2; 2 Id., 473, Sec. 92-95. Supervisors of Onondaga *vs*. Morgan, 2 Keyes, 237.)

Counties are public, as distinguished from private
corporations, and they are political as auxiliaries to the
Government of the State, and they are trustees of the
people, the inhabitants within their county. (North
Hempsted *vs*. Hempsted, 2 W. R., 109.) They are
sometimes called *quasi* corporations, because not in
terms declared by statute to be corporations, and have
a corporate capacity only for particular specified
ends. But so long as they are invested with corporate attributes, even if it be *sub modo*, the distinction
is without a substantial difference within the limits of
the corporate powers conferred. (2 Kent's Com., 278,
9; A. and A. on Corporations, Sec. 23.) They are
trustees only of the property held for public use.
They are not the guardians and protectors of the private and individual interests or property of the
citizen. They may not intervene by action to protect
or redress the individual citizen in respect to wrongs
or injury to his person or property. Their power as
well as duty is restricted to the protection and preservation of property possesed by them in their corporate
capacity. (Town of Guilford *vs*. Supervisors of Chenango; Mayor of Georgetown *vs*. Alexandria
Canal Campany, 12 Peters, 91.) This trustee-
ship and corporate power as a pecuniary fiduciary
relation extends to and embraces not only the tangible
property of the Corporation, but the franchises and
powers conferred for raising moneys and other means
for the support of the local government and the use of
the inhabitants of the county, and to the means realized

from the franchises and powers conferred. It is immaterial whether the grant be of fees and emoluments from licenses, excise duties, rents or the like, or of a power to levy taxes or borrow money. The grant is a money grant by the State to the extent of the power conferred and the money realized under and by means of it. The pecuniary ability of a county may consist entirely, as it does ordinarily, in the power delegated to it to levy taxes or create.a debt. The credit of the county, with granted power to use it, supported by the power of taxation delegated by the State, is a corporate right, and the fruits and avails of that credit, when exercised by the borrowing of money, are as much the property and rightfully belong to the treasury of the county as if the specific sum had been granted in terms and paid from any other source. In political and governmental matters the municipalities are the representatives of the sovereignty of the State and auxiliary to it in other matters relating to property rights and pecuniary obligations, they have the attributes and the distinctive legal rights of private corporations, and may acquire property, create debts and sue and be sued as other corporations, and in the borrowing of money and incurring pecuniary obligations in any form, as well as in the buying and selling of property within the limits of the corporate powers conferred, they neither represent nor bind the State.

The relation of principal and agent does not and cannot exist, for obvious reasons, between the State and the various municipal corporations, created with power to contract debts in respect to the exercise of the corporate functions. Debts contracted by municipalities by authority of the Legislature are contracted by them as principals, and not as agents of the State. If this were not so, they would be clearly within the prohibition of Section 12, of Article 7, of the Constitution, but that they are not was decided in "People vs. Flagg," 46 N. Y., 401. This agency must be established to entitle the State, without the direct sanction of the Legislature, to claim or control the fruits and proceeds of the legal pledge of municipal credit, and from such agency, once established, necessarily and logically results the liability of the State for the debts incurred, and this in face of the explicit prohibition in the State Constitution against the direct and indirect creation of a State debt. The State cannot claim the benefits and repudiate the obligations resulting from the relation of principal and agent. The claim of the State to funds and moneys thus acquired cannot be rested upon the general sovereignty of the State and its rights and duties as *parens patriæ.* The State may and must, in some cases, care for and protect those who are incapable of caring for themselves, as infants, idiots and the like; but a corporation with full power to acquire and hold property, create debts, levy taxes and sue and be sued, with a competent board of governors, is not within this class of incompetents in need of the exercise of this nursing quality of the State Government. Neither can I discern any just foundation for the claim of the State to these funds—that its action is necessary to the protection of the taxpayers of the municipality. The *cestuis que trust* of the corporate property consist of all the inhabitants within the territorial limits of the Corporation, including taxpayers and non-taxpayers; they are the corporators and their interests, as well the present as future inhabitants and corporators, are cared for and represented by the governing body for the time being as in other corporations. I incline to the opinion that money borrowed or raised by taxation for county purposes, and not wanted or used for the particular purposes for which it was raised, is applicable, by the action of the Board of Supervisors, to the payment of any county charge; but if this be not so, the want of power to appropriate it to public use, without legislative authority, does not work a forfeiture of the money to the State. It is not intended to deny the existence of plenary power in the Legislature to direct the appropriation of any money in the county treasury to any use or purpose for the benefit of the inhabitants of the municipality.—(Darlington *vs.* The Mayor, *supra.*) The same objection might be taken to the right of the State, for if the moneys were once in the State Treasury, it would require legislation to authorize their application or payment to any particular use. But whatever the Legislature might do in the way of revoking a grant of power or of using or controlling the property of a county, no power in that direction has been conferred upon the Attorney-General.

Much was said in the course of the argument of the position and rights of the taxpayers and the impossibility of justice being done them unless the State could by action recover and control the money in controversy. But the taxpayers as distinguished from other inhabitants of the county have no peculiar interests to subserve or right to or interest in the money. The *cestuis que trust* of a municipal corporation are all the inhabitants within the territorial limits, whether taxable or not; and although the taxpayer may be more immediately affected pecuniarily by a maladministration of the corporate and trust funds he has no rights except such as are common to all the inhabitants. One taxpayer for himself, or himself and all others or all the taxpayers combined, cannot have an action for the correction or prevention of a misappropriation or misuser of the corporate property. (Doolittle *vs.* Supervisors of Broome County, 18 New York, 155; Roosevelt *vs.* Draper, 23 Id., 318.)

When the State, in the exercise of the taxing power, or any of the political corporations in the exercise of a delegation of the same power, has collected taxes pursuant to law the amount levied has ceased to be the property of the taxpayers

and becomes corporate funds and money in trust
for public purposes. The result is the same if
the money is borrowed in anticipation of taxation and
to be levied of those who shall hereafter become tax-
payers. Neither the present nor prospective taxpayers have any special and peculiar interest in the fund
as distinguished from that of other citizens and subjects of the government imposing the tax or incurring
the debt. The borrowing of money to be repaid by
taxation in the future is but one form of exercising
the taxing power, and the character of the fund is the
same whether it has been collected of the taxpayer or
borrowed upon the credit of the government, State or
local. (People *vs.* Flagg, 46 N. Y., 401.) For all
governmental and public purposes, including that of
levying taxes and borrowing money for public use,
the corporation is regarded as perpetual, and no respect is had to the changing character of the constituency, and those liable to contribute to the support of
the government or the payment of its debts. If, by
mistake or error of any kind, taxes in excess of the
amount required for present purposes have been, pursuant to law, collected, they cannot be recovered back
unless there has been some irregularity or defect of
jurisdiction, which vitiates the assessment and levy.

Neither is the money a waif belonging to the State
or any one who may chance to obtain possession of it,
but it belongs to the municipal treasury, and is a trust
fund for public use by the corporate authority.

The result is the same if the money has been borrowed
in excess of actual wants, and it is enough that a binding
obligation has been incurred by the municipality to
repay the money. Whether the obligation was incurred strictly pursuant to law is not important. If
the public corporation having power to act individually
and in a corporate capacity has by its officers so acted
under the laws as to become bound by its obligation,
the debt has become a corporate and a county charge,

and the moneys, the fruits and proceeds of the obligation, are trust funds, subject to the control of the governing body of the corporation under the general laws
of the State. The validity of the bonds which are represented by the moneys sought to be recovered in this
action is conceded by the counsel for the appellants,
and if not valid the purchasers of the bonds are entitled to reclaim the money paid for them. If valid,
they are the obligations of the County of New York,
and the debt a county charge. The State is under no
obligation to pay the bonds or to provide for their
payment, except so far as a sovereign State is bound
to act in good faith toward those who have acted and
parted with their money on the faith of its laws and
policy. The State cannot in good morals do anything
to impair or diminish the ability of the county to
pay the bonds at maturity. The only security the
debtor has is the credit of the county, and the grant
of power to the county with direction in the act
to levy taxes for the payment of the debt. To this
extent the State may perhaps be regarded as contract-
ing with those who have taken the bonds, and to have
agreed that the grant of power shall not be revoked,
but this does not create an obligation to pay the bonds.
It only brings the transaction within the provision of
the Constitution of the United States prohibiting States
from passing any bill "impairing the obligation of
contracts," (Constitution of the United States, Article 1,
Section 10), and makes the grant of power irrevocable.
(Hoffman *vs.* Quincy, 4 Wallace, 535.) It is claimed
that the County cannot be sued upon these bonds and
a recovery had. That the Federal Courts would sustain an action upon these bonds against the County
can hardly be doubted in view of the past action of
these courts in similar actions. It has been held by
the courts of this State that for claims which by statute
are made a County charge, and for the auditing of
which provision is made by statute, counties cannot

be sued. (Brady *vs.* Supervisors of New York, 10 N. Y., 260; Martin *vs.* Supervisors of Greene County, 29 Id., 645.) Conceding that the rule holds, as to an absolute undertaking to pay a specified sum at a given day, it proves nothing. If an action will not lie upon the bonds against the County the holders have a perfect legal remedy by the writ of mandamus to compel the levy of the tax and the payment of the bonds, and whether the debt may be recovered by one form of civil procedure or another is not material. It necessarily follows that this money being the fruits and avails of a burden imposed pursuant to law upon the taxable inhabitants and property of the County of New York, for County purposes, of right belonged to the County of New York and its Treasury, and the County has an action against any one who has by fraud or force become possessed of it.

It would hardly be claimed that if after the avails of the bonds had been deposited with the County Treasurer, the alleged frauds in the audit had been discovered and the warrants withheld, or payment had been refused by the Treasurer, the State, by its Attorney-General, without legislation, could have compelled the payment of the moneys into the State treasury, or recovered the money of the County Treasurer. Neither would it be claimed that had the County Treasurer embezzled the funds his sureties would not have been liable as for county moneys received by him. Had the bonds been delivered to a purchaser without actual payment of the money, any proceedings for a recovery of the bonds or the purchase price would necessarily have been by the county. The fact that a larger sum was borrowed than was required to pay the just claims against the county, by reason of a fraud in the audit, does not, in my judgment, affect the question. The money has been raised, properly or improperly, upon the credit and at the expense of the county, and for its use, to be repaid by it.

The wrongful act of the public agents does not give to the State the rights and impose upon it the obligations of a principal in the transaction. Had only just claims been audited and allowed, and the precise amount required for their payment been raised, and that had been taken by force or fraud from the possession of the county treasury, the legal rights of the county and the relation of the State to the transaction would have been precisely the same as now, and yet the right of the county to maintain an action for the money would not, in the case supposed, have been doubted. The county would have been the rightful possessor of the money and the proper party to an action for its recovery. (Van Keuren *vs.* Johnston, 3 Denio, 183 ; Supervisors of Albany County *vs.* Durant, 9 Paige, 182.) The reversal of the decree in this case by the Court for the Correction of Errors (26 W. R., 66) was upon a ground not affecting the right of a Board of Supervisors to maintain the action, if a cause of action had existed.

If every county of the State should, by authority of law, levy by tax or borrow upon the credit of the county and a pledge of taxes to be levied in the future, a sum of money for the building of a court-house or other special purpose, no one would doubt the title of the county to the money so long as it remained unexpended in the hands of county officials, or its right of action for the recovery of it, if it should be tortiously taken or embezzled. If there should be a surplus remaining of the same money after the accomplishment of the special purpose for which it was raised, and it should be fraudulently or tortiously appropriated, the property of the county in such surplus and its right of action to reclaim it, to the exclusion of the State and every other corporate body would not be questioned. This case does not differ in principle and cannot be distinguished from that supposed. But for the importance given to it by eminent counsel I should not regard the source from which the money came as a controlling or even an important element in determining by whom the action should be brought. It was in the county treasury, and was paid from the treasury as alleged, and received by the defendant as the money of the county upon a claim against the county, and if such claim was fraudulent, and the pretence under which the money was obtained false, the defendant is necessarily liable to the county, either in an action for the fraud or for money had and received, and is estopped from denying the title of the county to the money or its right to reclaim it, if in fact it was falsely and fraudulently obtained.

These considerations lead to an affirmance of the judgment of the Supreme Court. While in view of some of the circumstances connected with the origin and history of this suit we might wish for the purposes of this action the law was different, we can but declare it as we find it. There is nothing in the transaction itself or facts alleged in the complaint to distinguish this case in principle from any other in which the funds and property of a county have been embezzled, stolen or tortiously appropriated, or tending to show that the right of action and remedy which would exist in such case in any county of the State, are not vested in or do not belong to the County of New York in respect to the wrong complained of here. Neither is it averred in the complaint that obstacles in any form exist to the prosecution of such remedy by the county, or that the corporate authorities have not prosecuted or will not and cannot effectually prosecute for the alleged wrong.

Were it believed that the remedy by and in behalf of the county was not plain, palpable and free from all doubt we might hesitate in giving the judgment to which our examination has led us lest a flagrant wrong might go unpunished. It was conceded by counsel for the plaintiffs upon the first argument of this appeal that the same reasons do not now exist for maintaining an action by the State rather than the county that were supposed to exist at the time of the commencement of this action. Reference was doubtless had in such concessions to the statements of the complaint stricken out by order of the Court below, acquiesced in by the plaintiffs, tending to show collusion between the county officials and the wrongdoers, and the difficulties, by reason of such collusion and complicity, in the way of an effective prosecution of an action by the county. Those statements are not now in the record, and the position and relation of the present government of the county to the defendants is supposed to have been changed. Whether this be so or not, is not material upon this appeal, as the record discloses no fact which will take this action or cause of action out of the general principle governing all like cases. It will not answer to ignore well established rules of law and invent new principles and modes of procedure solely by reason of the magnitude of a claim or the enormity of a wrong so long as there is a party in whom the cause of action is vested able and willing to prosecute, and established rules of law and familiar modes of procedure give an ample remedy to enforce the right and redress the wrong.

To sustain this action upon the ground that the individuals acting in the transaction under the statute were State agents, and not the agents of the county, would lead to serious results and greatly embarrass the State in respect to the many millions of municipal obligations which have been incurred under legislative authority, only differing in the form and method of execution from that exercised in this case. The State cannot make the actors State agents without assuming the position and responsibility of principal, especially if the agency is, as is claimed here, of a character entitling the State to the fruits and benefits of the agency. To sustain the action upon the ground of State sovereignty and a general State guardianship over municipal corporations and their rights and property interests without legislation upon this subject, and hold that for an invasion of the property rights of a public corporation an action will lie in the discretion and at the instance of the Attorney-General, in the name of the people, to the exclusion of or concurrent with a like right of action in the corporation damnified, would introduce a new and strange doctrine, subverting those by which the rights and obligations of that class of corporations have been governed, and lead to confusion and embarrassment in the future in the administration of the affairs and redressing of wrongs to the property rights of municipal corporations. The right to bring actions for injuries to their property is expressly conferred and given to counties by statute, and this necessarily excludes the right of the State to bring an action for the same cause. It is not intended to deny that a case may be made in which the Attorney-General may, in the name of the people, institute and maintain an action against a wrong-doer, and the public corporation whose rights have been invaded or threatened, and the governing body of such corporation, to enforce a right, or redress a wrong, or prevent a breach of trust where the governing body is faithless to its trust or a party to the wrong. Such a case is not made here, and the question is not before us. Judgment affirmed.

Judge ALLEN reads for affirmance; Judges GROVER, FOLGER, ANDREWS and JOHNSON concur. Judge RAPALLO reads for reversal; Chief Judge CHURCH concurs.

RAPALLO, J.

The main question in this case is whether, upon the facts stated in the complaint, admitting them to be true, the State is the proper party to maintain this action. By an Act of the Legislature, passed on the 26th of

April, 1870 (Laws of 1870, chap. 382, sec. 4), it was enacted as follows :

"All liabilities against the county of New York, previous to the passage of this Act, shall be audited by the Mayor of the city of New York, the Comptroller of said city and the present President of the Board of Supervisors, and the amounts which are found to be due shall be provided for by the issue of revenue bonds of the county of New York, payable during the year 1871, and the Board of Supervisors shall include in the ordinance levying the taxes for the year 1871 an amount sufficient to pay said bonds and the interest thereon. Such claims shall be paid by the Comptroller to the party or parties entitled to receive the same upon the certificate of the officers named herein."

The complaint alleges, in substance, that the auditors appointed by this Act between May and September, 1870, certified claims purporting to be of the character described in the Act, in favor of the defendants Ingersoll, Garvey and others, to the amount of several millions of dollars, upon which certificates revenue bonds of the county were issued in proper form by the Comptroller, as prescribed in the Act, and money was raised thereon from *bona fide* purchasers thereof, in order to pay the amounts so certified ; that this money was deposited in a bank to the credit of an account then kept by the Chamberlain of the city of New York as Treasurer of the county, and was afterwards obtained by the defendants Ingersoll, Garvey and Woodward, by means of Comptroller's warrants drawn upon the bank for the payment of the claims certified as aforesaid.

That the defendant Tweed, was, at the time of the passage of the Act of April 26, 1870, President of the Board of Supervisors of the county of New York, and consequently one of the persons by that Act appointed auditors ; that he assumed to act as such auditor, and that, in that capacity, he, as well as the auditors named in the Act, signed certificates of the audit and committed in obtaining it, cannot be questioned. That justice requires that such disposition shall ultimately be made of the money to be recovered as will relieve *pro tanto* the taxpayers, who will ultimately be subjected to the payment of the obligations upon which the money was wrongfully raised, is obvious. But in the absence of any machinery provided by law for a case so extraordinary, the Court should not undertake, whoever is plaintiff, to do more than to require that the avails of the recovery be placed in the treasury of the State, or other safe custody, to await further legislation.

Assuming the correctness of these propositions, which will be further substantiated in connection with the objections raised by the demurrant, it would seem sufficiently plain that the State is a proper party to invoke such a remedy as this case demands. The wrong complained of is the violation by an agent or appointee of the State of a trust and duty created by statute for a special purpose, through which violation of duty, he and the other defendants confederating with him, have obtained a large sum of money on obligations which must be paid by taxation under authority of the State. The damage resulting is to the fluctuating body of taxpayers of one of the divisions of the State, who, under the provisions of the Constitution of the United States, cannot be liberated from the burden to which the acts of the defendants have subjected them, by any means short of the State itself assuming and paying the bonds, the proceeds of which the defendants have wrongfully appropriated. On no other terms could any repeal of the Act directing the levy of the tax be sustained. The money which the defendants ought to replace will, by whomsoever recovered, be subject to the control of the Legislature. Even if recovered by the State and paid into the general fund, egislation will be required for its appropriation to any particular object. Unless it can be shown that under

existing statutes some particular officer or body is vested with the exclusive power of bringing the action in such a case, the interest of the people ought to be deemed sufficient to entitle them to intervene for that purpose, through their Attorney-General, who is, by statute, not only empowered, but required to prose-
. cute all actions in the event of which the people are interested.

(1 R. S. 179, Section 1.)

It seems to be conceded in all the discussions on the subject before and within the Court, that if the Attorney-General had been specially authorized by Act of the Legislature to bring this action, such authority would be valid and sufficient to sustain the action. This proposition necessarily concedes the interest of the State in the subject of the litigation.

If a special authorization in the particular case would have been sufficient to require the Court to entertain the action of the Attorney-General, on what principle can it refuse to do so in the face of the general statute, which not only empowers but requires him to prosecute all actions in the event of which the people are interested? Ordinary reasoning would lead us to the conclusion that this general statute is sufficient authority for his intervention in any such case, unless some special statute is pointed out which restrains his action in the particular case or grants the exclusive right to prosecute such action to some other officer or local body. No such statute has been pointed out, nor have I found any.

The cases in this State which deny the right of individuals to intervene simply on the ground that they are taxpayers whose burdens will be increased by the wrong complained of, proceed upon the ground that the general rule is that for wrongs against the public, whether actually committed or only apprehended, the remedy, whether civil or criminal, is by the State in

property or revenue of the county as such, but ultimately by means of the tax which the Supervisors of
the county were by the Act required to levy for that
special purpose in the following year, 1871. In order
to obviate delay in the discharge of the liabilities in
question a means was provided for discounting or anticipating the tax so authorized by the issue of the
bonds before referred to, and the amount necessary to
pay those bonds was to be raised by the tax.

The controlling question arising upon this demurerr
is whether, for any fraud, misconduct or breach of
trust on the part of any of the persons designated by
the Legislature for the purpose of carrying into effect
the provisions of this Act, which fraud, misconduct or
breach of trust has resulted in raising upon temporary
bonds issued in the form authorized by the Act a vastly
larger sum than was necessary for the discharge of the
liabilities provided for by the Act, and in transferring
the surplus into the pockets of the delinquent agent or
appointee of the State, and other persons confederating
with him to that end, an action will lie on behalf of
the State against the delinquent and his confederates
who have participated in the corrupt transactions and
their fruits. One material inquiry, in determining this
question is, upon whom will the loss occasioned by
these transactions fall? There can be but one answer
to this question. The bonds have been disposed of to
bona fide holders. They are directed by law to be
paid by means of a tax, to be levied on the taxpayers
of the county. The bondholders have the legal right
to enforce the levy of this tax. There is no property
of the county as such out of which these bonds can be
collected by legal process. The moneys, therefore,
which have been fraudulently raised upon these bonds
and appropriated by the wrong-doers, will have to be
collected under authority of the State out of the tax-
payers of the county, and the loss consequently falls
upon them. It is clearly shown by the authorities

cited in the argument that no individual can have a standing in court as a taxpayer merely for the purpose of obtaining redress for such a wrong ; and the reasons for this conclusion are too obvious to render discussion necessary. Among other reasons, it is evident in the present case it would be impossible to ascertain the extent to which any individual who was a taxpayer at the time of the wrong would be damnified, or even that he would be a taxpayer when the time should arrive for the levy of the tax. Who, then, is the proper party to appear as plaintiff and represent the fluctuating body of taxpayers, who, sooner or later, must be compelled by authority of the State to pay the money wrongfully obtained by the defendants on the credit of the tax to be imposed ?

The people of the State, through their Attorney-General, appear before the Court, claiming the right to intervene as plaintiff, and to compel their own unfaithful appointee and trustee, and those who have combined, conspired and shared with him, to replace the moneys which, under color of the authority conferred by the State, they have thus wrongfully obtained and applied to their own use, or to pay in the form of dam ages such sum as will compensate for the amoun. which by their wrongful acts they have obtained at the expense of the taxpayers. It must be conceded that the question presented is novel, but the law is not so defective as to be wholly destitute of remedy in such a case. The remedy required is, in the first place, to take out of the hands of the wrong-doers the fund which they have unlawfully obtained, or to compel them to pay an equivalent in the form of damages. The disposition of the money which the defendants may be adjudged to pay is not provided for by any existing law, and it is therefore impossible for the Court now to adjudicate what shall be its final destination. That the defendants are not entitled to retain it, and that they are liable in some form for the wrong allowance of the alleged claims which served as the foundation for the issue of the revenue bonds upon which the money in question was raised. That these claims were never in fact audited by the Board appointed by the Act of April 26, 1870, but that the certificates of the audit thereof were signed by the auditors separately and without investigation, in pursuance of a resolution adopted by them on the 5th of May, 1870, whereby the County Auditor, (then one James Watson,) was directed to collect all bills and liabilities against the county incurred prior to April 26, 1870 ; and it was resolved that the evidence of the same should be the authorization of the same by the Board of Supervisors, or its appropriate committees, on certificate of the Clerk or the President. The complaint then proceeds to allege that the accounts so pretended to have been audited were false, fictitious and fraudulent, and were prepared by fraud and collusion between the said Watson, (then County Auditor,) and the defendants Garvey, Ingersoll and Woodward, and put in such shape as to entitle them, by the terms of the resolution of the Board of Auditors, dated May 5, 1870, and before mentioned, to be certified under the Act of, April 26, 1870, without further investigation ; that after they had been so certified Watson obtained the Comptroller's warrants for their payment, and that the sums paid on such warrants were "pursuant to a corrupt, fraudulent and unlawful combination and conspiracy to that end by and between the said William M. Tweed, James Watson, Andrew J. Garvey, James H. Ingersoll and Elbert A. Woodward, agreed to be divided and were divided between the said James H. Ingersoll, Andrew J. Garvey and William M. Tweed," and other persons unknown, &c. The details of the transactions are set out in the complaint and schedules, and it sufficiently appears that these payments were made out of the fund raised by the sale of revenue bonds issued on the strength of the certificates of audit signed by the auditors appointed by the Act of April 26, 1870.

These facts which are admitted by the demurrer, establish that the State, through its Legislature, provided a method of discharging a specified class of the liabilities of one of its counties. That it appointed certain persons to carry out its enactments by auditing the liabilities, issuing bonds for the precise amount necessary to pay such liabilities when ascertained, and applying to such payment the proceeds of the bonds so issued. The State provided for the payment of these bonds by requiring the Board of Supervisors of the county to raise by taxation the amount necessary to pay them. The auditing of the claims was intrusted to three persons, not as county officers, but as special appointees of the Legislature to carry out the provisions of the Act. They were the Mayor and the Comptroller of the city of New York and the *then present* President of the Board of Supervisors of the county. His powers and duties as Auditor did not depend upon the continuance of his office of President of the Board of Supervisors. Instead of being personally named he was described in the Act as the then President of the Board. This was a mere designation of the person intended. He continued Auditor, notwithstanding the termination of his office of President of the Board of Supervisors, which, as is alleged in the complaint, occurred on the 4th of July, 1870. From the beginning he acted not in virtue of his county office, but as the repository of a special trust directly confided to him by the Legislature, and, together with the Mayor and Comptroller of the city, formed a commission appointed by the State for the performance of a special duty. This duty consisted in auditing and certifying the amount of the liabilities of the county up to a certain date, and, consequently, determining the sum which should be levied upon the taxpayers for the purpose of meeting those liabilities. The liabilities were not to be paid out of any fund its political character, or by some officer authorized by law to act in its behalf, and this is true whether the whole people of the State or only those of a particular locality are affected. Common nuisances, purprestures, usurpations of public offices and the improper exercise by public officers of their functions are recognized as instances of the application of this principle. The inconveniences which would result from any other principle, among which is the multiplicity of suits which would arise, are pointed out in those cases. No private person or number of persons can assume to be the champions of the community, and in its behalf challenge the public officers to meet them in the courts of justice to defend their official acts. *Their remedy is to invoke the action of the officer whom the law has appointed to sue in such cases.*

> Doolittle *v.* Supervisors of Broome County, 18 New York, 168.
> Roosevelt *v.* Draper, 23 New York, 818.

In the case last cited Judge Denio, in delivering the opinion of the Court, declares that "an act of administration likely to produce taxation is not a matter of private or individual concern. It is an affair altogether public, and the only remedial process against an abuse of administrative power tending to taxation which we can have, is furnished by the *elective* system, or *a proceeding in behalf of the State.*"

The grounds upon which the right of the State to presecute the action is denied are that the money which was taken by the defendants belonged to the county of New York. That the Supervisors of every county are empowered by statute to bring actions to enforce liabilities to the county and to recover damages for injuries done to the property or rights of the county, (2 R. S., 473), and that consequently the action should have been brought by the Supervisors of the county of New York. No other party is suggested as the proper plaintiff. Assuming that the provisions authorizing Supervisors of counties to bring actions are applicable to the county of New York (a proposition which is denied by the appellants) it is necessary to this defence to establish that the liability incurred by the defendants was to the county, or that the money taken by them was the property of the county. The only cases in which the Supervisors of a county are empowered by statute to sue are those before mentioned, together with some others which are foreign to the present case, such as actions on contracts made with the Supervisors for penalties and forfeitures, &c. (2 R. S., 473), and a county can neither sue nor be sued except by express power conferred by statute.

Hunter v. Mercer Co., 10 Ohio St. R. 520.
Hunsaker v. Borden, 5 Cal, 290.

It is worthy of remark, in passing to the consideration of this defence, that so far as appears upon the present record the right of the people to sue for and recover the money or damages in controversy is not challenged by the county of New York, and the question does not arise in consequence of any claim made by the county or on its behalf to the money or damages sought to be recovered. It is raised only by the alleged wrong-doers and as a means of defeating the action brought against them by the State. To be effective for that purpose it should appear not only that the defendants are liable to the county, but to that civil division of the State exclusively, and that a recovery by the State itself and satisfaction thereof would not bar a subsequent recovery on behalf of the county for the same acts.

The main points urged on the argument on the part of the demurrant in support of his defence that the money which he took belonged to the county, are these:

stituted in their place. To the assertion that if the Supervisors got the funds they might have exerted the physical power of applying them to the payment of those bonds. It is a sufficient answer in law that they had no legal right so to do, and, in fact, that they might have made some different disposition of them. To hold that where a fund raised as this was, under an act of the Legislature for a specific purpose, named in the Act, has not been applied to the purpose for which it was raised, the Supervisors of a county have the legal right or power to apply it to a different use, is too monstrous a proposition to be seriously entertained. It would be to allow the agent to overrule the principal.

It cannot be supposed that the Legislature ever intended that any such result should follow as that $6,000,000 should be raised on the credit of the taxing power of the State and placed at the disposal of the Supervisors of the county of New York, without any direction as to its application, especially in view of the fact that the Legislature has consistently denied to that county the unlimited power which is accorded to others, of raising by tax the amount deemed necessary for the expenses of local government, and has compelled the county of New York to come every year to the Legislature with a specification of the amount desired to be raised and of the purposes in detail to which the money so to be raised is to be applied. Not only has the general taxing power conferred upon Boards of Supervisors of other counties of the State been withheld from the county of New York, but for a long period the existence of the county as an organization was nominal merely. A record of the proceedings of the Board of Supervisors of that county covering a period of thirty years prior to the year 1840 is contained in a single small volume, and they show that it existed as a county more for the purpose of designation than for any substantial governmental purpose. The territory was the same as that of the city, and the latter exercised all the powers of municipal government. In 1857 and subsequently additional powers were from time to time conferred, and were often used for corrupt purposes, but the Act of 1870 stripped the Board of the most important of these powers and conferred them upon the special auditors. The proposition that the Supervisors, thus denuded of power, are the proper body to call to account the State agents who have superseded them, is a solecism unsupported by law or logic. The people of the State, through their Legislature, are the only power who can prescribe the ultimate disposition of this fund.

State of Md. v. B. and O. R. R., 12 Gill and J., 899, and S. C., 3 How. U. S. R., 534.

I can see no ground upon which the Supervisors of the county can claim the fund or damages in question to the exclusion of the State. The only purpose for which any party can claim to recover and hold this money is for the indemnity of the taxpayers, who are or will be burdened with the bonds. But there is no law creating the Supervisors trustees for any such purpose. Supervisors are not the representatives or guardians of the taxpayers. They are local officers whose duties are definitely prescribed by statute, and they cannot exceed the powers thus conferred upon them. The actions which they may bring are confined to such as are specified in the statutes and necessary to enforce liabilities or duties enjoined by law to them or to the body which they represent, that is, the county in its corporate character. They have no right to intervene for the protection of the general interests of the inhabitants or taxpayers of the county. (2 Denio, 464; 17 N. Hamp., 214; 6 Allen, 56; 4 Black [Ind'a] 256.) This duty specially devolves upon the State authority. (Davis v. The Mayor, 2 Duer, 663; S. C., 14 N. Y., 526; Attorney-General v. Eastlake, 11 Hare, 223.)

county government, according to their discretion. But the present case is entirely different. The money was raised for a specific purpose designated in the Act, and the Supervisors and all the county officers combined had no authority or power to divert a single cent of it from that specified purpose. There was no grant of the money in any form to the county. There was no surplus to arise in which the county could be interested, for no more was to be raised than precisely sufficient to pay the particular claims which should be certified by the auditors. There was no direction to pay the money into the County Treasury, nor was the least power or control over it given to the Supervisors, not even its custody. On the contrary, the State undertook, through its own direct agents named in the Act, to administer the fund to the exclusion of any action of the Supervisors. The claims were to be audited by the special board appointed by the Legislature and to be paid by the Comptroller of the city. There could not legally be any interference in the matter by the Board of Supervisors.

But it is said the credit of the county was pledged to the bondholders, and, therefore, the county should have the money. What is the credit of the county? It is not like the credit of an individual or a corporation having power to contract debts and property out of which they can be collected by legal process. The county is one of the civil and political divisions of the State. It holds property only for public uses, and no such property is liable on civil process for debts. The State in this case provided for the payment of certain debts of the county by directing the local authorities to levy taxes within the boundaries of their county, and in anticipation of the collection of such taxes authorized the issue of bonds. The creditors who took the bonds trusted the justice of the State and not the county, which was powerless to pay them, except through the means provided by the State. The obligations in question were not obligations voluntarily incurred by the county, or in consequence of any negotiation made by it, but were created by order of the State, for the purpose of carrying into effect a statute of the State, and the faith of the State is pledged not to withdraw its requirement that the local authorities shall levy the tax for the purpose of reimbursing to the bondholders the money advanced by them upon the bonds. The bonds amount to nothing more than legally authorized certificates of the amount which each holder is entitled to receive out of the tax which the State has directed to be levied, and on the faith of which tax the lender has advanced his money. The State, then, is the party by whose power and authority the money was raised and must be repaid. The county organization is the mere agency to carry out the will of the Legislature, and is compelled to do so. Can it be questioned that the State has an interest in protecting the fund, and recovering it or its equivalent in damages from those who have wrongfully possessed themselves of it by combining with the agent of the State? What right did the Supervisors of the county ever have to the possession of this fund? It is impossible to point to any law giving them such a right. What power of disposition would they have over it should they now recover and collect it? What could they do with it? If it were their money they could do anything they chose with it—apply it to the payment of the expenses of the Board of Supervisors, or to the erection of public buildings, or to any other purposes, or release it. But it is evident that any such use of the fund would be clearly in contravention of law. The authority to raise it was for the sole purpose of paying claims existing prior to April 26, 1870, and it could not lawfully be applied to any other. Those claims have been paid and overpaid. It is said the Supervisors might apply it towards the payment of the revenue bonds upon which it was raised, or of those which have been sub-

FIRST.—That the bonds upon which the money was borrowed were county bonds. That when a county borrows money pursuant to law upon its own bonds, the proceeds belong to the county, on the same principle as that upon which money borrowed by a natural person, or by a corporation authorized to borrow money, becomes the property of the borrower.

SECOND.—That the money so borrowed was actually paid into the county treasury, and that its abstraction by means of the certificates alleged to be fraudulent, was from that treasury ; and,

THIRD.—That such deposit of the borrowed money in the county treasury is alleged in the complaint to have been made in formal compliance with the statutes and usual modes of official proceeding in the city of New York.

The allegation that the deposit of the money in the county treasury was in compliance with the statutes, is matter of law and not of fact. It does not, therefore, conclude either party on demurrer. As matter of law no statute can be found authorizing the deposit of these funds in the county treasury. The only acts bearing upon the question to which we have been referred are, Laws of 1862, chapter 37, section 2, and 1 R. S., page 369, section 20, and page 370, section 29. The Act. of 1862 provides for the payment into the treasury of the county of moneys loaned upon revenue bonds of the county, issued in anticipation of the collection of the annual taxes of the county, to pay the ordinary charges and expenses under appropriations made by the Board of Supervisors for the support of the county government, and is expressly restricted to taxes authorized to be raised during the same year in which the money is borrowed. This Act is clearly inapplicable to the fund now in question. The Act of 1865 merely provides that all revenue of the city and county shall be deposited in the banks designated by the Chamberlain. The proceeds of the bonds now in question cannot be called revenue of the city or county. The mode provided by other statutes, which have been referred to, for drawing money out of the treasury of the county, do not affect the question—what moneys should properly go into such treasury? The only statutory provisions relevant to the question are 1 R. S., 369, secs. 20 and 29, which provide that it shall be the duty of the County Treasurer to receive all moneys belonging to the county, from whatever sources they may be derived, and that the Chamberlain of the City and County of New York shall be the County Treasurer thereof, and this brings us back to the original question, whether the fund raised by the issue of these bonds belonged to the county. If not, the mere deposit of them in bank to the credit of the Chamberlain did not invest the Supervisors with the exclusive right to such moneys. "The County Treasury cannot become the depository of any bonds but those that the law brings to it."

Jeff. Co. v. Ford, 4 Greene (Iowa), 370.

The only fact upon which the defendants can rely in support of their claim that these moneys belonged to the county is that the bonds upon which they were raised were county bonds. If a general power to borrow money for its own purposes had been given to the county, or if the money in question had been raised pursuant to law in anticipation of the annual taxes of the county to pay its ordinary charges and expenses under appropriations made by the Board of Supervisors for the support of the county government, which is the class of moneys to which the Act of 1862 relates, a title in the county might be made out. In that case the control and power of the disposition of the money would be conferred by law upon the Supervisors. They could appropriate and apply it to the expenses of the

The legal custodian of the fund which may be recovered in this action is not pointed out by any statute, and this is very natural. The existence even of such a fund was unanticipated, as it was not intended that any more money should be raised on bonds than should be paid out in regularly audited claims. But I think it a safe and a necessary doctrine that where moneys are thus raised under color of law, upon obligations which are a burden upon the taxpayers of the State at large, or of a particular locality, and such moneys are unlawfully appropriated by individuals, and there is no local authority or officer clearly vested by law with the right to sue for their recovery, the State must of necessity be held to be the proper party to prosecute. Were it otherwise public funds thus situated would be wholly unprotected and liable to be plundered with impunity.

But assuming that there was a right of action in the Supervisors as contended by the defendant, such right of action must have been founded upon some title to the fund conferred by the State. If the title to the fund was thus conferred upon them, it could only be held for public uses theretofore declared, or thereafter to be declared by the Legislature. It is impossible to conceive of any other kind of property they could have had in the fund. Certainly no individual right or interest in it. Supposing then that on some such ground the Supervisors had a right of action, but that they refused or neglected to prosecute. Was there, then, no redress? Could those who had taken the money retain it and be free from all responsibility for their acts? and must the taxpayers quietly submit to be taxed for the benefit of the wrong-doers? No one has as yet ventured to assert so bold a proposition. On the contrary, it seems to be conceded that in such a case the State might sue, but it has been suggested that, to entitle the people thus to intervene, they should have alleged in their complaint the refusal or neglect of the county officers to prosecute, and that with such an allegation the action might be maintained in behalf of the people. This necessarily concedes some interest on the part of the people in enforcing the claim against the defendants, for if they have none, the failure of particular persons or officers to prosecute could confer no right upon them. If, then, the people have an interest in the controversy, on what principle can it be claimed that they must defer to their subordinates and await their pleasure?

The case of stockholders in private corporations is claimed to be analogous. In such cases it has been frequently adjudicated that for the recovery of property belonging to the corporation, or of damages sustained for wrongs done to it by its officers or others, the stockholders, although being those ultimately injured by the wrongs complained of, will not be heard in Court, unless the persons who are appointed by law to represent their interests refuse to perform their duty, or are so far implicated in the wrongs to be redressed that it would not be safe to entrust the prosecution to their hands. Under those circumstances, Courts of Equity will entertain a proceeding by the stockholders in their own names. But the ground upon which stockholders are allowed to prosecute in the case supposed is totally different from that upon which the State claims to intervene in the present case. Stockholders have no interest to represent or protect except their own pecuniary interest in the property of the corporation; and it is necessary, before they can be heard, to show that their rights are not duly cared for by those whom the law has appointed to protect them. But the interest of the State, in the questions now at issue, is of a totally different description. It is not for the protection of a proprietary or pecuniary interest of its own in the subject-matter that it claims the right to intervene, but for the protection of a portion of its citizens against the wrongful act of its own appointees and their confederates, who have, under color of authority, conferred by the State, raised and appropriated, to their own use, a large sum of money, which must be repaid by the taxpayers of the division of the State where the money was raised. There is no similarity between the position of the State, in such a controversy, and that of a stockholder in a private corporation. To the State primarily belongs the power, and upon it devolves the duty of redressing just such wrongs; and unless it has in this instance delegated to some of its departments, not only the right, but the exclusive right, to perform this duty, it has not stripped itself of its own powers or rendered an application to its delegates, and a refusal on their part to act, a necessary preliminary to its own invocation of the action of the judiciary.

It is claimed on the part of the defendants, and this is the plea upon which they have expended the most of their force, that it would be placing too much power in the hands of the Attorney-General to allow him, without an express statute, to institute proceedings against public officers charging them with abuses of public trusts. This is a very feeble argument. As well might it be urged that a general power of attorney from one individual to another to prosecute and defend all actions in which the principal actually or in the judgment of the attorney had an interest was impolitic and void, as giving to the attorney too much power, yet this is the power of attorney which the State has given to its Attorney-General and requires him to execute. It must be borne in mind that the only power of the attorney is to bring the matters in dispute before the Courts in proper form for their adjudication. The attorney has no power to decide them, whether he be an attorney for an individual or for the State. His province is simply to lay the question in dispute before the Court. True policy would seem to dictate liberality in thus permitting controversies to be ventilated. The responsibility of deciding them does not rest with either party, but with the tribunals of justice before whom the cause is heard. The safety of the public is, in my humble judgment, better subserved by throwing open than by closing approaches to these tribunals for the remedy of public wrongs of the description disclosed in this action. The only substantial ground upon which the defendant in such a case might with propriety decline to answer at the suit of the Attorney·General, would be that a recovery by him and satisfaction thereof would not be a bar to a subsequent action for the same cause by the local authority.

If this could be made out it would be a perfect answer to the action. But it cannot. When the suit is brought by the Attorney General in a matter within his authority, no other involving the same questions can be instituted. And when a judgment is pronounced in such a suit, as the Attorney-General represents the public, all persons are bound by the decision. A judgment for or against the defendants in the present action would, consequently, be a perfect protection to them against any subsequent or other action against them for the same acts.

I have not referred in detail to the authorities upon which I have relied in confirmation of these views. They have been elaborately cited and discussed on the briefs and in the arguments of the eminent counsel on both sides who have argued before the Court, and references to them will be made by the reporter. It is sufficient to say that I have carefully examined them and discussed them with my fellow Judges, and that but for the prolixity which would be occasioned by an extended review of them and a demonstration of their applicability to the present case, I would cheerfully devote myself to that labor. I think it more useful to state the results. In my opinion the judgment should be reversed and judgment should be rendered for the plaintiffs on the demurrer, and leave to answer should be granted.

(A Copy.)

H. E. SICKELS,
Reporter.

The above opinions were delivered June 9th, 1874, and judgment given for the defendant Ingersoll accordingly.

At the election held in November, 1874, HON. THEODORE MILLER, the presiding Justice of the third department was elected in the stead of JOHNSON, J., who sat temporarily under an appointment to supply the vacancy occasioned by the death of the HON. RUFUS W. PECKHAM.

The opinion of MILLER, J., when thus presiding in the third department on giving judgment in favor of the State in this same case against the defendant Tweed, was as follows :

Supreme Court,

THIRD DEPARTMENT.

THE PEOPLE OF THE STATE OF NEW
YORK,
Plaintiffs,
against
WILLIAM M. TWEED and others,
Defendants.

Before MILLER,
POTTER &
PARKER, *JJ.*

CHARLES O'CONOR, SAMUEL J. TILDEN and
WHEELER H. PECKHAM, for the People.

DAVID DUDLEY FIELD, EDWIN W. STOUGHTON,
WM. FULLERTON, JOHN E. BURRILL, JOHN H.
REYNOLDS, W. O. BARTLETT, JOHN GRAHAM, ELIHU
ROOT and WILLARD BARTLETT, for defendant TWEED.

MILLER, *P. J.:*

The money which the plaintiffs claim to recover in
this action was realized under and by virtue of an Act
of the Legislature of this State, entitled "An Act to
make further provision for the government of the
county of New York," passed on the 26th of April,
1870. (S. L. of 1870, Chapter 382, page 875.)

By Section 4 of said Act it was provided that, "All
liabilities against the county of New York previous to
the passage of this Act shall be audited by the Mayor
of the city of New York, the Comptroller of the said
city, and the [then] present President of the Board of
Supervisors, and the amounts which are found to be
due shall be provided for by the issue of revenue bonds

of the county of New York, payable during the year one thousand eight hundred and seventy-one ; and the Board of Supervisors shall include in the ordinance levying the taxes for the year eighteen hundred and seventy-one an amount sufficient to pay said bonds and the interest thereon. Such claims shall *be paid by the Comptroller to the party or parties entitled* to receive the same, upon the certificate of the officers named herein."

It will be observed that the money raised by the issue of revenue bonds was to be paid by the Comptroller to the parties entitled to receive the same, upon the certificate of the officers designated. Although the complaint alleges that the money obtained upon the bonds issued was deposited to the credit of an account kept by the Chamberlain of the city of New York, as County Treasurer of said county, there is no statute authorizing or requiring any such deposit, and therefore this allegation is immaterial to make out a cause of action, and this case must be considered as if the money remained in the possession and under the control of the officer named, for the purposes designated in the Act, until otherwise lawfully disposed of.

The money claimed was in the hands of the Comptroller, to be paid by him, as required by law, to the parties who had a lawful right to the same, and the bonds upon which the money was obtained were subsequently taken up in pursuance of chapter 323, entitled "An Act for the Consolidation of the Debt of the County of New York" (S. L. of 1871, p. 631), and new bonds issued in the place of the old ones.

The injury complained of, and for which redress is sought in this action, is for issuing bonds to a larger amount than was required for the purposes named, viz. : the payment of liabilities against the county, and the appropriation of the excess of money which was thus raised by and for the benefit of the defendants.

There was no lawful authority to raise any amount of money beyond what was required for objects contemplated by the Act of 1870, before cited. The amount which was realized besides what was required for the payment of debts, was not for the benefit of the county or to pay its liabilities, or to be paid into the county treasury for any.purposes whatever. There is no law either for raising or appropriating any such fund beyond the liabilities of the county; for if six millions or any lesser sum could be raised in this manner, then one hundred millions, or any other unlimited amount, might be thus obtained.

So far, then, as the money appropriated by the defendants is concerned, it was procured without any lawful authority, and, in fact, in direct violation of law, as the Act under which it was supposed to be obtained does not sanction any such proceeding. It was only legal debts, honest and *bona fide* liabilities against the county which were to be audited and provided for by the issue of revenue bonds, and none but these demands would properly come within the provisions of the law.

The defendants, then, were in possession of funds without any legal sanction whatever. As they were not obtained for the benefit of the county, nor lawfully paid to its proper officer, I am inclined to think that the county was not the owner and never had lawful control over the money, and it never was within its lawful custody. While the county is liable to the innocent and *bona fide* holders of the bonds, issued by its proper officers in due form, acting under color of authority, it by no means follows that the funds thus unlawfully obtained, and which never had been lawfully paid over to the county for its benefit, were the property of the county.

Even if it be conceded that the county, in its corporate capacity, can sue, as it was neither the owner nor in the lawful possession of this money, it could not maintain an action of the character of the one now before us for its recovery.

The taxpayers can maintain no such action, nor in any form demand redress, as has been adjudicated by the Court in numerous cases. (Doolittle *vs.* Supervisors of Broome county, 18 N. Y., 155; Roosevelt *vs.* Draper, 16 How., 137; 23 N. Y., 324. See also 12 Peters, 100.) The future taxpayers who may be called upon to pay the bonds, who are at present unknown, and some of them not in existence, are the parties really interested, and they cannot prosecute for the reason that it is not known who they are or may be. Unless this action can be maintained, there is, perhaps, no remedy.

Assuming, then, as I think we must from the pleadings, that the money was unlawfully raised, and that it was unlawfully received and held by the defendants, the question arises, and is the main question to be decided in this case, whether the people can maintain this action?

It is contended by the defendants' counsel, that the power of the Attorney-General in England, as the representative of the Crown, to correct abuses or misapplication of trust funds, by an information in equity, was confined to trusts for charitable uses, and that funds of municipal corporations, which are not held for charitable purposes, are not considered as trust funds, but are regarded as the property of the corporations, the same as estates of private individuals belong to them personally, and in such case, the only remedy, prior to the English Act of 1835, for any misapplication or embezzlement, was by an action or proceeding in the name of the corporation.

Assuming that the money in controversy was the property of the corporation of the city and county of New York, which, as already stated, is at least exceedingly questionable, it is a matter of serious inquiry how far the English authorities sustain the doctrine contended for.

In The Attorney-General *vs.* Brown (1 Swanston, Ch. R., 265), which was decided in 1818, an information in equity was filed by the Attorney-General against Commissioners appointed by an Act of Parliament being authorized to levy a rate, not exceeding a certain amount, on the occupiers of all houses, &c., in Brighton, for paving, lighting and watching the town, and another rate on coal landed upon the beach, or otherwise brought into the town, for repairing or building works to protect the coast of Brighton against the encroachments of the sea, with power of distress for non-payment, &c.

It was alleged that the Commissioners had improperly applied a large portion of the rate collected, and had distrained the goods of the relator for non-payment of the duty, and the information asked for an account and an injunction against an undue levy, and a direction that they *replace any sums which they had applied to purposes* not warranted by the Act. A general demurrer, for want of equity, and a defect of parties, was overruled.

The Lord Chancellor Eldon, at the close of the argument remarked : "It is said that this is not a charitable use, and I am not disposed at present to consider it such ;" and in an able and elaborate opinion, after a full discussion of the case, he said, among other things : "I have heard nothing which prevents my concurring in the opinion that a parliamentary grant, destined to such purposes, *is a gift to charitable* uses. If that doctrine is contradicted, it must be done by higher authority than mine."

Although it is claimed that this case was decided on the ground alone that there was a charitable use, that such was not the fact appears quite distinctly from the case of The Attorney-General *vs.* The Mayor, &c.,

of Dublin, (1 Bligh, N. S. R., 312,) which is hereinafter particularly referred to.

The next case, in the order of time, bearing upon the question, is The Attorney-General vs. Heelis, (2 Simons & Stewart, 67). This case was decided in 1824, by the then Vice-Chancellor, Sir John Leach, who had been counsel in the case of The Attorney-General vs. Brown. It was an information and bill in which ten persons were the relators and plaintiffs, on behalf of themselves and all the other tenants and occupiers of houses and other premises situate in Great Bolton, in the county of Lancaster, subject to the rates of assessment, and entitled to the benefit of certain acts of Parliament, under which a common was enclosed and vested in Commissioners upon trust, to apply the rents for the improvement of the town, with power to them to levy a rate on the inhabitants in case the rents were insufficient. An account was asked of the rents, alleging misapplication, and that a rate levied was unnecessary. A general demurrer was interposed, for want of equity, which was overruled, on the ground, among others, that funds supplied from the gift of the Crown, or of the Legislature, or of private persons, *for any legal public or general* purpose, are charitable funds, to be administered by Courts of Equity. The case of the Attorney-General vs. Brown is referred to in the opinion of the Vice-Chancellor, Sir John Leach, who had been counsel against the information in that case, and the views expressed appear to have been based somewhat upon an erroneous construction given by him to the authority in the Attorney-General vs. Brown, which case, as will be seen, sustains a different doctrine.

In The Attorney-General vs. The Mayor, &c., of Dublin, (1 Bligh, N. S. Rep., 312) decided in 1827, an information and bill was filed in behalf of the inhabitants of Dublin paying water rates against the corporation, stating various acts of mismanagement and misappropriation of funds arising from the rates, submitting that the corporation were trustees under the Act for the rates thereby given, for uses which were charitable in their nature, and charging that the conduct of the corporation amounted to a breach of trust, and praying, among other things, for a declaration and execution of the trust, and that accounts might be taken of the rates received by the corporation and the application thereof, that the wrongdoers be decreed *to replace the moneys* they had wrongfully taken or misapplied, &c. It was submitted in the answer that the purposes specified in the Act were *not charitable uses*, and held, (reversing the judgment of the Court below), that the Court had jurisdiction to entertain the information and bill.

The decision of this case is not put upon the ground that it came within the statute in regard to charitable uses. Lord Redesdale, who wrote the principal opinion, at p. 341 says : "It is expedient in such cases that there should be a remedy, and highly important that persons in the receipt of public money should know that they are liable to account, in a Court of Equity, as well upon the misapplication of as for withholding the funds. Suppose even the case of a public accountant, clearly within the Act, who, having embezzled or misemployed the public moneys, had rendered accounts which were imperfect or fabricated ; could not the Attorney-General. upon discovery of the fact or the fraud, proceed by information *to recover the moneys* so fraudulently withheld or misappropriated ?"

Again he says : "A similar remedy is applicable, as I conceive, to any person having the trust and management of public money ; any public accountant of any description."

At page 347 he further remarks, "We are referred to the statute of Elizabeth with respect to charitable uses, as creating a new law upon the subject of charitable uses. The statute created only a new jurisdiction—it created no new law," &c. * * * "In the process of time, indeed, it was found that the commission of charitable uses was not the best remedy, and that it was better to resort again to the proceedings by way of information in the name of the Attorney-General. The right which the Attorney-General has to file an information is a right of prerogative. The King, as *parens patriæ*, has a right by his proper officer, to call upon the several courts of justice according to their several jurisdictions, to see that right is done to his subjects who are incompetent to take care of themselves, as in case of charities and other cases."

The Lord Chancellor (Eldon) in the course of the argument, at page 334, observed that "The case of the Attorney-General *vs.* Brown, whether ill or well-decided, was not decided solely upon the ground that it was a charitable use. Upon reflection I thought so, but the *judgment rested upon other grounds.*" Again he remarks, "In the *Attorney-General* vs. *Brown*, the question was much argued whether the fund was to be applied to a charitable use. After the argument it appeared to me that it was a charitable use. But *that* was not the *ground of the judgment* in that case, whether it was well or ill founded; because I was of opinion that the Court of Chancery had jurisdiction in that case, *whether it was or was not a charitable use.*" He also remarks, at page 335, that the case of the Attorney-General *vs.* Heelis weakens the authority of the Attorney-General *vs.* Brown, because much of the doctrine in the former case is not reconcilable with the principle of the decision in the Attorney-General *vs.* Brown. That in neither of those cases did the Court look sufficiently into the old law upon the subject; and that the research which has been made, confirms the decision in the Attorney-General *vs.* Brown. At page 357, he further states that, in the Attorney-General *vs.* Brown, he " was of the opinion that it was not *necessary* that it should be a *charitable use*, to give the Court of Chancery jurisdiction upon the subject."

The case of the Attorney-General *vs.* The Mayor, &c.,

of Dublin, is a strong and decided authority for the
doctrine that jurisdiction.exists, in all cases of public
trust of the character indicated, in favor of the Crown.

I think that the cases already referred to, as explained in 1 Bligh, must be regarded, up to that time,
as holding that a charitable use is not essential to
maintain the action to reach moneys misappropriated
under the circumstances stated.

In 1835, the case of the Attorney-General *vs.* The
Mayor, &c., of Dublin, was followed and sustained by
the Attorney-General *vs.* The Mayor, &c., of Liverpool
(1 *Milne & Craig*, 171), where it was held that the
Court had authority, under its general jurisdiction, to
interfere for the protection of property vested in the
corporation of a borough, upon the ground of a breach
of trust committed or threatened.

The case from 1 Bligh is cited, and at page 201 the
Master of the Rolls remarks: "Nobody ever questioned the right of a Court of Equity to interpose in
order to see that the public duties were discharged,
and that the trusts upon which the corporation held the
property were duly performed."

The injunction issued was dissolved, because the
construction of the statute was doubtful, and the injunction would deprive parties of the opportunity to
exercise a right.

The information filed in the last case cited was
amended, and the same case is reported in 1 Keene,
513, under the title of The Attorney-General *vs.* Aspinwall, where the demurrer was again allowed by the
Master of the Rolls.

Upon an appeal to the High Court of Chancery, the
decree of the Master of the Rolls was reversed (2 M. &
Craig, 613).

It should be stated that the information in this case
was filed for the purpose of setting aside a mortgage
and an appropriation of moneys raised by the corporation of Liverpool to endow certain clergymen offici-

ating in that city, made by the old corporation before the election of officers under the new organization, and it was held that, where property is devoted to trusts which are to arise at a future day, and to be exercised by trustees not yet *in esse*, an intermediate act done by the holders of such property, inconsistent with the security of the property, or the performance of the trusts when they shall arise, will be set aside; and if the *trusts are of a public nature, the Court will entertain this jurisdiction upon an information* of the Attorney-General, notwithstanding that the Trustees, after they come into *esse* themselves, decline to interfere. The Lord Chancellor said, p. 623: "I cannot doubt that a clear trust was created by this act for *public*, and therefore, *in the legal sense of the term, charitable purposes*, of all the property belonging to the corporation at the time of the passage of the Act."

The doctrine laid down in the case last cited is in accordance with the decisions in the previous cases, to which reference has been made, as explained in 1 Bligh. It may be remarked that the last case was subsequent to the English Reform Act of 1835 (5 and 6, W. 4, ch. 76), by which corporate funds were declared to be trust estates and funds of a public character, and the corporations' or local officers becoming trustees for the benefit of the public, who become beneficiaries under the provisions of the Act, and involved the construction of some portions of that Act. This fact does not, however, alter the law, as settled by previous cases, as to the right to maintain the action, even if there is not a trust in the nature of a charitable use, and does not impair the full and direct approval of the Lord Chancellor Eldon of the doctrine which had previously been enunciated. Since the passage of the Act of 1835 the right of the Attorney-General to bring actions of a similar character has been repeatedly adjudicated in the English Courts. (See Attorney-General *ex rel.* the Mayor, &c., *vs.* Wilson *et al.*, 1 Craig & Philips, 1; The

Attorney-General *vs.* The Corporation of Poole, 2 Keene, 190; same case, 4 Milne & Craig, 17; also, 8 Clarke & Finelly, 409; Attorney-General *vs.* Eastlake, 11 Hare, 205; the same *vs.* Barrett, 3 Irish Rep., N. S. Chan. R. Eq., 392; the same *vs.* Compton, 1 Younge & Collyer, 417.) I do not consider it important to review these cases at length, and will only refer to one of them, which directly bears upon the questions discussed.

The Attorney-General *vs.* Eastlake (*supra*), was an information filed at the relation of two of the rate-payers of Plymouth against a majority of certain commissioners, appointed under a local Act, who were authorized to levy rates for paving, lighting, &c., the streets of a town, and it was held that as the object was beneficial, not only to the inhabitants subjected to the rates, but also to other persons having occasion to visit the town, the purpose was *public* and *charitable* within the meaning of the statute of charitable uses, and the question depends, not on the source from which the funds were derived, but the *purposes* for which they were applied. In this case the earlier authorities are examined and discussed at length by the learned Vice-Chancellor, who considered that the case of Heelis was overruled, and that of Brown sustained by 1 Bligh. He argues, at page 216, that "all the cases agree that not only the particular *public or general purposes* expressed in the Statute of Elizabeth are charitable, but that all other *legal, public* or general *purposes* are within the equity of the statute.

After stating a case where an Act of Parliament is passed for a private purpose, and for the benefit of individuals who are dealing with their own property, he remarks, at page 222, &c., "but when you come to the purpose of paving and lighting a town, which is for the benefit of all the inhabitants, &c.," **** "one does not need to look at this recital, by which we are told that, amongst other things, there will be benefited *The Royal Naval Hospital, The Royal Barracks* and other public establishments. It is sufficient to say it is a *large and general purpose* for this town, although not beyond the limits of the town, and for that purpose certain moneys are to be levied. I cannot see *that the source* from which these moneys are here derived, namely, from *taxation, can make any difference as to the charitable or public nature*, and which would be attributable to the funds if they proceeded from a more limited sphere of bounty ; and if there be no distinction on that ground, the Attorney-General is the proper person to represent those who are *interested in that general and public or charitable purpose.*'' This case, then, virtually and really holds that all *public* uses are in legal effect *charitable* uses, and that funds raised for the general purpose of the public are within the rule. If rates raised for the paving of a town are within the rule, moneys realized under an Act of the Legislature, to pay debts incurred in the government of a great city, and in making public improvements for the benefit of its inhabitants and others who may have business there, are clearly embraced in the principle decided. The analogy is striking between the two cases, and I am unable to discover any real ground of distinction.

The case of The Attorney-General *vs.* The Corporation of Carmarthan (Cooper's Chan. Cases, 30), cited by defendants' counsel, is not in opposition to these views. In that case a demurrer was interposed for multifariousness, which was allowed, and the case was decided in 1805, long prior to the decisions before cited, which uphold the doctrine that an action may be maintained by the Attorney-General, even if there is not a charitable use. A careful review of the English cases establishes, beyond controversy, that whenever an individual or a corporation have been authorized by a statute to administer *public funds* for *public purposes*, such person or body is liable to an action by the Attorney-General for any misapplication or misconduct in the performance of the trust. I am not aware of any reason why the same principle should not control in this case.

The defendants' counsel rely upon the case of The People vs. Miner (2 Lansing, 396) as an authority in their behalf, which, it is claimed, being a General Term decision of this Court, is decisive of the question. The action in that case was brought in the name of the People against the defendants, as railroad commissioners, to restrain them from issuing certain bonds, under an Act of the Legislature of this State, for railroad purposes, and it was held that neither the Code confers upon the Attorney-General the power to prosecute in the name of the People, nor has he such power at common law. The learned Judge who wrote the opinion maintains the position that the only cases in which, at common law, the Attorney-General was authorized to interfere to restrain corporate action, or was a necessary party for that purpose, were those in which the act complained of would produce a public nuisance or tend to a breach of trust for charitable uses.

In this I think that he is entirely mistaken, so far at least as relates to municipal corporations, and he does not sufficiently discriminate between public and private corporations, the difference between which should be borne in mind in the examination of questions of this character.

It is also apparent that he has entirely overlooked the case of the Attorney-General vs. The Mayor of Dublin (1 Bligh, W. P., Rep., 312), to which he refers at page 407, and says: "I have thus referred to all the cases cited in the opinion of Duer, J., except that in 2 Bligh N. R., 312, which I have not been able to find."

The case is wrongly cited in 2 Duer, 668, as well as in 2 Lansing, and hence was not at all considered by the learned Judge. As this case, thus omitted, gives a construction to the prior decisions, and, as already shown, settles the law up to that period, its omission destroys the force of the People *vs.* Miner as a binding authority, even if it were applicable here. The fact that no effect is given to The Attorney-General *vs.* The Mayor of Dublin, and the latter case not having been examined, discussed or considered, the case last cited is not decisive of the question now before us.

It may also be remarked that the opinion begins with a decision that the merits of the action were against the plaintiff, thus rendering it unnecessary to decide the question, which was fully discussed, and therefore it is *obiter*.

This case also holds substantially that a taxpayer is the proper party to bring such an action, which, if not erroneous, is at least doubtful, as the General Term in the Fourth Department have recently held the other way. (See Mans. opinion. Ayers *vs.* Lawrence.)

With all respect which I entertain for the distinguished jurist who gave the opinion referred to, and with all the consideration which should generally be given to a General Term decision, it would not be in accordance with well-established rules to hold that this case, under the circumstances, was controlling and decisive.

In the case of The Attorney-General *vs.* The Utica Insurance Company, (2 John Ch. R., 371,) also cited by defendants, the right of the Attorney-General to maintain an action against a private corporation was considered, but that authority does not, I think, decide the question here involved. It merely related to the jurisdiction of the Court over offenses against a public statute, in regard to the business of banking, which arose on a motion made by the Attorney-General upon an information filed by him. The remarks at page 384 were not necessary to the decision of the case, and the authorities cited mainly looked the other way. But conceding that the opinion expressed is entitled to consideration, it is worthy of observation that the principle claimed to be upheld has been overruled in the English Courts by numerous subsequent cases. This case was decided in 1817, while those which we have already cited, as decisions of the law, were all determined at a far later period.

The defendents also rely upon the language of Davis, J., in the People *vs*. Booth (32 N. Y., 398). This is not an analogous case, and the remarks there made were not called for in deciding the case, and therefore must be considered as an *obiter dictum*.

It has been held that the Attorney-General may prosecute on behalf of the State, or the State itself, where a preventive remedy is called for by the circumstances. (Davis *vs*. The Mayor of N. Y., 14 N. Y., 526 ; The Same *vs*. The Same, 2 Duer, 663. See also 11 Hare, 223.)

In 2 Duer, 666, 667, 668, (*supra*), the right of the Attorney-General, in the name of the people, to maintain an action for a public wrong is fully and ably vindicated, and although the authority of the last case is questioned in the People *vs*. Miner, I am inclined to think that the views expressed by Duer, J., can be upheld, as we have already seen, both upon principle and authority.

In the People *vs*. The Mayor, &c., (32 Barb., 102), it was held by Hogeboom, J., at Special Term, that where there was a clear violation of law, or a clear misuser or abuse of corporate powers, the people, as representing the general public, the body of citizens who are aggrieved, are the proper parties to enforce the remedy.

In the People *vs*. Lowber (7 Abb., 158), Ingraham, J., intimates an opinion, that in such a case as was then before him the Attorney-General might maintain the action.

In the People *vs*. The Mayor (9 Abb., 253), the same views are expressed by the same learned Judge. In the People *vs*. The Mayor (10 Abb., 144) T. R. Strong, J., holds the same opinion.

Although the views of these distinguished Judges are not entirely decisive, yet they are entitled to great consideration.

There are also several cases which have come to my knowledge, which are not reported, which are directly adverse to the People *vs.* Miner, and which involved the precise question which there arose; that is, whether the people could maintain an action restraining railroad commissioners from issuing bonds.

In the People *ex rel.*, Leonard Proctor *vs.* Swarthout, *et al.*, which, I understand, was a similar action, Justice Mason, as Referee, held that the action could be maintained, and in his opinion he says: "This action is properly brought by the Attorney-General in the name of the People, on the relation of Proctor. The right to prosecute and maintain this action is given by statute," &c. "The Attorney-General has the right to maintain this suit independently of the statute at common law;" and cites Story's Eq. Pl., Secs. 8 and 49; Mitford's Eq. Pl., 21, 24, 32; Bart., 102; Barbour on Parties, 367; Edwards on Parties in Eq., 60 and 61; Calvert on Parties, 301–308.

In the People *ex rel.*, Thompson *et al.*, *vs.* Benedict *et al.*, railroad commissioners, and others, which was an action to declare void certain bonds alleged to have been unlawfully executed by said railroad commissioners, a demurrer was interposed by the complaint, and sustained at Special Term. Upon an appeal at General Term in the Third Judicial District, before Justices Hogeboom, Peckham, and Ingalls, in March, 1870, Hogeboom, J., delivering the opinion, it was decided that the action was properly brought in the name of the People, and the demurrer overruled. The learned Judge said: "I think, under our statutes authorizing suits to be commenced by the Attorney-General to restrain *corporations* from exercising unlawful powers and individuals from exercising *corporate* rights and privileges not granted to them by any law of the

State, and under the well-established powers of a Court of Equity, this suit is well brought in the name of the people.

This case involved the same question as the People *vs.* Miner, and is similar in its leading features The ac tion could not be maintained without a decision of this very point in favor of the plaintiff, and as it is not apparent that any consideration bearing upon the question was overlooked, I am at a loss to see how it can be disregarded as a binding authority. It is, at least, entitled to as much weight as the People *vs.* Miner.

After a careful examination of the cases bearing upon the question considered, my conclusion is, that the action is properly brought by the Attorney-General in the name of the people, and can be maintained in its present form.

Where a public right is infringed upon, the State, by the Attorney-General, may bring an action for the benefit of the people at large, or of a portion of the public. Such a rule cannot be confined merely to public nuisances. Many wrongs may exist without a remedy, except through the intervention of the State, and it seems to me that there is nothing inconsistent with the principles upon which our government is founded and administered, to allow the chosen officer of the people, in their own name, to prosecute an action of this character, having in view the protection of the interests of the public against those acting as trustees on the behalf of a municipal corporation. There is no provision of the Revised Statutes, or the Code, inconsistent with such course of procedure, and I apprehend no danger can arise from the abuse of such a power, as it is always the subject of legislative restriction and regulation. This is the extent to which it is necessary to go to sustain the plaintiff's action.

Nor is there, in my opinion, any substantial ground for claiming that the action cannot be maintained in equity because a money judgment is demanded.

The Code has abolished the distinction between law and equity, and the equitable character of the claim is not less apparent because money was unlawfully raised and misappropriated.

That the recovery of money may be a part of the relief demanded in an equitable action, is also abundantly established by authority. This was a part of the relief demanded in the Attorney-General vs. The Mayor of Dublin ; and Lord Redesdale, in his opinion, as we have already seen, puts the question whether the Attorney-General could not proceed by information "*to recover the moneys* so fraudulently withheld or misappropriated." See, also, Attorney-General vs. Compton, 1 Younge & Collyer's R., pp. 417, 426, 427.

If an accounting can be demanded in such a case, it seems quite clear that where no accounting is required, because the amount misappropriated is fixed and determined, that a recovery of the money in the hands of the parties may be demanded. If money could not be demanded in an action in equity, in cases of public trust, the equitable remedy would fail in many cases.

If the views expressed are correct, then it is not necessary to consider the question whether the Board of Supervisors or the County, even if there was a right in either of these bodies to sue, has authority to bring an action on behalf of the County.

In The Attorney-General vs. Wilson, (1 Craig & Philips, 1,) before cited, where the wrong-doers were officers of the borough of Leeds, the Lord Chancellor expressed an opinion (at page 23) that although the Attorney-General might assert the right of the public in an information, "if, before the Act passed, a corporation might, in a proper case, institute a suit for the purpose of setting aside transactions fraudulent against it, though carried into effect in the name of the corporation, that right cannot be affected by the Attorney-General having a power to complain of the transaction." According to this intimation there may, per-

haps, be two rights of action which are not inconsistent.

It is not, however, necessary to determine this point,
and it is of no consequence, whether the county has the
power to sue, if that right exists in the People.

It is quite enough that the action can be maintained,
in its present form, in the name of the People, to uphold the complaint.

Nor is it, in my opinion, necessary that the county
should be made a party in order to maintain this action, were they entitled to the money. In most of the
cases cited, which related to the rights of municipal
corporations, these municipalities were not made parties. Such was the fact in reference to Dublin, Brighton, Liverpool and Leeds.

The averment of collusion in the complaint was not
essential, and this, as well as such portions of the complaint as set forth facts not material to sustain the cause
of action, upon the grounds already discussed, are redundant, irrelevant and immaterial. They furnish no
ground for demurrer, and might have been stricken
out, if a motion had been made at the proper time, or
may now be disregarded as surplusage.

The question raised, as to the disposition to be made
of the money which may be realized if a recovery be
had, is of no importance, if, as the authorities hold,
the action can be maintained. It may, however, be assumed, I think, that the Legislature of the State, in its
wisdom, will make such provision for its appropriation
as will be just and proper, and the circumstances of
the case demand.

Some other questions are raised by the defendants'
counsel, but these are not of sufficient importance to
demand discussion.

The order appealed from must be affirmed with costs,
with leave to amend in twenty days after service of
order, upon payment of costs.

The decision of the case of The People *os.* Connolly

depends mainly upon the questions already discussed, and as no additional points are presented, which authorize a reversal of the order in the latter case, it must, for the reasons stated, be affirmed, and the same order made in all respects.

POTTER, *J.*, wrote for affirmance, and
PARKER, *J.*, for reversal.

COURT OF APPEALS.

THE PEOPLE OF THE STATE OF NEW YORK,
 	
    Respondent,
 	
  agst.
 	
THOMAS C. FIELDS,
    Appellant.
	Statement for FIELDS,
	the Appellant.

Appeal from a judgment of the General Term of the Third Department, affirming a judgment in favor of plaintiff entered upon a verdict directed by Hon. Peter S. Danforth, at the Albany Circuit in May, 1873 (fols. 78, 137), under exception by defendant. The verdict was for $554,062.73. The jury also found specially under the direction of the Court " that no sum beyond $50,000 had been found due under the Act of 1869, before the passage of the Act of 1870." (Fol. 138.)

Judgment was entered and filed July 1, 1873, for $554,062.73 damages and $9,589.07 costs. (Fol. 83.)

The action was brought to recover the moneys for which judgment was recovered, upon the allegation that they were unlawfully and fraudulently paid by the Comptroller of the City of New York to the defendant, as the assignee of several parties who claimed pay as members of certain engine companies of that city, under an Act of the Legislature passed May 12, 1869 (fol. 22), and a supplementary Act passed April 26, 1870. (Fol. 27.)

Various allegations of fraud were made in the complaint, all of which were denied in the answer, and of which no proof was given on the trial.

The complaint charged collusion between the several officers of the city and county and the defendant, to shield him from prosecution for the recovery of these moneys (fol. 34). This was denied by the answer (fol.

61), and was unsustained by any proof upon the trial.

The complaint further charges that defendant was a member of the Legislature of 1870, and voted for the Act of that year, and organized measures for procuring its passage (fol. 31). The answer admits the alleged membership and vote, but avers that the provision in question was a section of the city tax levy, and that his vote was for the General Act, without knowledge that it contained the section in question (fol. 57). It denies the allegation that defendant arranged or organized measures to procure the passage of the Act (fol. 60). No proof was given upon the subject.

The sections of the Acts of 1869 and 1870 are as follows : "The Comptroller of the City of New York is hereby authorized and directed to audit and adjust and pay the claims, not to exceed the sum of $50,000, of members of Engine Companies Numbers 36, 37, 38, 39 and 40, and Hook and Ladder Companies Numbers 13, 14 and 15, which were organized under the direction of the Commissioners of the Metropolitan Fire Department, between the 10th and 31st days of October, 1865, and described in the Report of said Commissioners for the years 1865 and 1866, as 'suburban companies.' The said Comptroller is hereby authorized and directed to raise the money necessary to pay the sum or sums which *may be found due* said members of said Fire Department on said claims, as aforesaid, on the stocks of the City of New York, issued in the usual form, said stock to be called the 'Fire Department Stock,' payable thirty years after its date, and to bear interest not to exceed seven per cent. per annum." The section then directs an annual tax to pay interest and create a sinking fund. (2 Laws 1869, p. 2,131.)

"The Comptroller of the City of New York is hereby authorized and directed to pay the claims *which have been found to be due* to the members of Engine Companies Numbers 36, 37, 38, 39 and 40, and Hook and

Ladder Companies Numbers 13, 14, and 15, under the provisions of Section Seven, Chapter 876, Laws 1869, and to raise the *additional amount required for such purpose*, by the issue of stocks of the City of New York in like manner as provided by said Section Seven, of Chapter 876, Laws 1869, and the interest and principal thereof to be raised also in the manner therein provided." (1 Laws 1870, p. 892.)

It appears by the complaint (fol. 9) and answer (fol. 43) that the Metropolitan Fire Department and the Engine and Hook and Ladder Companies mentioned in the quoted sections of the Acts of 1869 and 1870 were organized under the Act of 1865—the latter in October of that year—who continued in service until January 1st, 1868.

The claim of these firemen was that they were entitled to the same rate of compensation as was paid to the firemen of the city generally. It was so allowed and paid (fols. 101, 127). (See also the Schedules.) The rate of compensation was ascertained "from the Report of the Fire Commissioners and the law which fixed the rate of compensation." (Fol. 120.)

The averments in the complaint relative to the Report of the Commissioners of the Fire Department (fol. 10, &c.), and to the communication of such department to the Legislature of 1868 (fols. 15 to 22), are denied by the answer, except as to the amount involved in the claim of these companies which is admitted (fols. 44 to 47), and are entirely unproved.

The allegations, that there was nothing due to these claimants (fols. 14, 28), are denied (fol. 53). Nothing properly appears upon the case, beyond the laws above recited, enabling the Court to determine, as an original question, upon the validity of the claims thus made and adjusted, unless it be the proof that the claimants were paid at the rate allowed other firemen, that being ascertained from the Report of the Commissioners, and the law by which it was established (fol. 120). In this respect the plaintiff's case seems to rest altogether upon the theory that the payment of the claims was not authorized by the Acts of 1869 and 1870.

The City was made a defendant and answered. The answer was subsequently withdrawn (fol. 67). No judgment was entered against it. (Fol. 82.)

At the close of the evidence defendant moved for a non-suit, which was denied and exception taken (fol 134). Defendant asked the Court to rule that he was not liable beyond the money he received for his compensation. This was refused under exception (fol. 136). The Court was requested to submit to the jury the question as to the amount found in the Comptroller's office to be due claimants under the Act of 1869. This was also refused, and defendent excepted (fol. 136). The Court had previously rejected evidence to show that defendant acted as an attorney in the collection of these moneys, and paid the surplus beyond his agreed fee to his clients. (Fol. 132.)

POINTS.

I.—No right of action against the defendant, of any character, in favor of any party, was shown on the trial.

First : The case, as presented by the evidence, is a simple action, brought by a debtor against the attorney of his creditor, to recover back money paid him as such attorney, upon the ground that the claim upon which it was paid was unfounded ; and this, after the attorney had accounted with his client.

The professional relation of defendant and his settlement with his clients must be assumed, under the offer to prove those facts (fol. 132), for the purpose of this proposition.

The unproven allegations of collusion and fraud, of which the complaint is largely composed, will not be suffered to embarrass the case. They answered their temporary purpose, and are sufficiently characterized by the circumstance, that although prominent and influential upon popular and judicial judgment, not the slightest effort was made on the trial to sustain them. An effort was made to prove that defendant officiously pressed the claims in the Comptroller's Office, but it signally failed (fol. 125). He appears to have acted legitimately as an attorney, manifesting certainly no more ardor than properly belonged to one uniting the incompatible but lawful relations of attorney and assignee.

The denied charge, that defendant falsely and corruptly fabricated these claims (fols. 29, 54), is not only without evidence, but the testimony on the part of plaintiff repels it. The proofs presented to the Comptroller (fol. 183, &c.), show that the claimants were paid only for actual service rendered at the compensation fixed by the Metropolitan Fire Commissioners. The oral testimony affirms the same fact (fols. 101, 120). Each claimant verified his term of service, and testified to non-payment of his claim.

In the absence of all other proof, a legal and just demand, to the full amount paid, was established. The Court will take judicial notice of the official character of defendant, and it was proven that he appeared before the Comptroller "as counsel and advocate of the claims." (Fol. 124.)

Irrespective, therefore, of any aid derivable from the Statute of 1870, it appears only that defendant, as attorney, presented to the proper city officer claims on behalf of clients, received payment, and delivered proceeds to his principals. The propriety of the first payment of $49,277.34 (fol. 93), under the Act of 1869, is not disputed. The Comptroller had ample power by virtue of his office to make the additional payment

of 1870, without the authority of the Special Act of that
year. (1 Laws of 1870, p. 374.)

Second: The proposition is therefore maintained,
that defendant has been adjudged to repay money
collected by him as attorney for another, after it
passed to his principal, upon the unsupported allegation that the claim and payment were unfounded and
fraudulent. If this be so, it is manifest that the recovery is upheld by no principal of law or justice.

Third: Assuming that defendant, as attorney, presented the claim and obtained payment under the law
of 1870, without legal right, and that the Comptroller
paid under a misapprehension of the Act, and without
authority, defendant was not then liable.

(1st.) There is not the slightest proof or justifiable
suspicion that defendant doubted the integrity of the
claim. He believed it collectable without legislative
aid (fol. 58). There is not even evidence disputing
its validity. Granting, however, its invalidity, and
that defendant was conscious of its injustice, is the
doctrine to be affirmed that an attorney is civilly liable
for money he collects and pays to his client upon a dis-
honest demand?
The question is not changed by the circumstance
that the payment was obtained from a municipal
officer. Application to him for payment was regular.
He was the financial officer of the city. There is no
charge in the complaint of collusion with him prior to
the payment. The judgment must be sustained, if at
all, upon the extreme theory that an attorney is liable
to an action for money collected by him for another
upon an inequitable demand.

(2d.) Concede, further, that defendant knew the claim
to be fraudulent, and as attorney, nevertheless under-

took its collection and enforced it, without resort to collusion or device, by simple diligence and energy, however unprofessional and reprehensible such conduct may be, there is no law rendering him liable to a civil action. Counsel often doubt the uprightness of their cause. Not unfrequently they consider it iniquitous. Whatever may be their various conceptions of duty under such circumstances, no court has adjudged that the rule of action approved and practiced by *Lord Brougham* exposed them to liability for all the money they unrighteously recovered.

(3d.) In the entire absence of all evidence of fraud, without any impeachment of the honesty of the claims collected by defendant, he cannot, at any rate, be made responsible beyond the sum in his hands. If he acted uprightly and conscientiously as attorney for these claimants, in good faith, asserting rights he believed to be legal (and there is no substantial dispute of that assumption), the utmost limit of his obligation, moral or legal, would be to return what he has retained. Neither morals or law justify that exaction. But the most fastidious judgment would not require him to become sponsor for the honor and responsibility of his clients.

Fourth : Granting, again, that the claim was unfounded, plaintiff and all others are estopped from claiming reimbursement. At the least, the demand was colorable. It was apparently supported by law and equity. It was presented by parties who had served the city, and who claimed and received pay at the rate of compensation allowed to others. The application was made to the proper financial officer of the city government. Acts of the Legislature empowered him to adjust and pay the claim. If it shall be concluded that these Acts did not authorize the extent of payment made, that will, probably, be found a debatable, and, at the worst, a dubious question, about which lawyers might reasonably differ.

The case then assumes the aspect of a doubtful claim urged by an attorney for his client, before a city officer authorized to audit and pay its just amount, followed by deliberate and protracted investigation and final adjustment and payment, without complicity or fraud. It is submitted that this constitutes a stated and settled account, conclusive upon all parties. There is no mistake to be rectified. No fact was misunderstood. No miscalculation occurred. If there was any error, it was purely one of law.

Fifth: It may be added, argumentatively, that had it been proved, as alleged, that the companies composed of these claimants, had been awarded by the Commissioners and paid an inconsiderable amount (fol. 13), their demand for further pay can scarcely be stigmatized as fictitious and fraudulent, in face of its ostensible fairness and of the Act of 1869. The latter, at least, adjudges an equity to the limit of $50,000. And no reason has yet appeared why it should not be allowed to the amount paid other firemen, as fixed by law (fols. 101, 120).

Sixth: If the preceding views be incorrect, the action cannot be maintained, for the reason that the moneys claimed were demanded and paid by the authority of the Legislature expressed in the Act of 1870.

(1st.) Plaintiff insists that the Act of 1869 limits the compensation to be made to the sum of $50,000, and that the Act of 1870 is either a nullity, or must be deemed to apply only to the balance of $722.66, remaining at the time of its passage unpaid, as required by the Act of 1869.

(2d.) In the construction of these Statutes, it is to be considered : *First:* That the Legislature were fully

apprised of the amount of the claim (fols. 20, 46.
Second: That if the claimants were entitled at all,
they were so to the full amount, there being no evidence of any discrimination as to pay, between them
and the other firemen.

(3d.) Under these circumstances, the words, "*not to
exceed the sum of* $50,000," will be accepted as a limi-
tation, only upon the sum *then* to be paid by the
Comptroller. The provision appears in the annual
city tax levy, designed only to furnish means to maintain its government for the current year. The justice
of the claims is recognized. The Comptroller is directed to audit and adjust them, and to pay not to exceed $50,000. The restrictive words do not, necessa-
rily, refer to the audit. They may be satisfied by application to the payment then to be made.

(4th.) If it were the intent of the Legislature to extinguish a claim of more than half a million, appropriate words to that end would have been employed.
The payment would have been declared to be in satisfaction. The idea of a compromise would have been
suggested in some form.

The requirement of an *audit and adjustment* is inconsistent with this idea. If a claim of this large
amount was to be satisfied by the payment of an ascertained and declared sum, there was not the slightest
need or propriety of an audit, involving a laborious
and dilatory accounting. It cannot be supposed that
the Legislature contemplated a possible reduction of
the claim below $50,000, through the process of an ad-
justment by the Comptroller. The aggregate of service by the changing members of these companies was
unquestioned and is admitted by the pleadings (fols.
9, 43). The only point made is as to the rate of compensation. These claimants demand pay according
to the allowance made to the regular firemen. They
were entitled to that or nothing, as the proofs stand.

(6th.) All doubt as to the intent of the Legislature and the effect of the Act of 1869 is resolved by that of 1870. It directs the Comptroller to "pay the claims which *have been found to be due* to the members" of the named companies, under the Act of 1869.

(*a.*) The evidence incontestably establishes that the whole amount claimed had then been found due. The affidavits presenting the claim were filed with the Comptroller prior to the Act of 1870, with the exception of two taken on the day it passed (fols. 1188–1206), and five filed subsequently in the same month (fols. 1161, 1181, 1182, 1184, 1198). The great bulk of them had been submitted, from time to time, months before the first payment (fols. 183 to 790). It was exceedingly laborious and tedious to gather them, many being procured from distant Counties and States. The precise time of their presentation is unimportant, if it shall appear that the Comptroller settled the principle and mode of his audit.

Plaintiffs introduced what is called "the summing up or bill" (fols. 92, 142). That was the first paper read, and to it were attached the voluminous schedules which follow (fol. 99), excepting Exhibit 5 (fol. 796), and including the statements from fol. 804 to fol. 1157. It will be observed that the members of each company are tabulated in two forms, the one of which exhibits in columns the total service of each fireman—the whole amount claimed—the amount paid and the balance due. These were prepared, as shown by the cross-examination of *Mr. Storrs*, under the Act of 1869 (fol. 99, &c). Additional claims were afterward submitted by affidavit, and some errors were discovered in the computation. After the Act of 1870 new schedules were prepared, adding the new claims and correcting the mistakes, being merely in review of the first, and substantially the same. (Fols. 103, 117.)

It is plain, therefore, that the audit and adjustment,

under the Act of 1869, included all the claims, except the few added after the Act of 1870, and that they were recognized by the Comptroller to their full amount. He directed the preparation of the schedules (fol. 120). And *Mr. Storrs*, Deputy Comptroller, at the time of the first payment, announced that "the Comptroller could then pay only ten per cent. of the amount *then found due*" (fol. 107), the payment being substantially at that rate. (Fol. 100.)

(*b.*) The Act of 1870 assumes and declares that the claims in question "*have been found to be due*" under the Act of 1869.

Its provisions indisputably show that the Legislature of 1870 did not understand their amount to be limited to the $50,000, directed by the Act of 1869 to be paid, or intend the Act of 1870 to be restricted to the balance remaining unpaid under that of 1869, because, *first*, the Act of 1870 directs the Comptroller " to raise the *additional amount* required " for its purpose by the issue of stock. If no claim beyond $50,000 had been found due, it is plain that no " *additional amount*" was necessary to be raised by the issue of stock, or otherwise ; *second*, if only $50,000 had been found due, there was no need for the supplementary Act of 1870, as that of 1869 gave full direction and authority for the audit and payment of that sum, and provided means for its satisfaction. The result, therefore, of the construction sought to be given by complainant nullifies the Act of 1870, contrary to a cardinal rule of interpretation ; *third*, it is ludicrous to suppose that the Legislature would not only multiply needless commandments to the Comptroller to pay an audited claim, but direct the issue of city bonds running thirty years to enable the payment of $722.66.

(*c.*) The Act of 1870 thus becomes an absolute recognition of the entire claim, and is a positive direction for its satisfaction. At all events, it is an implied affirmation that, under the Act of 1869, more than the sum of $50,000, for which it provided, had been found due, and that amount is demonstrated by the evidence to be that ultimately received by the defendant, less the five claims presented subsequent to the passage of the Act. This must be so, or the Act of 1870 must be annulled by judicial construction. The folly must be imputed to the Legislature of enacting a law without a subject on which it could operate. The fundamental canons of construction, that effect must be given to a statute, if possible, and that an absurd conclusion must be avoided, if it can be, must be disregarded.

If there be any question upon the evidence as to the amount found to be due by the Comptroller, under the Act of 1869, it was error in the Court below to direct a verdict for plaintiff. Defendant requested the submis-mission of that question to the jury. (Fol. 136.)

Seventh : Hence it would seem to be incontestable that the Comptroller of New York paid and defend-ant received the moneys charged to have been fraudu-lently and illegally obtained under the authority and by the unequivocal declaration of the Legislature. This action presents the singular paradox of an ar-raignment for fraud by the Attorney-General, in the name of the people, of a citizen acting by the authority of the people, through their Legislature.

Eighth : It is needless to discuss the pertinency and effect of the circumstance that defendant was a member of the Legislature of 1870. There is no testi-mony raising any imputation of corrupt conduct or neglect of duty in that station. The complaint states no facts justifying any such charge. There is an ob-scure suggestion to that purport (fol. 31), but it is met by the answer (fols. 58, 60), and is unsustained by proof.

Ninth : There is no pretence in the evidence for the suspicion that defendant practiced any fraud or device, or exerted any influence upon the Comptroller or his subordinates. The proceedings in that office appear to have been wholly uninfluenced and rigidly accurate. An unfortunate attempt was made in that . direction. (Fol. 124.)

II.—If any right of action against the defendant appears, it is not vested in the people or State. The plaintiff is not the real party in interest.

First : The plaintiff certainly was not, at the time of the alleged misappropriation, the owner of, or pecuniarily interested in, the fund charged to have been fraudulently obtained. It belonged entirely to the City or County of New York, and for the purpose of the argument it is immaterial which.

The several laws affecting the question of title leave it somewhat confused. The fund was destined to the payment of the members of the Fire Department. That was created by the Act of 1865 (L. 1865, p. 395), which constituted the Cities of New York and Brooklyn, "the Metropolitan Fire District of the State of New York," to be governed by four Commissioners. By it (§ 12) the Comptroller of the City was to borrow, on the credit of the city, the money necessary for its maintenance during the year 1865. By § 16, the Board of Supervisors of the County is directed to raise annually by taxation the sums of money required by the estimates to be furnished by the Commissioners, which were to be deposited with the Treasurer of the State to the credit of the department, and drawn by its treasurer. All property pertaining to the Fire Department of the city was to be turned over to the new organization, the title remaining in the city. (§ 17.)

It was under this Act that the Commissioners, by regulation and estimate, provided for the payment of firemen, although it confers no express authority to that effect.

The right of this Metropolitan Fire Department to the fund in question (§ 22) might be plausibly argued, were it not for the Acts of 1869 and 1870. These award additional compensation to specified companies, against whom (it would seem) the Commissioners had made a discrimination claimed to be unequal. They direct it to be paid by the Comptroller of the city, through the issue of city bonds, which were to be retired by a tax imposed by the Board of Supervisors of the county upon the taxable property of the city and county. They exclude the possibility of right in the Metropolitan Fire Department, or its treasurer, or the Treasurer of the State. The object to which the fund was devoted was the protection of the inhabitants of the City and County of New York. It was contributed by them through taxation upon their property. It was to be dispensed by their officers. It was theirs originally, and continued theirs except for the special use to which it was devoted.

This title was not personal to the individual taxpayer. It was vested, like as any other collected tax, in the county representing its inhabitants. The legal title was in the county, the beneficial interest in the tax-payers. In support of the intervention of the State by this action, it has been said that the tax-payers being the parties really interested, there was an imperative necessity for the interposition of the State ; that changing population and the vicissitudes of society forbid the ascertainment of the real beneficiaries and the equitable distribution of the fund when recovered. The answer is that the county represents all its inhabitants in their county interests. The succession of generations, changes of residence, deaths and births, have no intelligent bearing on the argument.

It is to escape these embarrassments that the corporation is created. It neither dies or absconds. It is the same legal entity through all changes, losing no capacity or power, and representing always the fluctuating population within its borders. It neither acquires or loses any right when a citizen dies, or removes, or a new dweller is acquired. Removal or death may affect the rights of individuals, but does not impair or enlarge the rights of the aggregate population claiming through its legal organ. Otherwise it would be impossible to maintain government. The constant and manifold alternations of society would effectually prevent the ascertainment of legal right, if individuals are to be regarded. In every conceivable case where a municipal corporation should assert a legal right and remedy, this suggestion of changed personal interests would interpose a barrier to relief and invoke the aid of the State.

It has been asked, on the supposition that the Legislature had forbidden the payment of this money, after it was raised, to whom would it belong, and answered by the querist "not to the County or the Supervisors. They had no lawful authority to apply it to any purpose."

This is an extraordinary proposition. By command of the Legislature, the Supervisors raise money by tax for a special object. Before its application, the object is removed, and counsel argue that the fund does not belong to the Municipality but to the State. Certainly it is the property of the county. Its bonds, on which the money was procured, are outstanding, and are to be paid by the county. Can it be plausibly contended that the State may seize the fund and leave the county to tax its citizens for the payment of its bonds? The State cannot thus confiscate property. Obvious justice and strict law demand the appropriation of the fund to the redemption of the bonds. If not, it would still be county property—proceeds of its credit—a licable to its use.

Second: Whether the money 'belongs to the Metropolitan Fire Department or to the City or County, either was competent to sue for its recovery. The power in each case is conferred by express Statute.

The County of New York derives its organization from the same Act forming the other counties of the State. These "civil divisions" were re-affirmed by the Revised Statutes. New York is designated a County in the same section and manner as the others. (1 R. S., p. 83.)

Each County thus created has capacity, as a body corporate (among other things), to purchase and hold lands for the use of its inhabitants—to purchase and hold personal property—*to regulate and dispose of its corporate property—and to sue and be sued in the name of its Board of Supervisors.*

By the Constitution of 1846 the City and County of New York was constituted into four Senate Districts (Article 3, § 3). The County of New York was treated as such, in the apportionment of Members of Assembly. (§ 5).

The Legislature has repeatedly provided for the government of the County of New York, recognizing it a County. By an Act passed in 1870 (p. 481), the Mayor, Recorder and Aldermen of the City were made the Board of Supervisors of the County. The Finance Department of the City was, by this Act, charged with the like powers and duties, "in regard to the fiscal concerns of the Board of Supervisors," as it exerted for the city. And all vouchers for moneys, drawn by the Board, were to be allowed by the Auditor and approved by the Comptroller. By § 2 of another Act of the same year, provision was made for actions and judgments against the County (p. 878). And by § 4 of this latter Act, the capacity of the County to contract and incur liabilities is recognized.

It is manifest that the County of New York is a corporate body, empowered to hold real and personal property, and to regulate and dispose of it; to sue and be sued, and to assert its legal rights in every capacity pertaining to an individual citizen. In these respects it has the same rights and privileges, with the same power of assertion and protection, as belongs to the City of New York.

If it be supposed that the city and county are so blended by territorial identity, community of officers and common interests, as to supersede the latter organization, a new mode of repealing Statutes is discovered. A merger like this would not aid this action. If the city has absorbed the county, by representing the same population and interests, it has adequate ability to sue. The Court of Appeals, however, recognizes the Board of Supervisors of the County of New York as a competent party to an action.

The People v. Supervisors, 34 How., 379.

The People v. Supervisors, 32 N. Y., 432.

Bank of Commonwealth v. Meyer, 43 id., 187.

Newman v. Supervisors, 45 id., 676.

Perfect title and perfect ability to assert it are therefore shown in one or the other. If this be so, it is difficult to imagine any principle entitling the State to prosecute. Upon the argument on Demurrer at General Term, it was supposed to be found in English authorities, maintaining the authority of the Attorney-General of England to enforce the observance and performance of public trusts. The analogy is imperfect, and the principle inapplicable for several reasons:

(1st.) The doctrine was upheld on the ground of necessity, because there was no other party able or willing to enforce a remedy. Hence it was argued in this case that the tax-payers were the parties in interest—that neither they or the County could sue—and it was the duty of the State, through the Attorney-General, to interfere for their protection. Under the allegations of the complaint, admitted by the demurrer, this seemed to be so. Conspiracy, collusion and fraud were charged and undenied. Assuming the complaint true, the local authorities were paralyzed; the tax-payers could not maintain suit, as the law then was, and the alleged plunderers rejoiced in impunity. This was the main ground of the decision of the General Term upon the demurrer.

The case now presents entirely different features. There is no pretence of combination between the defend-ant and city or county officials. There is no proof of fraudulent representation or artifices practiced by defendant. And it would seem to be indisputable that either the city or county might enforce the trust.

(2d.) Granting, in the fullest sense, the power claimed for the Attorney-General of England, it by no means follows that like authority is vested in the State of New York, or its Attorney-General. The former flows from royal prerogative. The latter rests upon statutory conferment. The essential difference in the forms of government of the two countries distinguishes the functions of the two officers. The one represents the king, as *pater patriæ*, possessing " all the rights which the king hath, as Chief of the Kingdom and as trusted with the execution of the laws." (Tomlin's Law Dict., Title Prerogative.) Upon his own volition, in the exer-cise of this broad authority, he may move any pro-ceeding of a public nature. The other is an officer of limited and express powers. He represents no sover-eignty. The Legislature is the only omnipotent agent of the people. The State, as a body politic, is but an aggregation of officers and agents, each with defined duties and limited powers. The Attorney-General has no plenary authority. He can only act as the law authorizes him. There is no original, inherent author-ity in the State or any of its officers. All are but creatures of the people, having power only as it is ex-pressly bestowed. From what source does the Attor-

ney-General of New York derive his right to bring this
action ? The Legislature has not directed it. No
statute confers it. It is made his duty "to prosecute
and defend all actions, in the event of which the people
of this State are interested." But the people have no
interest, in the sense of the statute. Doubtless they
are interested in preserving the purity of public office
and promoting the prosperity of every division of the
State. This is not the interest forming the foundation
of a civil action. Neither [the State or the Attorney-
General is constituted the guardian of public morals,
or possesses inherent power over public trusts.

> The People *v.* Mayor, 27 How. Pr., 84.
> The Same *v.* Booth, 32 N. Y., 397.
> The Same *v.* Clark, 53 Barb., 176.
> The Same *v.* Miner, 2 Lan., 396.

(3d.) Undoubtedly, at Common Law, the Attorney-
General may bring actions to restrain *purprestures*
and *nuisances* upon public property.

> Davis *v.* Mayor, &c., 14 N. Y., 506, 526.
> The People *v.* Vanderbilt, 26 id., 287.

This class of authority gives no countenance to this
action. A *purpresture* is an invasion of the right of
property in the soil, while the same remains in the
king or the people. A *nuisance* is an injury to the
jus publicum or common right of the public.

> The People *v.* Vanderbilt, 26 N. Y., 293.

The definition illustrates the question under discussion. In these cases the Attorney-General may sue,
because either the property of the people or their common right is invaded.

And in the last cited case, *Justice Selden* declares
that "the title to the land being vested in the city,
there could be no *purpresture*, and as the defendant
acted under the authority of the city, &c.," it was
necessary to show a nuisance in fact. Judgment passed

for the people on the ground that they had resumed the title temporarily vested in the city.

The case maintains that while the *title* was in the city, although for public purposes and in trust, the people could not maintain an action for *"an invasion of the right of property."*

It is a direct adjudication upon the principle here involved. The right of action is made to depend upon the title. No one will claim any title or right in the people at large, or the State to the property sought by this action.

The people must have a direct interest, either by ownership or by common right, before their Attorney-General can sue; as in case of *purpresture—a title* invaded—and in case of *nuisance—a common* right disturbed.

In the present case no such title or *jus publicum* exists. This action relates exclusively to personal property. It makes no difference to the State whether it be reclaimed or lost. The City and County of New York must pay their bonds in either event. The pledge of taxation for that purpose must be redeemed.

Von Hoffman v. City of Quincy, 4 Wal., 535.

(4th.) Another distinction, of considerable moment, is apparent. The power of the Attorney-General of England, in all the authorities cited on the other side, is directed to the preservation and proper application of public trust funds. The interest of the true beneficiaries is sought. The prayer is, that the fund be appropriated according to its design. Equity power is invoked.

But this is a strict action at law. And if the people recover, to whose benefit does the recovery enure? Not to the City and County of New York or the unfortunate tax-payers of that misruled region. The State puts money in its purse, to which it has no shadow of right, and there is no law by which it can be gotten out.

Besides, the defendant is not protected by the judgment. The county is not a party. The tax-payers are not, and no judgment is entered against the city. Neither is estopped from suit.

If the people can maintain this action, upon identical principle, they can sue for any fraudulent perversion of a public trust fund. Bank and railroad corporations are governmental agents, exercising a public trust. The Attorney-General may investigate their administration, and sue to recover misapplied moneys, not for the use of stockholders, but for the enrichment of the State. The importance of the Attorney-General, as a public functionary, is dangerously enlarged, if this doctrine be sound. He becomes a despot, governed only by his arbitrary discretion, gaining power by absorption, and accountable only to himself.

W. A. BEACH.
Counsel for Appellant.

STATE OF NEW YORK.

IN THE COURT OF APPEALS.

THE PEOPLE OF THE STATE OF NEW YORK, *Plaintiffs and Respondents,* *against* THOMAS C. FIELDS, impleaded with the MAYOR, ALDERMEN and COMMONALTY OF THE CITY OF NEW YORK, *Defendant and Appellant.*	STATEMENT and POINTS *for the Plaintiffs.*

STATEMENT.

This is an appeal by the defendant, Thomas C. Fields, from a judgment on verdict in favor of the plaintiffs for $554,062$\frac{73}{100}$, together with $9,589$\frac{7}{100}$ costs and disbursements, rendered at the Albany Circuit, before Danforth, J., entered July 1, 1873 (fol. 84), and affirmed at a General Term for the Fourth Department, March 10, 1874, before Miller, Bockes and Boardman, JJ., with 79\frac{68}{100}$ costs. (Pages 1, 2 and 3.)

The defendant Fields appealed to this Court March 23, 1874 (page 1). There are duplicate pages, 1 to 4 inclusive.

The defendants, the Mayor, Aldermen and Commonalty of the City of New York, suffered judgment to pass against them by default for want of an answer (fols. 67 to 71). The defendant Fields put in an answer. (Fols. 42 to 65.)

FACTS.

Prior to March 30, 1865 (Laws, p. 395), when a paid fire department was established, there had always been in the City of New York volunteer fire companies, who not only served without compensation, but paid a large part of the expenses attendant upon their operations. The paid system then inaugurated required the paid firemen to devote their whole time to the duties of their employment. The new system was organized under what was familiarly known as the Metropolitan Fire Department. (See 32 N. Y. R., pp. 377 to 398.)

This new department did not think fit to extend their *paid* system over that part of the island, City of New York, lying north of 59th street, until January, 1868 (Complaint, fols. 9, 10 ; answer, fols. 42, 43). But in the interim, that is, from October 1, 1865, until January 1, 1868, they retained in this so-called suburban district eight pre-existing volunteer companies, by virtue of an agreement with them, allowing them a certain stipulated reward (Complaint, fols. 11, 12). This was nothing like full pay, but the reason is apparent. The companies were retained essentially on the basis of the old volunteer system, not being required to devote any more time to the duty than had been usual under that system. This, of course, left the men as before, free to pursue their ordinary business avocations. It is indeed probable that these still continuing volunteers in the fire companies received nothing personally, as the $1,000 paid each company may have operated no further than to relieve the privates from their usual contributions to the company fund.

On this basis the eight suburban companies served until January 1, 1868, when they were disbanded, and the *full pay* and *full time* system was extended over the whole island. During that period, *i. e.*, from October 1, 1865, to January 2, 1868, these suburban companies received in full their whole stipulated compensation. The employers honestly paid the laborers their wages ; the laborers cheerfully received the same, and were fully satisfied. All parties were contented, until Thomas C. Fields, the defendant in this suit, got up, for his own profit, a claim, as he called it, against the public for full pay to these suburban firemen, about 250 in number, for this whole term of volunteer firemanship, as if they had been full members of the paid fire department, devoting their whole time to the service. This claim was presented to the Legislature in 1868, but was opposed by the fire department and rejected (Complaint, fols. 14 to 22; answer, fols. 45 to 51). Fields became assignee of these claims, and was to receive and did receive half the amount for his own use. (Complaint, fols. 31 to 34; answer, fols. 48 to 51, 56, 57, 60.)

Fields' advocacy was continued, and at last it became effective, for the Legislature of 1869 incorported in what is commonly called the city tax-levy of that year a section in these words:

"§ 7. The Comptroller of the City of New York is hereby authorized and directed to audit, and adjust and pay the claims, not to exceed the sum of fifty thousand dollars, of members of engine companies numbers thirty-six, thirty-seven, thirty-eight, thirty-nine and forty, and hook and ladder companies numbers thirteen, fourteen and fifteen, which were organized under the direction of the Commissioners of the Metropolitan Fire Department, between the tenth and thirty-first days of October, eighteen hundred and sixty-five, and described in the report of said Commissioners for the years eighteen hundred and sixty-five and eighteen hundred and sixty-six, as 'suburban companies.' The said Comptroller is hereby authorized and directed to raise the money necessary to pay the sum or sums which may be found due said members of said fire department on said claims as aforesaid, on the stock of the City of New York, issued in the usual form, said stock to be called the 'Fire Department Stock,' payable thirty years after its date, and to bear interest not to exceed seven per cent. per annum. The Board of Supervisors of the County of New York are hereby authorized and directed to order and cause to be raised by tax, upon the estates by law subject to taxation, within the City and County of New York, an amount sufficient in each year to pay the interest on the stock herein authorized, and also an amount sufficient to pay and redeem said stock at its maturity."

On and prior to Nov. 1, 1869, action was had in the Comptroller's office under this section, by which (except a trifling amount paid to another) the defendant Fields received $49,277$\frac{84}{100}$. The precise shape of this action will be hereafter stated. But it may here be noted that of the $50,000 appropriation so made by the Legislature of 1869, there remained unapplied the sum of 722\frac{66}{100}$. This is supposed to have been the slender basis on which the enactment of 1870, hereafter mentioned, was obtained.

Thomas C. Fields, the defendant, was elected to the Assembly of 1870. He was interested to the extent of one-half in whatever might be obtained on this claim. Cotemporaneously with his election, Nov. 3, 1869, his agent or assistant in this business, Mr. Parsons, a Notary Public, began to take supplementary affidavits to enlarge the claim. (See first date at fols. 1185 and all these affidavits, fols 1157 to 1213.) The annual city tax levy, passed April 26, 1870 (page 892), contained another seventh section in the following words:

"§ 7. The Comptroller of the City of New York is hereby authorized and directed to pay the claims which have been found to be due to the members of engine companies numbers thirty-six, thirty-seven, thirty-eight, thirty-nine and forty, and hook and ladder companies numbers thirteen, fourteen and fifteen, under the provisions of section seven, chapter eight hundred and seventy-six, laws eighteen hundred and sixty-nine; and to raise the additional amount required for such purpose by the issue of stock of the City of New York, in like manner as provided by said section seven of chapter eight hundred and seventy-six, laws eighteen hundred and sixty-nine, and the interest and principal thereof to be raised also in the manner therein provided."

Subsequently to the passage of this Act of 1870, fresh action was had in the Comptroller's office, under which the defendant, Thomas C. Fields, as assignee of these claims, received from the Comptroller, June 3, 1870, the further sum of $459,977$\frac{19}{100}$ (fol. 39). These proceedings will hereafter be more particularly stated.

The plaintiffs claimed that the Act of 1870, like that of 1869, limited the allowances to $50,000.

They also claimed, as a matter of fact, that no claims had been "*found due*" prior to the enactment of 1870, to any amount exceeding $50,000. Upon the pleadings, this was the only actual issue; and it was the only matter of fact contested at the trial.

There was no conflicting evidence; and the verdict was for the amount received by Fields, less $50,000, with interest on the balance.

The proceedings of the trial present no question except in reference to the issue, whether the Comptroller had, before the passage of the tax levy of 1870, "*found due*" or audited and allowed, under the Act of 1869, claims exceeding $50,000.

The oral evidence is contained between fol. 89 and fol. 132. The documents showing the action had in the Comptroller's office prior to the Act of 1870, occupy the case from page 47 to 239, and are as follows:

DOCUMENTS OF 1869.

Hook & Ladder Co. No. 13, from p. 48 to 78; summation as to each person on p. 55.

Hook & Ladder Co. No. 14, from p. 78 to 102; summation as to each person on p. 83.

Hook & Ladder Co. No. 15, from p. 102 to 116; summation as to each person on p. 105.

Engine Co. No. 36, from p. 117 to 145; summation as to each person on p. 123.

Engine Co. No. 37, from p. 145 to 166; summation as to each person on p. 151.

Engine Co. No. 38, from p. 166 to 198; summation as to each person on p. 172.

Engine Co. No. 39, from p. 198 to 217; summation as to each person on p. 198.

Engine Co. No. 40, from p. 217 to 238; summation as to each person on p. 217.

Three Engineers on p. 238.

The above summations of each Company are, in each instance, in two columns. One column is in ink and the other in pencil. The pencil sums are, in each instance, one-tenth of the inked sums. None of these columns are added up.

On page 47 is an account dated Oct. 30th, 1869, in favor of Thomas C. Fields as assignee. The pencil or ten per cent. column in each of the summations is here set down; a deduction is made of a sum "paid," and the balance is carried into a column which is footed up $43,339.62.

This is followed by an unsigned certificate of its correctness, and a receipt by the defendant Fields to the Comptroller for the sum last above mentioned, bearing date Nov. 1, 1869. The check on the Chamberlain in favor of Fields for this sum appears on p. 239.

The papers given in evidence at the trial, and inserted in the case, do not exhibit any further action in the Comptroller's office in the year 1869. The testimony of Storrs, the Deputy Comptroller, however, shows that in some way, not distinctly appearing from the documents printed in the case, there was paid $49,277$\frac{34}{100}$. (Fol. 94.)

The complaint (fol. 26) states that claims to this amount were presented under the Act of 1869, and "audited, adjusted and fully paid"; also "that the defendant Fields, by himself and his agent, conducted the whole business of presenting such claims, and received from the said Comptroller, in two separate sums, all the moneys so paid by him, except the sum of $245, which was so paid to one John Hart." The defendants' answer at fol. 51 "admits and states that, by himself and his agents, aided by many of the said claimants, the whole business of presenting such claims was conducted, and that the said sum of $49,277$\frac{34}{100}$, excepting $245 paid John Hart, was received from the Comptroller by the defendant."

DOCUMENTS OF 1870.

As far as papers in the case or any evidence goes, the preceding statement exhibits all that was done in the Comptroller's office in 1869. But it appears that Fields' office assistant (fol. 129), Mr. Parsons, as Notary Public, between Nov. 3, 1869, and April 26, 1870, obtained affidavits from persons who had belonged to these suburban companies, and who probably had straggled away and could not be found when the first set of accounts was made up. These additional affidavits occupy the case from p. 312 to 329.

On the basis of the documents so made up prior to Nov. 1, 1869, and the new additional affidavits, 35 in number, so obtained after that date by Mr. Parsons, one D. P. Smith, an assistant in the Comptroller's office, *subsequently to the Act of* 1870, proceeded to make up other statements of the claims. The detailed accounts then made up are printed in the case from page 241 to page 312. The summing up is on page 240. It is essentially similar to the account of 1869, on page 47, except that it is larger, and deducts from each company's new total not only what was deducted in the account of 1869, but all that was then paid on that account. It is footed up $459,977$\frac{19}{100}$. And here appears the only formal official allowance to be found anywhere. It bears date June 3, 1870, and on that date Thomas C. Fields receipts for this whole sum. (Pages 240, 241.)

There being no evidence that there had been any official audit or finding by the Comptroller before the Act of 1870, for any sum exceeding $50,000, the jury were directed by the Court to find for the plaintiffs the whole amount received by the defendant Fields, less $50,000, and the jury found accordingly. The defendant Fields did not sum up or ask leave to do so, but asked the Judge to submit the question of fact to the jury. He also claimed, 1st, a right to the moneys received; 2d, that the plaintiffs had no title, and 3d, that having acted as attorney for the claimants he was not chargeable. The Court overruled all these points, and the defendant Fields excepted. (Fols. 133 to 139.)

POINTS.

FIRST POINT.—The liability of the defendant Fields to some party is perfectly clear.

I.—The first Act, A. D. 1869, p. 2131, § 7, contained no authority to the Comptroller to "audit or adjust" any claims beyond $50,000.

1. The limitation, in plain terms, applied alike to the auditing and adjusting as well as to the payment.

2. The latter portion of the section confirms this construction, for it expressly directs the Comptroller "to raise *the* money necessary to pay *the* sum or sums which *may be* FOUND *due* said members of said fire department."

3. There is no limitation on the amount to be

raised, except the amount found due. This proves
that no more than $50,000 could have been found due
under the authority to audit. The first branch alone
would require this construction. The second confirms it.

4. The amount treated as due and payable and
actually paid by the Comptroller, in fact and as appeared by the records and accounts of his office, was
$49,277$\frac{34}{100}$ (Complaint fol. 27). This, it will be noted,
was all the money the Comptroller had power to raise,
for he could only raise the sum necessary to *pay* what
he *found due*. It must be presumed that he, in fact,
raised no more; doubtless such is the fact.

5. The duties charged upon the Comptroller by the
Act of 1869, as to raising and paying, may well have
been and possibly were unperformed in April, 1870,
to some extent. Here was aliment for the Act of 1870,
without imputing to it the monstrous construction
acted on by Comptroller Connolly and Fields.

II. The Act of 1870, Laws, p. 892, § 7, under which
$459,977$\frac{70}{100}$ were paid, is expressly limited to "the
claims which *have been* found due * * *under*" the
Act of 1869. Now, as no more than $50,000 could
have been found due under the Act of 1869, the obvious purpose was to enjoin payment of some unpaid
balance "found due" under that appropriation.
There might have been in fact such a balance, *i. e.*,
722\frac{66}{100}$. The only word in the whole of this very
verbose and repetitious Section 7 of 1870, affording
color to the Fields-Connolly construction, is the word
"additional." But that word has full operation, if
applied to the balance of 722\frac{66}{100}$ of the $50,000 appropriation of 1869, which remained as yet not raised
or paid.
In such mere private acts as this *gift* is, the courts

have no guide to the construction, except the letter. They must be taken strictly, and it is a general rule that grants by the sovereign power, of every description, must be taken strictly as against the grantee, and most favorably to the government. (Charles River Bridge *vs.* Warren Bridge, 11 Peters, U. S. Rep., p. 420.)

III. There was no authority under Section 7 of 1870 to audit or allow any claims. It is merely a direction to pay claims already *found* to be due under the authority given in the prior Act. It was shown that there was, in fact, no such *finding* to any extent beyond the sum before paid. The Act could only operate upon claims audited and adjusted before its passage.

IV. The Court is bound to adopt the construction which preserves the limitation of $50,000, otherwise the Comptroller and Fields might have given away more money than the fee simple value of the city, the State or the Union.

SECOND POINT.—The corporate body known as the Mayor, Aldermen and Commonalty of the City of New York was not interested in the matters in question.

I.—The moneys were raised by order of the State through a special Commissioner directed by statute to raise them. The Comptroller, as such Commissioner, had no power to raise one cent beyond the claims audited by him. There could be no surplus or balance to go into the corporate treasury. Even if the pretended claims were valid and bound the City Corporation, they have been fully paid ; so the City Corporation has suffered no prejudice. If the so called claims were sham and the payment a gift, the State made the gift, and consequently the City Corporation had no concern in the matter.

II.—The city stock directed to be issued is expressly provided for by the State. Both the interest and the principal are, through the State's taxing power, charged on the tax-payers of the city and county. They are not charged in any way on the funds of the City Corporation. The Board of Supervisors are directed to levy the amount needed. How can the City Corporation ever suffer?

The most fertile imagination can suppose but a single case. In ordering its Commissioner to issue city stock, perhaps the State *forced* the City Corporation to become the State's surety. Even so, the only interest that the City Corporation could have in the matter would arise from a conjecture that perhaps the State might fail to levy the taxes, and so leave its surety, the City Corporation, liable to the bondholders. An action *quia timet* by the City Corporation, as surety, against its principal, the State, and Fields, would be an odd proceeding, especially as the State is not suable.

III.—In a word, the State's authority to charge the tax-payers of future times has been corruptly, fraudulently and illegally employed, to the injury of no one except those very future tax-payers, and the State is their only guardian in the premises. The City Corporation is nowise concerned, save as surety for the payment. The State has itself undertaken to pay. The Supervisors were never to have anything to do with the matter, except the ministerial duty of levying the taxes. When levied, the Supervisors could have nothing to do with the collection of them, the safe keeping of them, or the disbursement of them. If it could be imagined that between their collection and payment over to the stockholders the money might temporarily remain in some local treasury, the future temporary duty would never constitute a grievance to the custodian, which could make such custodian the proper plaintiff against Fields.

IV.—It should be remembered that, if these volunteer firemen had had any claims, they would have been against the State or against the Fire Department Corporation, and in no sense against the City Corporation. (Laws 1865, p. 395, §§ 2, 23, 5, 3, 22, 10, 11, 16, 12 ; Laws, 1866, p. 719, ch. 315.)

And the State appropriated the moneys raised under these laws precisely the same as other moneys in the treasury. (Laws 1867, p. 1460. See also General Term Brief on the Demurrer, pp. 8 to 11.)

THIRD POINT.—If the City Corporation, whose corporate name was used in the bonds, could therefore be supposed to be not only a proper party, but *prima facie, the* proper plaintiff, the distinct and admitted allegations of collusion and neglect on its part justify the action by the State.

> *See printed brief of plaintiffs on re-argument in* Ingersoll's case, pp. 25, 47 to 51, inclusive ; 63, 64, 77, 119, 120, 121, 173 to 181, 189, 190.

(*a*) In respect to private corporations and trustees, the doctrine is familiar that if the corporation or trustee refuses to sue, or intentionally omits to sue, or is in collusion with the alleged debtor or wrongdoer, the *cestui que* trust or stockholder can sue, making the corporation or trustee a party defendant.

> Abb. Digest Corp., p. 781, § 121, *et seq. ;* Robinson *v.* Smith, 3d Paige, 222 ; Cunningham *v.* Pell, 5 Paige, 607 ; 3d Edwards, ch. 127 ; Code, § 119.

While the individual corporators of a Municipal Cor-

poration are in a certain sense the *cestui que* trust, yet
it is well settled that they are not so in such sense as
will enable them to sue.

Doolittle *v.* Supervisors, 18 N. Y., 159.
Roosevelt *v.* Draper, 23 N. Y., 324.

The taxpayer or individual corporator not being able
to sue, it follows that the Attorney-General must be
the proper party, for there is no other. It devolves on
him, in cases of Municipal Corporations, as representing
the general public, to take the place that in a private
corporation would be taken by an individual stockholder.

(*b.*) The question whether the State or City Corporation should be the party plaintiff, is one which the defendant Fields cannot raise.

The cause of action belongs to one or the other;
both are parties to the suit, and both are barred by
this judgment from maintaining any further action for
this cause.

If the City Corporation might have complained, it is
sufficient to say that it has not appealed.

The judgment should be affirmed, with costs.

D. PRATT,
Attorney-General.

COURT OF APPEALS.

THE PEOPLE OF THE STATE OF NEW
YORK,
Respondents,

vs.

THOMAS C. FIELDS, Impl'd, &c.,
Appellants.

WILLIAM A. BEACH, for Appellants.

D. PRATT, (Att'y-Gen'l), CHARLES O'CONOR, and
W. H. PECKHAM, for Respondents.

FOLGER, J. : The first inquiry is this : is the appellant liable to any party for the moneys, or any part of them, obtained and received by him ?

He is not liable unless those moneys were paid him without authority of law. There was no authority of law for the payment, unless it is found in the Acts of 1869 and 1870 ; without those Acts the members of the fire companies, whose assignee the appellant was, had no legal claim for any personal compensation.

A brief statement will make this plain. By the Act of 1865 (Laws of 1865, chap. 249, p. 395), there was erected the Metropolitan Fire District of the State of New York. The City of New York was comprised within this Fire District, (§ 1). Four citizens, residents of the District, were to be appointed by the Senate, upon the nomination of the Governor, to be "Metropolitan Fire Commissioners," (§ 2). They were to form a Metropolitan Fire Department. They were to possess all the power and authority conferred upon or possessed by any officers of the then existing Fire Department of the City of New York, and other power conferred by the Act. By this grant of power they had the right to exercise all powers for the management and direction of the existing Fire Department of the City of New York, its premises and property; and they had the sole power and authority thereafter to extinguish fires in that city. The Commissioners were appointed, and in the exercise of these powers they, in October, 1865, organized these fire companies, to perform duty only on alarms of fire, and for an annual compensation to each of the companies of one thousand dollars. No compensation was provided, or meant to be, for any fireman, as an individual. The duty to which he was called was considered to be but an occasional one. It was thought to be rewarded by any privileges and exemptions which all firemen might claim, and by the $1,000, given as a whole sum to each company, in gross. There was no provision made by these Commissioners for payment of any money to any of these firemen, as individuals, and hence there was no provision of law to that end until the Acts of 1869 and 1870.

It may be insisted that the facts upon which this conclusion rests were not proven at the Circuit. There was no testimony given thereto. It is, however, substantially averred in the complaint, wherein the substance of the report of the Commissioners thereupon is stated, and the truth of that report is alleged. To be sure, the appellant's answer avers that he has no knowledge or information sufficient to form a belief as to that report; but he does not specifically deny the averment in the complaint, of the truth of the statements, as set out in the complaint thereupon, as he should have done to raise issue and require proof from the plaintiff.

Nor does the general denial at the close of the answer apply to this averment of the complaint, for that denial includes only those allegations of the complaint " not specifically answered unto." Moreover, it is plain that there was no contention as

to these facts, at the trial, and the case proceeded
upon the recognition, tacit or otherwise, by
both parties, of the existence of the facts which are
averred in the complaint, as to the organization, compensation and disbanding of these companies. Prior
to the Act of 1869, then, there was no law upon which
those men could found a claim for any recompense to
themselves for services as firemen. The Legislature, in
passing that Act, must be presumed to have known this ;
to have known that it was acting upon an assertion,
merely, which had no such support, in law or in equity,
as would enable the claimants to maintain an action
in any court. When, then, that Act used the word
claims, it did not mean that which was due of right
and could be maintained as such. It meant no more
than something which was asked for, or asserted to be
due, for which a pretence was set up. As, then, there
was no basis in law or equity, for a demand of payment as of right, it follows that the purpose of the
Legislature was to give. In doing this, it could fix
what sum should be given ; and so it did, by the declaration, that it should not exceed the sum of $50,000.
Nothing can be more clear, than it willed to give, but
to give no more than that amount, nor does the restriction as to the amount apply only to the act of payment. The words audit and adjust, in the Act, are as
much affected by it as the word pay. The Comptroller
could no more audit and adjust, in the sense of ratify-
ing and allowing a sum greater than that paid, than
he could pay more than that. He was required to
audit, to hear the claimants as to their claims, for this
was needed to ascertain who were the persons who
came within the description of the beneficiaries under
the Act. He was required to adjust the amount of the
gift of $50,000 to the number of claimants and their
relative interest therein, so that each should receive his
fair proportion, and no more ; and furthermore, though
doubtless, the Legislature was apprized of the amount

claimed, it is not so unusual that the amount demanded falls short of the amount which can be well based upon the pretence for the demand, that it may well be supposed that the Legislature meant to direct the Comptroller to ascertain whether indeed the claims upon the gift did in fact come up to its amount, even upon the unreal foundation asserted for them. It might be, that even upon the basis upon which they were put by the claimants, and notwithstanding their apparent amount, an investigation into them would keep them within the sum bestowed by the Legislature. Though they might go beyond it, and that fact be apparent upon the examination of them, made by him, yet he had no power from the Act to allow them above that amount, nor thus to ratify them at any sum above it, nor to impose nor to admit an obligation greater than that. He had no power, by any act of his, either of audit, adjustment or payment, to declare or find due from the Fire Department, nor from the city, nor from other source, more than the sum of $50,000. Due means owing, and owing must come of a right. There was no right save that created by the act making the gift. That was limited to a sum named ; and so no more could be found owing, no more could be found due, than that sum. With the purpose plainly declared of paying no more than $5 ,000, it cannot be that the Legislature meant to authorize an audit and adjustment which would find due more than that, which would create an obligation upon which payment of more than that could be lawfully demanded. Whatever may be the accurate philological definition of the words audit and adjust, we find them in a connection which affects that meaning. As placed in this statute in the circumstances in which it was passed, they mean the act of receiving from all these men the statement of their claims, and of the facts making them beneficiaries of the State, and the apportionment of the gift among them. The Legislature did not, by the Act of

1869, intend to declare the legality of the claims, nor to empower any official person to so act, as to make them an obligation due. The Act of 1870 comes in as a supplement to that of 1869. There is no direction in it for a further audit and adjustment. That which has been found due on the audit and adjustment under the Act of 1869, is authorized and directed to be paid. The Legislature did not, in that Act, mean that the Comptroller should so audit as to admit as due and thereby create a debt for more than $50,000. No more did it, by the Act of 1870, mean to assume that more had been admitted or found to be due than that sum. The language of the Act of 1870 is, to pay the claims which have been found to be due under the provisions of the Act of 1869. Now the argument of the appellant rests upon these words— "which have been found to be due," as if they meant that which presented itself to the attention of the Comptroller, on his examination under the Act of 1869, and that as he did perceive that upon the facts produced to him, if they were a legal ground for a claim, there was due and owing the sum subsequently paid to the appellant, so as matter of law and of fact, that was the sum which was found to be due. But the Acts are to be read together. They are in *pari materia*. The words and phrases used in one are charged with the same meaning when found in the other. "Which have been found to be due," in the Act of 1870, is a phrase of the same import as "which may be found to be due" in the Act of 1869. We find in the latter Act, authority and direction to the Comptroller to raise money by the issue of Stock of the City necessary to pay the sum or sums "*which may be found due*" on these claims. As he might not, by the express limitation of the Act, pay more than $50,000, he might not issue stock for more than that amount. As he might not pay more than that amount, nor issue stock for more than that amount, and yet, as he may and is required to issue stock to an amount of all "which may be found to be due," it is plain that the Legislature subjected that phrase to the same limitation, and meant that no more than $50,000 should be found to be due, by any audit and adjustment under it. When, in the Act of 1870, it uses the similar phrase, "which have been found to be due," and adds to it the particularization of when and where and how, by saying under the provisions of the Act of 1869, it is plain that the phrase was used in the same sense, and within the same limitation.

The Act of 1870 goes no farther than that of 1869. It is to be borne in mind, that in construing these acts, we are looking for the intention of the Legislature. That is to be learned from the words used by it, as affected, explained and limited, the one or more by all the rest. When, in the Act of 1870, the Legislature refers to the Act of 1869, and speaks of that which may have been found due under its provisions, we are taken back to that Act and can but see that in 1870 it did not mean to declare that any more was due or had been found due upon those claims than would rise in amount to the limit fixed by the former Act. Nothing was due, that is, owing, to those men, to which they had a legal right, before the Act of 1869. On the passage of that Act, the directions contained in it made due and owing to them a sum no greater than $50,000. The exact amount thereof, up to that limit, was to be arrived at by the Comptroller's audit. It is the amount arrived at by that audit, not exceeding that limit, and not already paid, of which the Act of 1870 authorizes and directs the payment. This was the intent of the Legislature, as shown by the language of the two Acts. That there might have been another intent on the part of the promoters of this legislation is probable, from the facts shown upon the trial. But these facts do not show through the language of the enactments, nor does it appear that they were in the possession of the Legislature.

There are some considerations ingeniously urged which are not in harmony with this view. Thus, the Act of 1870 gives authority to raise "the additional amount" required for the purpose of paying the claims which have been found to be due. This, it is urged, should be construed to mean an amount in addition to the sum fixed by the Act of 1869. But it cannot be. It is an additional amount needful to pay the claims which may have been found due under the provisions of that Act, whereby no more than $50,000 could be found due. It is further urged, that if no more was still to be paid than the unpaid portion of the $50,000, there was no need of further legislation. This is true. But that an enactment to one end is not strictly necessary thereto is not so strong a reason that it must have been intended for another end, as to overcome the evidence of intention derived from the language used by the law makers. It is said that it is ludicrous to suppose that the Legislature would not only multiply needless commands to the Comptroller to pay unaudited claims, but direct the issue of city bonds running thirty years to enable the payment of $722.66, which it appears was the amount not paid of the sum of $50,000. Indeed, there is a ridiculous disparity between the amount of this unpaid residue and the financial machinery proposed for meeting it. But not greatly more so than in the case of the Act of 1869. For the City of New York, to supply its treasury with the sum of $50,000 in the year 1869, surely did not need the issue of a thirty years' stock, unless in the absence of any other lawful mode of raising or obtaining that sum, and for that municipality, with its great resources and its great credit, to be put to such means to raise so small a sum, to wit, as $50,000, does indeed seem unnecessary, unless a necessity arose from the want of any provision of law enabling its financial officers otherwise to procure that sum for that purpose. If such necessity existed the provision is no longer ludicrous, and as it existed, if at all, in 1870 as well as in 1869, it is no more ludicrous to apply it to the unpaid residue of $722.66 than to the sum of $50,000. Furthermore, it may be presumed that the Comptroller would not issue stock in bonds of uneven amounts, but would act in accordance with the ways of financial men, and that he had already prepared, before the Act of 1870, the stock for issue to the even amount of the sum authorized by the Act of 1869. The ten per cent. allowed and paid by him upon the claims presented was arbitrary. It did not fully comply with the Act of 1869. It was evidently adopted for the convenience of his office in making calculations of amount due to each of so many claimants. So that the authority in 1870 is not necessarily to be read as for an issue of new stock to the sum of but $722.66, but for an issue of so much as was unused in 1869 or for an application of moneys already derived from an issue of stock under the Act of 1869 for the whole even sum of $50,000. Thus, there is not to be imputed to the Legislature the absurdity which the appellant contends would belong to it if the view of these statutes is not adopted which we have set forth.

It follows that a payment by the Comptroller to the appellant and the receipt by him of more than $50,000 was entirely without authority of law.

It will be seen that we have placed this conclusion upon the official inability of the Comptroller to audit and find due and owing, and allow upon these claims any more than the sum of $50,000. Any action beyond this was *corum non judice* and void. It is claimed by the appellant that as a matter of fact the Comptroller did find that there was due upon these claims more than that sum. We think that the testimony shows that there did appear before the Comptroller, in 1869, such statements from the claimants, of the time for which they had acted, as, when measured in money, by the wages paid to the hired members of the Fire Department, would amount to more than the sum awarded by the Act of that year. But we are not inclined to think that, as matter of fact, the Comptroller ascertained, as an official, conclusive result, that there was more due than that sum. The official and binding result arrived at was, that the claims were enough in amount to cover the sum awarded, and so much as that was officially found due. upon them. It is not necessary to do more, however, than to hold that as there was no authority in the Act to audit at a sum greater than that named in the Act, so there could have been no official finding to be due more than that amount.

The payment to the appellant was illegal. Is there, for this reason, a right of action, somewhere, to recover from him the whole or a part of the moneys he received?

There are allegations in the complaint of false and fraudulent intent and conduct on the part of the appellant in relation to these claims, the presentment and payment of them, and in his action as a member of the Legislature which passed the Act of 1870. There are also allegations of acquiescence, with knowledge of this fraudulent intent and conduct, on the part of the city of New York and its officials, and of collusion and connivance on the part of the city and its officers with the appellant.

These allegations are all denied by the appellant's answer. There seems to have been no direct proof made upon them. Can it be inferred by the Court, as matter of law, or as so plain that it need not be left to a jury, from the fact of the payment having been made and received without authority of law, that the appellant received it fraudulently and corruptly? In one of the briefs submitted to us on the part of the plaintiffs, it is conceded that this action is not founded upon any theory of the civil liability of the appellant for his acts as a member of the Legislature. They are alleged only as characterizing the act of presenting the claims to and receiving the money from the Comptroller. But the appellant, while admitting that he voted, as a member of Assembly, for the Act of 1870, denies that he knew of its purport and provisions in respect to these claims. The case, so far as the allegations of fraudulent conduct against the appellant are concerned, rests upon the facts that there was never any legal claim of his assignors against the Fire Department nor the city; that the legislation of 1869 and 1870 gave no legal claim nor right to them to an amount over $50,000; that it may be presumed against the appellant that he knew that these were the facts o the case, and hence knew also that the Comptroller, the financial officer and agent of the city, paid this money with no authority in fact from his principal, and no authority in law from any source. If it be doubtful whether there is enough here to make out fraudulent action on the part of the defendant in so clear a manner as to warrant the Court in directing a verdict, we have to say that it is not needed that we pass upon that question. An action may be maintained on other ground. The payment was made and received without any lawful power in the Comptroller to make it. The defendant is chargeable with knowledge of this. It was a payment by an agent who had no authority as such to make it. It was, then, no payment by the principal in mistake of law or ignorance of facts. The principal, in legal view, had no part in the payment, and it was made against its will. It was equivalent to an appropriation, by the appellant, of the moneys to his own use, with the acquiescence and help of the officer of the city, who was authorized to pay them out, not otherwise than in accordance with law. Having made the payment unlawfully, it was an act not within the scope of his agency, and does not bind his principal. (United States v. Bartlett, Davies, 9; Stevenson v. Mortimer, Cowp., 805; Taylor v. Plumer, 3 M. & S. 582.

There is for these reasons a right of action somewhere against the appellant to recover the whole or a part of these mortgages.

It is urged that the appellant received this money as the attorney for these men, and that as he has paid over to them the share agreed upon between them, he ought not to be liable for more than the share retained by him. There is proof that he acted as attorney and counsel for them. The proof is that he received the whole money as assignee of the whole of it. There is no proof of any agreement between him and them, nor of any payment by him to them. Evidence thereof was offered by the appellant and rejected, under exception by him, as immaterial. If it was material it was error to reject it, so that the case may be considered as though the evidence had been received. We do not think that the proof would protect the appellant. If it was illegal to receive the money, it was illegal for him to dispose of it, save to return it to the city treasury. If he knew that it was illegal to receive it, and that it was a wrong for him to do so, and he is therefore liable for that part retained by him, he also knew that it was illegal for his clients or principals to receive, and that it was wrong for him to pay over any part of it to them. He cannot thus defend himself from liability for the whole. (See Stephens *v.* Elwall, 4 M. & S., 259; Snowden *v.* Davis, 1 Taunt., 359; Sharland *v.* Mildon, 5 Hare, 469.)* This is not like the case of an attorney at law who knowingly prosecutes an unfounded claim in the courts, by the forms and processes of the law, and, recovering judgment, receives and pays over the avails. There, when final judgment has been rendered, it is the law of that case, for the parties to it, and it is the law itself which delivers the avails of the judgment to the recipient. It is not so here. The inquiry is, *second*, whether the appellant is liable to the plaintiffs in this action?

The question here presented has been of late much considered in this Court, in the case of *The People* v. *Ingersoll, impld.*, decided June 9, 1874. The appellant claims that the judgment of this Court in that case is conclusive in this case. The respondents suggest features in this case which materially distinguish it, as they claim, from that.

One of these is, as is urged, that the money received by the appellant was the property of the State, or the State had such a right and title therein as to afford ground for a right of action to recover it. It is no more in this than in that case alleged in terms that the money belongs or belonged to the plaintiffs. In this case as in that, the appellant is not sued as an express trustee, but as a wrong-doer in obtaining the money, and for a completed wrongful act. It is explicitly held in that case, that unless there is a right of property in the State to the money so received, there is no right of action. This is to be taken with the qualification, that the question is there reserved and not passed upon, of whether the State would not have a right to interfere in case of a refusal to sue, and of collusion with the wrong-doer on the part of the municipal or other body in whom was the title to the money and the primary right of action therefor. Though title in the State to the money is not alleged in terms, it is suggested in argument that the facts averred, and proved or admitted, show a title. These facts do not differ from those in *Ingersoll's case* (*supra*), save that the legislative direction was to raise money for the purposes of a statutory civil division of the State differing in extent from the City of New York, whose expenditures were ordinarily provided for by taxation ordered by the State, the avails of which passed into State Treasury, and were paid from thence in the ordinary course of disbursement of that civil division. So that the moneys raised for that civil division did ordinarily go into the State Treasury and come under its control, with a right thereto in the State, and had they been wrongfully received therefrom or intercepted on their way thereto, the State might maintain an action therefor. But the moneys here sued for were not raised for the purpose of that civil division. The very ground of the action is that the purpose for which the moneys were raised was an illegal, false and fictitious purpose, and was not the purpose of the Fire Department. They were not raised in the manner directed by the Act creating that civil division (see Sec. 10 of Act of 1865). The Legislature directed the raising of these in a new and different manner. Hence they never became its moneys. They were not raised by taxation, but by the bonds of the city, and they passed into the treasury of the city, and not into the treasury of the State (Sec. 16 of Act 1865), and there being no claim upon them for any legitimate purpose of the Fire Department, they became and were an unexpended and unappropriated surplus, the funds and property of the city, as much so as if upon any other unfounded pretence of authority the Comptroller had issued the stock of the city and obtaining for it half of a million of dollars had deposited it with the City Treasurer. The facts of this case make no material distinction of it from that referred to, and that is, in this respect, controlling upon this. Another distinction suggested is this: It is alleged in the complaint that ever since the payment of the money to the appellant, the City of New York and all of its officers who might or could exercise any power or authority in the premises, have with full notice and knowledge of the facts, acquiesced in the misapplication of the moneys, and colluded with the appellant in protecting him from responsibility by any judicial means or remedies. This allegation is denied by the answer of the appellant. There is no direct proof made of its truth. The city of New York is a party defendant to the action. It made answer to the complaint, but withdrew it, and is without an answer upon the record. The material allegations of the verified complaint are to be taken as admitted by it. We think that the question is thus fairly raised in the case, whether if a municipality has a right of action for its money wrongfully received from its treasury, and refuses to prosecute for a recovery, the State may, in its character of *parens patriae*, bring action nominally for itself, but really in behalf of the individuals or body of citizens who are presently or ultimately to be affected by the wrongful payment and misapplication. It is true that the averment of the complaint is denied by the answer of the appellant. It is admitted by the city. It stands upon the record, so far as it is concerned, undenied. The judgment by default which has been, or may be, taken against the city, will always be an adjudication settling that fact as against it. And this adjudication will always be available, not only to the people who are the plaintiffs in the action, but also the appellant, the co-defendant, as a final determination of that question against the city. So that, if that fact gives a right to the State to interfere and bring an action, it is admitted by the city to have existed when this suit was commenced, and an adjudication based upon that admission will always enable the appellant, notwithstanding he has put the fact in issue, and it has not been proven upon the trial against him, to interpose a judgment in this action against him and the city, of a recovery of these moneys, in bar of another action by the city against him for a recovery thereof. Being a fact admitted of record, it binds all parties to the action, the party defendant who has admitted, and also the party co-defendant, because it takes from him the opportunity of saying that if recovery is had in this action against him, he is still liable to his now co-defendant in another action for the same cause.

The money of a municipal corporation has been illegally paid by its officer, and illegally received by

the appellant. The municipality and its officer refuse to sue for a recovery thereof. This presents the
case of a fund held in trust for the public purposes of
the members of a municipal corporate body which has
been unlawfully despoiled, and the official trustees of
which, with whom is the primary right of action,
refuse to act for its protection and reinstallment, and
for the redress of the injury to the body of the tax-
payers, present or future, who are in a sense the *cestuis
que trust.*

An individual tax-payer or a number of tax-payers
may not maintain such an action. *Doolittle* v. *Supervisors*, 18 N. Y., 159; *Roosevelt* v. *Draper*, 23 *Ib.*,
324. They do not represent and may not assume to
act for the whole public body injuriously affected.
Hence, in case the municipality and its officers refuse
to act, there is no party to approach the Courts unless
there is some other and superior trustee for the public,
who may rightfully interfere. There can be no other,
unless it is the State. Can the State thus interfere?

In the *People* v. *Ingersoll*, this Court purposely re-
frained from deciding or even intimating an opinion
upon this question. There, as here, the action was to
recover a sum certain, the avails of the bonds of a
municipal corporation, issued by authority of the State
Legislature, to provide means for the payment of
municipal liabilities. The bonds in both cases were to
be redeemed at maturity by municipal taxation. The
avails of these bonds, it was alleged in each case, had
come to the possession of the defendant by means of
fraudulent devices and practices of himself and others
associating with him. The moneys realized by a
sale of the bonds of the county, in that case, were regarded and treated as the moneys of the county, to
the same extent and subject to the like control as if
they had been raised for the same special purpose by
present taxation, and paid into the county treasury,
or were in the possession of any other of the county

agents. The sale of the bonds was an anticipation of the tax, and *the issue of the bonds* was an exercise of the taxing power in one form. The burden was and is upon the taxpayers of the locality, and whether the money was levied presently or borrowed upon its credit and levied thirty years thereafter, could make no difference in passing upon the question of the ownership of the money. In either case, as this Court held, the moneys were the moneys of the municipality.

It was conceded in the *Ingersoll case*, as well by the counsel for the plaintiffs, as in the dissenting opinion in this Court, that the Court could not in that action adjudicate what should be the final destination of the money in controversy. Such concession seemed to be the yielding of the question to whom the money belonged, and an admission that it did not belong to the State, the plaintiffs in the action, and in connection with the position of the most eminent of the counsel for the plaintiff, that the question: " Who owns the money ?" was but another way of putting the question, " Who can maintain the action ?" and that the party regarded in the law as the technical owner of the money, was the party to maintain the action was fatal to the claim of the plaintiffs to recover. The two positions are not consistent with the claim to recover, and the difficulty in finding a solid ground, on which to rest successfully a right of the people of the State by the Attorney-General to maintain the action, is made very apparent by a bare statement of the admission and positions so absolutely incompatible with the theory of the action.

It was possible in that action, if it had been allowable upon the facts alleged in the complaint, and a liability of the defendant, Ingersoll, to account to the people of the State for the money alleged to have been fraudulentiy obtained and illegally received by him from the County of New York, would have been established, to give judgment in such form as to enforce the liability. The Court below had not in that action given force and finality to the remedy, and if the plaintiffs were, upon the complaint, entitled to any relief, if they should have had any standing in Court as against the defendant, the judgment would have been reversed and the cause remanded, to the end that the proposed relief, legal and equitable, might be granted. It, was because the plaintiffs did not, by their complaint, make a case for any relief, legal or equitable, that the demurrer was sustained and judgment given for the defendant. Upon this appeal we are shut up to the question whether the plaintiffs, the People of the State, are entitled to a judgment in their favor for the money illegally and fraudulently taken from the City of New York. They have recovered a money judgment, by which they are adjudged to be entitled, as owners, to the sums awarded. It is not a recovery in trust, or for the benefit of any person or corporation. The judgment does not recognize, but, on the contrary, is inconsistent with, any right or interest of any other party in or to the money. The judgment is that the plaintiffs recover the amount specified, and that they have execution therefor, and no other or ulterior disposition of the fund is made or is consistent with the record. It is a legal judgment, founded upon a supposed legal and technical right of the plaintiffs to the money, in their own right. The fact that the Corporation of the City of New York, in whom is the legal right to the money and the cause of action, is a party to the record as a defendant, and has not defended the action or controverted the claim of the plaintiff, does not avail the latter. Such an omission of the corporation to assert its legal rights, cannot work a transfer of the fund and right of action to the plaintiffs. It may be that it was a breach of trust and of duty on the part of the managing body and official representatives of the municipality, but cannot operate as a forfeiture of the rights of the constituents, the *cestuis que trust*, or confer upon the plaintiffs a legal right to the money, or authorize the People, by their Attorney-General, to take the place in Court in pursuing the wrong-doer and asserting a right to the money which the law gives to the legally-entitled custodian and trustee. The corporate authorities of the city of New York can no more donate or transfer, without consideration or authority of law, the property of the city to the State, than they can to the defendant or any stranger. Every act of that kind would be *ultra vires*, and would confer no legal right upon the transferee. But the city authorities did not, by omitting to defend the action, admit or concede the title of the plaintiffs.

No judgment was demanded concluding their rights, and, whether by reason of the transactions alleged in the complaint, the plaintiffs had a legal cause of action against the defendant, did not concern the City of New York. Does then, the averment, regarding the same as proved or admitted, that the several officers of the city as well as of the county of New York, "if any, who might or could exercise any power or authority in the premises, have, with notice and full knowledge of such payment and of its fraudulent nature, acquiesced and still do acquiesce in such fraudulent misapplication of the said moneys, and at all times since such application, were and still are colluding with the said Thomas C. Fields, in the fraud aforesaid, and in protecting him from responsibility for the same by any judicial means or remedies," give to the plaintiffs a right of action which, but for these facts thus averred, they could not have. It is noteworthy that there is no assertion anywhere in the complaint that this action is prosecuted for or in the interest of the city. Neither is it expressly or impliedly admitted, in the clause alleging collusion of the city officials, that the money or the rights to the same, are now, or ever were, in the city, or in any person or body, other than the plaintiff. Those who are now put forward as the *cestuis que trust*, and in whose interest it is sought to sustain the recovery, are nowhere averred to be the real parties in interest, and the relation now assumed by the plaintiffs, of trustees, is not averred in the complaint. It is a fact, not wholly without significance, that the distinguished counsel for the plaintiffs did not deem it important to resist, by appeal, the striking out of a similar clause from the complaint in the Ingersoll case, as it is likely they would have done, had it been considered that the facts in that clause averred were essential to give to the plaintiffs a standing in court, as trustees or otherwise, if every other claim of right should be denied. But neither counsel nor parties are estopped or foreclosed by this implied admission of the immateriality of the facts now relied upon, and the question must be passed upon as if no such admission had been made.

Notwithstanding the caution of the Court, in its reference to the question now under consideration, in disposing of the *Ingersoll case*, we cannot but regard the decision in that case, and the reasons upon which it went, as decisive of the present question. Most certainly the fraud and collusion of the City officials alleged, could not and did not deprive the City of New York of its property rights, or confer title to the money in dispute upon the State. Such an idea would be preposterous, and is not put forth by any one. The loss to the City by the misfeasance or malfeasance of its official representatives and agents, could only be such as naturally and necessarily resulted from the omissions or acts, and not such as could form a forfeiture of legal rights, and because loss might ensue to the City, as the consequence of the neglect or wrongdoing of its servants or agents, it would by no means follow as a legal or logical sequence, that the title to the money and what might be saved, became vested in the State, or any other body, whose representatives would be more vigilant in protecting or pursuing or reclaiming it. But the judgment in the action does accomplish just that, and awards the money to the plaintiffs to the exclusion of the City.

The prerogative rights of the State, as sovereign over municipal corporations, and their civil and property rights, and the extent to which they could be asserted, by the administrative or executive officers of the State government, were necessarily considered in the *Ingersoll case*, and the judgment of the Court was that while the absolute sovereignty of the State over the municipalities of its creation was conceded, its actual exercise was limited by the legislation upon the subject and that no power was delegated to the Attorney-General or other State officer, to assert any such right of sovereignty over the property of municipal corporations, in the absence of express legislation to that end. We there held, that corporations of that nature could not be deprived of their franchises or property by implications of power, either in the Attorney-General or other officer. The money sought to be recovered in that case had been obtained by fraud, and by the collusion and neglect or breach of duty on the part of the city agents, and so far as appeared no claim was made to the money by the county, or effort put forth to recover it; and every intendment was necessarily in favor of the plaintiffs. Substantially every element was in that case, that is to be found in that now before us, with the additional circumstance favorable to the plaintiffs, that they could have had any relief to which by the case made they were entitled. The Court adjudged that the plaintiffs had no standing in court, and dismissed the complaint. If there is any right or authority in the Attorney-General representing the State to maintain this and the like actions, or any action to recover corporate or trust funds fraudulently misappropriated or converted or to call defaulting official trustees or wrong-doers to account for moneys thus diverted from their proper destination and use, such right exists concurrently with a like right in the municipal corporations, and does not depend for its exercise as against a wrong-doer upon any want of fidelity or willingness to prosecute of the municipal authorities. Att'y-Gen'l *v.* Wilson, (1 Craig & Philips, 1). The averment of collusion or neglect to prosecute does not give vitality to the authority, nor is it necessary to put the Attorney General in motion. In other words, it has no materiality. It is not necessary to refer to the cases from the English reports in which the Attorney-General has intervened to enforce the performance of trusts by corporate authorities and official trustees, or the reasons upon which the decisions have proceeded, or the foundation upon which, in England, the jurisdiction of the Courts and the right of the Crown rest. They are considered sufficiently in *The People* v. *Ingersoll.* It suffices to say here that all those actions are in equity, and brought directly to enforce a trust and compel the application of trust funds, by the appropriate trustee, to the objcts of the trust, and such other incidental relief, either against the guilty trustees or those to whose possession the trust funds had come, as the circumstances of the case asked for. There is no parallelism in those cases and this, and if the same existed and the same practice prevailed here as in England, they would have no relevancy upon the question before us. The case is not distinguishable by any material circumstance from *The People* v. *Ingersoll,* and must be adjudged accordingly.

"Folger, J., reads for reversal and new trial; Grover, Andrews and Johnson, J.J., concur; Church, Ch. J., and Rapallo, J., dissent; Allen, J., absent, not voting."

A copy.

H. E. SICKLES,
Reporter.

It is the interest of all mere partisans to prevent laws from being made, or judicial decisions forming precedents pronounced, which might be inconvenient to themselves or their friends. Here the tricksters of both parties meet on a common ground.

That sort of forensic reasoning which is often more sharp than wise, early discovered that the abstraction of an employer's money by an agent could not easily be punished as a crime. In a great degree this technicality was early gotten rid of in respect to private servants by the statutes rendering embezzlement indictable. But no law of this sort has ever been extended, in our State, to *public* agents. The revisors of 1830 proposed so to extend it; but the astute Legislature of that day rejected their proposition. It may be found in the Revisor's Reports, 3 R. S., p. 820, Sec. 58, Second Ed., and is as follows:

"If any officer of this State, intrusted with moneys belonging to the people of this State, or to any county, town, city or village, by virtue of his office, shall fraudulently or corruptly apply such moneys, or any part thereof, to any purpose incompatible with the duties of his office, whereby the people of this State shall sustain any loss, he shall, upon conviction, be imprisoned in a State Prison not exceeding ten years, or shall be fined not exceeding ten thousand dollars, or both, in the discretion of the Court."

Had this law been enacted, it might have been easier to convict Tweed; and perhaps his indictment would not have been extended to the "monster" dimensions so often complained of. At all events, it would have afforded some facility in the prosecution of delinquent officials.

A bill to this same effect is now before the Legislature, A. D. 1875. It seems to be thought too severe, and its passage is doubtful.

Instituting civil suits against the New York City peculators in the name of the State has sometimes been spoken of as an ingenious device. There is no ground for so regarding it. There was no other practicable remedy. (*See pages* 29 *to* 35 *inclusive.*) Had its availability been very doubtful, it would still have been an imperative duty to try the experiment. Nothing could have excused the Attorney-General's assistants in omitting to make it, unless indeed they had been possessed of a perfect conviction that it would fail. So far from this being the case, the English precedents were clearly in its favor. How these precedents happen to be inapplicable here has not yet been shown. In order, however, to naturalize them, and thus avoid the inconvenient results of the decisions in the Ingersoll and Fields cases, a bill has been prepared as follows :

An Act concerning Judicial Remedies for Peculation and other Wrongs Affecting Public Moneys and Rights of Property. Passed   1875.

The People of the State of New York, represented in Senate and Assembly, do enact as follows :

SECTION 1.—Where any money, funds, credits or property held or owned by this State, or held or owned officially or otherwise, for or on behalf of any public or governmental interest, by any municipal or other public corporation, board, officer, custodian, agency or agent of any city, county, village or other division, subdivision, department or portion of this State, has been heretofore without right obtained, received, converted or disposed of, and not actually recovered back and restored, previously to the passage of this Act, unto the proper and lawful official receiver, depositary and custodian thereof, either in specie, or by full and lawful compensation for the same duly made, all such money, funds, credits and property, together with all right, title and interest in the same, and all suits and actions, and cause and causes, right and rights of suit and action for the same, and for any damages or other compensation due, recoverable, or that might be had on account, or by reason of any and every such obtaining, receipt, conversion or disposition, and all claims and demands for such damages and compensation, shall be deemed and taken to be vested in the people of the State of New York, and, so far as may, in judgment of law, be necessary to effect such investiture, are by force of this Act transferred to and vested in the people of this State accordingly. And any Court in which any action in the premises may be at the passage of this Act, on appeal or otherwise, in the name of any plaintiff before entitled to prosecute the same, shall, on the application of the Attorney-General, direct the same to be continued in the name of the people of this State.

SECTION 2.—Where any such money, funds, credits or property as aforesaid shall be hereafter without right, obtained, received, converted or disposed of, and shall not, within one month after such wrongful obtaining, receipt, conversion or disposition thereof, be so actually recovered and restored as aforesaid, then and from the expiration of that term all such money, funds, credits and property and all such right, title and interest in the same, and all such claims, demands, rights and remedies in respect thereof, as in the first section of this Act are in like cases mentioned, unless previously so vested by law, shall, in like manner, by force of this Act, be transferred to and vested in the people of the State of New York.

SECTION 3.—The Attorney-General on his own motion may, and, on the written request of the Governor, he shall, prosecute all such suits, actions and judicial proceedings as may be necessary or expedient for enforcing the interests, rights and remedies of the people of this State in this Act mentioned.

SECTION 4.—On petition filed against the Attorney-General as respondent by any corporation, board, officer, agency or agent, for or on behalf of any city, county, town, village, division, department or portion of the State in the first and second sections of this Act mentioned, the Supreme Court, at any Special Term thereof held in the County of Albany, on summary proceedings after the recovery and actual receipt by the people or into the State Treasury of any property, money, funds, credits, damages or compensation in this Act mentioned or referred to, which, if this Act had not been passed, would not have belonged to the State, may make such order and judgment as may be just and equitable for the disposition of the proceeds of such recovery, so as to reinstate the lawful custody which was disturbed or impeded by the wrong complained of, after reimbursing the State Treasury, out of such proceeds, for all expenses that may have been incurred by the State in the premises. This section shall apply to actions now pending, and such summary orders and judgments shall be subject to appeal in like manner and to the same extent as judgments in actions.

SECTION 5.—On the application of the Attorney-General, any trial, motion, appeal or hearing in any action by the people for any of the causes mentioned in the first and second sections of this Act shall, in all the Courts of this State, and without reference to its order on any calendar, be entitled to a preference over any other business whatever.

SECTION 6.—No Act or part of any Act which may be inconsistent with the provisions of this Act shall be of any effect to prevent the full operation of this Act.

SECTION 7.—This Act shall take effect immediately.

The Mayor of the City of New York having announced to the Corporation Counsel, January 2, 1875, an intention to remove him, the eldest of the counsel named on page 29 (*ante*) presented to the Mayor (January 29, 1875) certain observations on the counsel's answer. His concluding remarks were as follows :

VII.—Although the amounts are more impressive in the metropolitan city, precisely such frauds as those perpetrated by Tweed, Connolly and Fields occur in the interior. An instance may be instructive. Over $54,000 were awarded by the Legislature to a remote county in the North Woods, whereupon its faithful Supervisors granted the whole sum to the person who acted as *their agent* in the application. This happened in 1871, the memorable year of Tweed's fall. The agent received the money in the same summer, and whilst the $6,000,000 of the Court-house fraud was being paid out to the New York conspirators. A State action was brought by the Attorney-General against the Supervisors and the agent ; but the decision in the Fields case is a controlling precedent, and must be fatal to it. Four of the seven Appeal Judges hold that the Supervisors can alone prosecute any legal remedy. This, of course, as to all local frauds, virtually establishes a long rogues' holiday. True it is that one of the Judges who united in that opinion was dropped by the people at the late election, and a competitor entertaining opposite views was chosen in his place ; but there is still a majority in favor of the doctrine which thus affords to knaves a practical impunity. A pertinent remark occurs at § 736 of Judge Dillon's leading American Treatise on Municipal Corporations : " Since experience has shown how liable these corporations are to be betrayed by those who have the temporary management of their concerns, it would never do for the Courts to hold that relief against illegal acts could *only* be had by an authorized suit brought by and in the name of the Corporation."

As we have seen, the supposed technical rule, now finally sanctioned in the Ingersoll and Fields decisions, together with the virtual possession of the City Law Department through an appointee of their own, has, from the outset, formed the Ring's machinery for saving their assets from the just consequences of their political bankruptcy. When this cavil was first ventilated in October, 1871, our eminent fellow-citizen, Mr. Evarts, remarked that its investigation was superfluous. "If," said he, "there should be any doubt as to the adequacy of existing remedies, the Legislature will immediately remove it." This idea had its origin in his extensive knowledge of legislation in purer times, and his confidence in the uprightness of the coming men. It was creditable to him as a jurist, although, as we shall see, his confidence was unmerited, and, consequently, his prediction was not verified.

A Republican Legislature was elected under the banner of official reform ; and, on its meeting in 1872, Mr. Tilden brought into the Assembly a bill framed in conformity with Mr. Evarts' conception. It proposed to recognize a right of action in the State, effectually guarding, at the same time, all local interests. If enacted, this bill would have obviated all technical difficulties and secured substantial justice, but it did not become a law. Next in this history we find official reform checked by the decisions in favor of Ingersoll and Fields ; but despair was not yet justifiable. The Republicans had hitherto controlled ; yet, almost cotemporaneously with those inconvenient decisions, the other political party seemed to be coming into power, and thus another resort was afforded. The unsuccessful effort made by Mr. Tilden in 1872 might be renewed under other auspices. Accordingly, his bill was drafted anew for the incoming Legislature (*see the new draft, ante,* page 321); and then it was that proceedings were initiated for the removal of the Ring's appointee from the head of the City Law Department, that his place might be supplied by an energetic foe of official malversation and corrupt jobbery. The Tilden bill above alluded to was desirable in 1872 to obviate technical objections then deemed utterly futile and sure, as it seemed, to be repudiated in our highest Court, and indeed by all enlightened and impartial jurists. But now, *i. e.*, in the Autumn of 1874 the proposed law had become a necessity. Not only had judicial learning in the interim uncovered to view the crying evil that existing laws, just as the Ring and their professional advocates had astutely contended, did commit to the thieves themselves and their associates the exclusive right to be heard in courts of justice against such local thefts as we are contemplating; but other events had occurred greatly increasing the need of some such clearing-up enactment. Nearly all the chief wrongdoers had withdrawn themselves beyond the limits of our State, and doubtless had also carried with them their ill-gotten gains. It is evident that great difficulty must attend any attempt to establish before foreign Courts the title of local boards or officers to maintain actions for these public moneys. Counsel considerably versed in our laws, and with large experience in applying them, have differed with reference to this question, nor have our highest judges been unanimous in their interpretations. If the right to the stolen funds were vested in the State by statute, the remedy in all cases and in all courts and places would be plain and effectual. Besides, the State of New York would be more readily recognized in foreign countries as a suitor and more fully respected than any corporate or *quasi* corporate official body claiming to represent the interests of a local constituency. Yet, from information received since your charges were presented, it seems probable—indeed, it is certain—that neither the Tilden remedial enactment above described (*ante*, p. 321), nor any other of like or similar efficacy, will be adopted by the Legislature of 1875. Attachments against assets which have been transported to foreign climes, and writs of arrest under the code of procedure against persons who have fled to Belgium or Brittany, are indeed proposed ; but this is simply "a mockery, a delusion and a snare." Our ancestral jurisprudence is denied us by a lean majority of one,* overruling CHURCH, our universally reverenced Chief Judge, RAPALLO, the chosen representative of our great metropolis, and MILLER, the most recent recipient of our people's favor. Legislators will not reinstate it, and, for the present, the people are remediless.†

It was desired that the perpetrators of the flagitious thefts discovered in 1871, should be pursued even to the ends of the earth with the most efficient instrumentalities attainable and stripped of their plunder ; it was also desired to avoid raids on the Treasury through false claims at law, combined with weak defenses. Recovering public money or inflicting personal incon-

---

* In the Ingersoll opinion (*ante, p.* 208), the Court comments most felicitously upon the pernicious effects of a modern contrivance, i. e., the forming in government of what it aptly terms "a hybrid body." The *first* experiment of this kind, in our experience, was Tweed's Board of Supervisors. Some materials for an instructive history of the *second* are furnished in this book.

† The Court of Appeals admits it to be desirable "that the law was different" from the rule which, unhappily, they were bound to "declare." (*Ante, p.* 221 & *p.* 200.)

venience upon any individual was not the object in either case. The aim was, by making examples and instituting safeguards, to deter from such evil practices as have obtained, and thereby to save from official rapacity the money which still remains in the possession of our citizens, as yet unstolen.

From the time when Mr. Tilden, now our Governor, engaged my professional aid for this purpose, in 1871, until, in the present year 1875, it became evident that, whatever political party may be in the ascendant, the peculators, past and prospective, have such influence that the arm of remedial justice, paralized by the action of the Courts, cannot be re-invigorated by needful legislation, my hope for official reform and my confidence in its practicability were unshaken. That animating impulse led me to advise and strongly to desire the removal now under consideration; giving that advice involved an obligation to aid, if requested, in consequent inquiries; and, for this last reason alone, the task of examining the respondent's answer has been performed. It is presumed that no further service of the kind will be required. By whomsoever prosecuted, civil suits against the Ring will be embarrassed by technicalities arising from the numerous existing laws prepared in their interest;* and, meanwhile, the statute of limitations will be apt to cover their frauds with its mantle of oblivion. It is plain to my mind that unless there shall be introduced hereafter some great and vital change in administration, not now practicable, even one dollar of the stolen $30,000,000 will never be recovered; nor is it likely that the continuous jobbery of certain classes can otherwise be arrested. In my judgment, these circumstances render it unimportant to the public whether or not the suggested removal shall take place; and, as personal aims have never weighed in considering the

---

* See page 208.

question, the interest I once felt in it has wholly ceased. My inclinations do not tend, however, either to indolence or despair. Terrible as are the evils engendered by political tergiversation and now overspreading the land, this great people are too intelligent and too greatly blessed by the natural advantages of their glorious country to be irremediably ruined by selfish factions. The pressure of these very evils must ere long stir to needful efforts, for their own deliverance from misrule, the tax-paying and burden-bearing classes who are neither place-hunters, nor politicians by trade. When they shall arise and institute a movement of sufficient power to compel needful legislation, without regard to the interests of "our friends," my good wishes will accompany it. Nor shall any service in my power be withheld from it. At the very next election an entirely new Legislature is to be chosen. Perhaps then, or at some other period not far distant, we may hope to see expelled from control the rival factionists who, as the fabled brothers divided immortality, hold, in alternate enjoyment, the ever active privilege of swindling the public with impunity through the forms of law.